MEDIA LITERACY
for CITIZENSHIP

MEDIA LITERACY *for* CITIZENSHIP

A Canadian Perspective

Kirsten Kozolanka and Paul Orlowski

CANADIAN SCHOLARS

Toronto | Vancouver

Media Literacy for Citizenship: A Canadian Perspective
Kirsten Kozolanka and Paul Orlowski

First published in 2018 by
Canadian Scholars, an imprint of CSP Books Inc.
425 Adelaide Street West, Suite 200
Toronto, Ontario
M5V 3C1

www.canadianscholars.ca

Copyright © 2018 Kirsten Kozolanka, Paul Orlowski, and Canadian Scholars.

All rights reserved. No part of this publication may be reproduced, stored in a retrieval system, or transmitted, in any form or by any means, without the prior written permission of Canadian Scholars, under licence or terms from the appropriate reproduction rights organization, or as expressly permitted by law.

Every reasonable effort has been made to identify copyright holders. Canadian Scholars would be pleased to have any errors or omissions brought to its attention.

Library and Archives Canada Cataloguing in Publication

Kozolanka, Kirsten, author
        Media literacy for citizenship : a Canadian perspective / Kirsten Kozolanka and Paul Orlowski.

Includes bibliographical references and index.
Issued in print and electronic formats.
ISBN 978-1-77338-079-7 (softcover).--ISBN 978-1-77338-080-3 (PDF).--ISBN 978-1-77338-081-0 (EPUB)

        1. Media literacy--Canada--Case studies. 2. Mass media--Canada--Case studies. 3. Case studies. I. Orlowski, Paul, 1957-, author II. Title.

P96.M42C3 2018   302.23   C2018-903440-8
                                       C2018-903441-6

Text and cover design by Elisabeth Springate
Typesetting by Brad Horning

18 19 20 21 22   5 4 3 2

Printed and bound in Canada by Webcom

CONTENTS

Preface *vi*

Introduction *viii*

Chapter 1: Ideology Critique and the Media in an Era of Neoliberalism 1

Chapter 2: Building an Inclusive Society: The Role of Alternative Media 24

Chapter 3: Democracy in a Changing Landscape of Media Sources 44

Chapter 4: Media Literacy in an Era of Fake News and Alternative Facts 70

Chapter 5: The Public Media Challenge in a Fractured Media Society 99

Chapter 6: The "Science" of Climate Change and the (Mis)Informed Citizen 119

Chapter 7: The Other: The Canadian Mosaic Hits a Roadblock? 145

Chapter 8: Indigenous Representation in the Media 164

Chapter 9: War and Terror: Militarization and the Fearful Citizen 193

Chapter 10: The Role and Future of Journalism in Society 210

Glossary *228*

About the Authors *234*

Index *235*

PREFACE

So much information; so little time. The pace of life seems to move faster every year, and there are always exciting new things to try and to share with those around us. It wasn't so long ago that mailed letters and daily newspapers delivered directly to households showed us new vistas and gave us almost everything we needed to know. Now we use as landmarks the new version of a Samsung Galaxy or an Apple application.

All of this brings new meaning to what we always called "media," but that now has become so many exciting ways of connecting with each other—the simple and pure enjoyment of communication. We share this wonder.

Although we didn't know it at the time, this book project had its beginning when one of us (Kirsten Kozolanka) edited an issue of *Our Schools/Our Selves*, the journal of the Canadian Centre for Policy Alternatives, on "Media Education and Educating Media" (2007), and the other (Paul Orlowski) submitted a chapter called "Bob Dylan Was Right—It *Is* a Political World: The Case for Critical Media Literacy."

As educators, both of us saw the importance of media literacy in a challenging, quickly moving world. And what better way to understand media literacy than by connecting it to something we both believed to be the essence of media literacy: citizenship. How could we write about media literacy if we didn't connect it to who we are as citizens? As citizens, we inhabit the same place and, likely, have the same sense of place, share the same sense of belonging. If we are to understand media literacy, we need also to see ourselves as citizens.

ACKNOWLEDGEMENTS

Kirsten Kozolanka

I would like first and foremost to thank Paul Orlowski, who, as an education professor, was able to share incredible knowledge that made the project more insightful. I also thank him for the pure enjoyment of our long chats that often had nothing to do with the book itself, but made the long process of writing delightful. I also thank my patient life partner, Charles Brabazon, and our awesome daughters, Honor and Greer.

Paul Orlowski

I would likewise like to thank Kirsten Kozolanka. It has been a unique and harmonious relationship to co-author a book with someone who lives thousands of kilometres away. Although we have had numerous phone calls, we have never actually met in person. There are a few other people who deserve special mention: my daughter, Katrina, and my sister Sarah for their love and support; my University of Saskatchewan colleagues and friends Mike Cottrell, Howard Woodhouse, and Jonas Kiedrowski; University of Saskatchewan law professor Sákéj Youngblood Henderson for pointing me to some excellent resources for Chapter 8; and lastly, Stephen Colbert (yes, *that* Stephen Colbert) for helping me remain relatively sane during the Trump presidency.

We both very much appreciated the work of the four manuscript reviewers. This was an arduous task. In particular, the comments we received from Professor Nicole Cohen of the University of Toronto and especially Professor Eric Spalding of the University of the Fraser Valley were very insightful. Finally, we were very fortunate to be in the good hands of Natalie Garriga at Canadian Scholars/Women's Press, along with everyone else we worked with there. Thank you, all.

INTRODUCTION

Democracy doesn't spring from nowhere or grow all by itself, but is renewed by the trust we as citizens have in the information that we get from our country's leaders, most of it through the media. Journalism is a key element in this state-citizen relationship in building and maintaining democracy. Despite excellent and groundbreaking investigative journalism like the Panama Papers, much of the mainstream media currently find themselves on financially shaky ground. Social media like Twitter and Facebook pose a serious threat to traditional media outlets, but their positive contributions to a vibrant democracy are muted against seriously negative traits. Alternative media outlets are ubiquitous and often produce trenchant journalism, but many have difficulty growing large enough audiences amid the cacophony of voices, some serious while others are mere entertainment and well financed.

Public trust in the mainstream media is on the wane in recent years, and by corollary, mistrust in the media and in public institutions in general appears to be on the rise. Results of this new-found mistrust were evident in the 2016 referendum known as Brexit, in which British voters eschewed the position of the Establishment and demanded an exit from the European Union. A compelling argument could be made that the election victory of Donald Trump as president of the United States in November 2016 is the apex of what mistrust in the media can bring to a society.

The Trump presidency, however, may be merely a harbinger of what mistrust in the media and other public institutions such as government and the justice system will create. Although fake news is not an altogether new phenomenon, social media enable these stories to go viral—and *this* is a very new development. Powerful vested interests are fuelling a climate change denial movement, pun intended, and a growing mistrust in scientific research has found a political home with Trump and many conservative politicians in Canada and especially the US who dismiss the human-caused heating of the atmosphere. This turn away from scientific research suggests that a return to pre-Enlightenment perspectives is a possibility. The implications of this are frightening.

It is also of immense concern that Canadian society and especially American society appear increasingly divided between progressive and conservative factions. The ideological fault lines of the past are transforming into huge crevasses in which one set of values and perspectives has very little in common with the other. Protest movements like Idle No More and Black Lives Matter form the backdrop for the nativist anger evident among Trump supporters. The so-called alt-right protest march in Charlottesville, Virginia, in August 2017 in which a counter-protestor was killed, was a frightening expression of this White anger. As many readers will recall, President Trump had difficulty putting blame on the White nationalist and neo-Nazi protesters for the violence that erupted. Canada is not immune from these trends. In 2016–17, a leadership candidate for the Conservative Party of Canada utilized divisive discourses about race, religion, and culture to garner support for her ultimately unsuccessful campaign.

Middle- and working-class citizens demanding an end to neoliberalism and its mean-spirited policies of austerity live among others who support Trump and blame economic problems on immigrants, refugees, and women. In other words, while some citizens have a class analysis to explain the growing wealth gap, others point to race, culture, and gender as reasons for their social and economic anxiety. Social movements such as Occupy Wall Street and the Tea Party are manifestations of these respective anxieties. Again, similar ideological differences appear to be widening in Canada as well.

Even with the plethora of cultures and diversity of viewpoints that comprise a nation like ours, however, there is only one society in Canada. A strong civil society is a goal worth striving for—understanding each other's perspectives and experiences is the best way to maintain and strengthen such a society. Likewise, it is also vitally important to always remember there is only *one* atmosphere that everyone on the planet, indeed, all living creatures, must share. All of these problems will be much more easily solved with an informed and engaged citizenry, and media literacy is one of the most effective ways of fostering this type of citizen, one who is knowledgeable and politically conscious. Further, media literacy is the best way to combat the abundance of fake news that Trump and others promote with reckless abandon. The fake news strategy will likely outlast President Trump, and citizens need to be vigilant around what constitutes a fact versus made-up, bold-faced lies. Indeed, media literate citizens are much less likely to be duped into a false political consciousness that leads them to vote against their own best economic interests, or ignore climate change, or support unnecessary wars, or turn a cold heart toward fellow citizens of another race, religion, culture, or sexual identity.

Media Literacy for Citizenship highlights a critical viewpoint in that it examines issues at a far deeper level than many other textbooks on media literacy do. In particular, the case studies included in some chapters are designed to foster a critically thinking citizenry that understands various social and ecological issues facing Canada and the world today. We are living in perilous times, and an argument could be made that informed and engaged journalists or educators are required now more than ever. They and their future students may be inspired to become as informed as possible and participate in our democracy more than ever before. It is worthwhile for Canadians, indeed, for all citizens of the world, to bear in mind the slogan on the online masthead of the *Washington Post*: "Democracy Dies in Darkness." Citizens need to be informed, they need to demand that their elected representatives be as transparent as possible and not keep important information secret. If citizens do not hold politicians to these ideals, a withering democracy is on the horizon.

An intended goal of the book is to assist journalists and citizens in articulating a critique of the powerful forces that work *against* the attainment of civil society. It *is* a complicated world, and becoming ever more so. A media literate citizen is better positioned to deconstruct discourses intended to obfuscate the issues, such as the oft-heard trickle-down economics of neoliberalism, and the so-called hoax of climate change. The wealth gap is increasing in Canada and the United States; the Earth's atmosphere is getting warmer, and the extreme weather events more severe. It is the burning of fossil fuels that poses a major threat to our future well-being, *not* Islam, feminism, or the rights of LGBTQ+ people. As this book demonstrates, a media literate citizen would understand these things. Indeed, media literacy in the context of this book is understanding the role of the media as a hegemonic device, and seeing its potential as a counter-hegemonic force.

The book aims to impress upon students important questions and ideas to aid in the comprehension of trends and events in Canada, the United States, and the world. It is our contention that Canadians must be aware of how the media addresses social, economic, and political issues in the United States, not only in Canada. Geopolitical forces influence what occurs in Canada—it is wise to be aware of them and to understand them. Media literacy is a powerful instrument in the service of these aims. The book's subtitle, *A Canadian Perspective*, refers to how we view the role of the media from our vantage point as Canadians. For the most part, the book focuses on Canada, but by necessity it also frequently concentrates on American media coverage of politics in the United States. The chapters on fake news and the climate change denial movement are examples of our Canadian perspective on our neighbours to the south.

The 10 chapters of *Media Literacy for Citizenship* examine print journalism and social media more than television and radio. Some important topics have out of necessity over space concerns been given short shrift. Blogging occasionally enters the discussions, but not to an in-depth extent. The first five chapters are explorations of the landscape of the media today—some are more general, while others are more specific. Chapters 6 through 9 each examine in a comprehensive manner how the media present a specific issue. All of these issues are of vital importance to civil society. The final chapter addresses the role and future of journalism in contemporary Canadian society.

At times, the mainstream media is presented as an obstacle to strengthening civil society. This criticism is not to suggest that we do away with the mainstream media. Rather, it is to advocate for journalism to strive to attain its most noble function, which is to strengthen our democracy, to foster an informed and engaged citizenry. *Media Literacy for Citizenship* asks the media and educators to help foster a politically conscious citizenry able to think critically and solve the serious problems that threaten our society and the planet's well-being. This is a tall order to be sure, but one that is both necessary and possible.

CHAPTER 1: IDEOLOGY CRITIQUE AND THE MEDIA IN AN ERA OF NEOLIBERALISM

Orwell, Huxley, and Marcuse were concerned that democracy was not going to live up to its promise because it requires an informed citizenry. Each described a different but valid threat to democracy. All assumed that knowledge is socially constructed, and upon reflection it is not difficult to see the validity in this position, especially as it pertains to the media. The issues the media focus on, the ways in which groups are represented or not represented, the language used to frame debates, and what is omitted from these debates are some of the ways in which knowledge is socially constructed. Further, all knowledge is ideological and, therefore, has political implications. Understanding the importance of this statement is the goal of this chapter. Indeed, an informed citizenry that comprehends the political implications of what constitutes knowledge is the basis of any truly democratic society. Only a media literate citizenry can possibly understand the forces aligned to dismantle hard-won victories like public healthcare, public education, and other components of the commons.

There are various forms of media literacy. The type of media literacy most required for an informed citizenry, and the focus of this chapter, is concerned with understanding the political ideology behind corporate media. Political ideology is also socially constructed. Citizens must comprehend the major political ideologies in Canada and the US in order to become media literate. These ideologies are conservatism, liberalism, and social democracy. Media literacy is a valuable asset in combatting false political consciousness, or the notion that some people who consider themselves politically aware nevertheless vote against their own best interests. Media literacy is necessary to stop neoliberalism, which in its most blatant expression is the corporate takeover of society. Its main tenets are the deregulation of the private sector, the regulation of the public sector, corporate tax cuts, privatization of the commons, and combatting the collective bargaining rights of workers. The chapter investigates the neoliberal assault on one key component of the commons, namely, the public education system, and includes pedagogy for teaching about political ideology.

CHAPTER 2: BUILDING AN INCLUSIVE SOCIETY: THE ROLE OF ALTERNATIVE MEDIA

While the mainstream media play a strong and important role in conveying information and opinion to citizens, such media do not cover very much beyond the norms and the availability of mainstream society. Yet the reams of information and the issues that do not make it into mainstream media leave a huge lacuna of interesting and inspiring information and ideas that suggest broader and more complete understandings of society, along with new issues not previously noticed before.

The inclusion of alternative views from such media into our society is easily accomplished, should we wish to engage with them, and in fact provides different positions on issues covered in the mainstream media. This chapter includes a list of prominent alternative media in Canada; most or all of the views that the alternative media have show a different, broader, or entirely new point of view.

In addition, social movements have strong connections to alternative media. In fact, a social movement often creates its own media, even if it is a simple newsletter, either online or in hard copy. The "new" social movements (which just means that they are online) also use social media instead of, or along with, online media. A key question to consider when reading this chapter is: do social media as a communication device reach enough of the audience and supply enough of the information that social movements need to be effective?

CHAPTER 3: DEMOCRACY IN A CHANGING LANDSCAPE OF MEDIA SOURCES

Most citizens today are aware that in recent years traditional newspapers are having difficulty surviving financially at the same time as they must compete with social media sites such as Twitter and Facebook. This chapter explores the quickly changing dynamics in contemporary journalism and its evolving effects on citizenship and democracy. It explores some of the reasons why public trust of mainstream media has been waning in recent years. Mainstream journalism has an important role in a vibrant democracy, yet it can also act as a hegemonic device. Since the ascent of neoliberal economics in the 1980s, corporate media are rarely supportive of economic policy or politicians that do not adhere to this doctrine.

Social media advocates, by comparison, claim that new media offer different news to the public on topics and perspectives intentionally or unintentionally omitted in the mainstream media. According to this line of reasoning, the corporate media are *not* offering the public the important news stories they need to become informed citizens. By comparison, social media outlets are able to provide multiple perspectives on almost every issue imaginable. Hence, the reasoning goes, democracy is strengthened by Twitter, Facebook, and other media formats found on the Internet. But is this actually true?

Do social media outlets strengthen or weaken our democracy? Does our political economy pose limits on the extent to which social media are allowed to strengthen democracy? The chapter suggests that social media do indeed provide space for voices and perspectives generally shut out of the public discourse in the mainstream media. Yet there are also democratic shortcomings with social media that only an economically secure mainstream media can provide. A vibrant democracy requires a mainstream media committed to investigative journalism based on an ethos of ethics. Some of the issues covered in this chapter are discussed in greater depth in subsequent chapters.

CHAPTER 4: MEDIA LITERACY IN AN ERA OF FAKE NEWS AND ALTERNATIVE FACTS

Chapter 1 discusses the social construction of knowledge, a concept that makes it virtually impossible for *any* citizen or journalist to be truly objective. Indeed, how a story is framed, and the decisions over who and what to include and exclude are just a few of the ways that bias is inherent in all journalism. Chapter 4 extrapolates upon this notion. Partisanship in the media is usually more overt than bias, and propaganda even more so. In recent decades spin doctors have become more influential in how information is managed and how media presents policy. This trend away from objectivity, however, seemed to take a quantum leap with the election victory of Donald Trump in November 2016. Two new terms quickly entered the public lexicon: *fake news* and *alternative facts*.

Trump is the first president to have his media relations aides invoke the term "alternative facts" when presenting the White House perspective to journalists in the mainstream media. The general consensus is that the Trump administration created the term *alternative facts* merely as a creative way of referring to outright lies. The usage of the term *fake news* is somewhat more complex. Trump is adept at utilizing two variations of the fake news strategy—one is to dismiss negative stories about him by investigative journalists as "fake news," and the other is to completely fabricate stories about his political opponents as a distraction for the media and especially the public to ponder. The former is part of his attack on mainstream media (with the exception of the conservative Fox News) and therefore democracy itself, while the second is an egregious affront to an informed citizenry and our democratic traditions. Further, social media, including Trump's penchant for Twitter, enable fake news stories to go viral.

The focus of this chapter is necessarily on the contemporary United States, although there are signs that right-wing politicians in Canada are also engaging in this obsequious practice. The implications for democracy and civil society are dire as these tendencies toward a post-truth world are left unchecked. The chapter ends with ideas and websites designed to resist this troubling fake news trend.

CHAPTER 5: THE PUBLIC MEDIA CHALLENGE IN A FRACTURED MEDIA SOCIETY

Public media have long been revered and are seen in this chapter as a key element in Canada becoming Canada. To an extent, we can say that, as Canada grew as a nation, public media made that possible—and vice versa. This chapter also connects public media with the public interest, a goal that was clear from its very beginning in the British Broadcasting Corporation (BBC) in England. However, most students have been growing up in a media world of abundance, with little understanding of the meaning of "public media."

In this chapter, we explore Raboy's take on public media—specifically, public broadcasting—in which he extends public media beyond the simple exchange of information that we see in all non-public media. He instead suggests that there is something particular to Canada that binds us together with public broadcasting. Instructors might ask if this is enough to bring us together as a country: Does public broadcasting still have a role to play? Nation building is one thing; surely, having built a nation by now, we can let CBC go? How is it different and unique from other media? One of the keys to continuing public broadcasting could be that, as Raboy has pointed out, it is not so much the broadcasting itself (that is, the technical possibilities that all media have now) that is significant, but instead the experience Canadians have through communicating with each other through public media.

CHAPTER 6: THE "SCIENCE" OF CLIMATE CHANGE AND THE (MIS)INFORMED CITIZEN

Scientific evidence has led to 97 percent of climate scientists concluding that human-caused climate change is happening. Indeed, there is a growing acceptance among climate scientists that in order to mitigate the potential effects of climate change–related catastrophes on living species, the temperature increase must not reach 1.5 degrees Celsius. Chaotic weather patterns, including severe droughts, are becoming the norm. Demonstrable evidence points to melting polar ice caps. Despite the science, however, there are many people in Canada and especially in the United States who do not believe the science, who contend that talk of human-made climate change is a "hoax."

This chapter explores why significant numbers of people believe there is serious disagreement among scientists regarding climate change, when in fact there is not. It examines the role that political ideology plays in the acceptance of climate science. It analyzes the mainstream media's role in explaining this myopia, including the access given to climate change–denying organizations. The chapter gives special attention to these organizations and where their funding comes from. It makes the link between climate change deniers and vested economic interests from fossil fuel industries in both countries. Neoliberal politicians with links to the fossil fuel industries are also implicated. Civil society requires politicians who understand and accept climate science research. Only an informed citizenry will be able to withstand the misinformation coming through mainstream media outlets. This misinformation plays on public fears of a collapsing economy if society dares to confront the fossil fuel industries. This chapter offers suggestions for potential roles that may foment resistance to the powerful lobby of climate change deniers.

CHAPTER 7: THE OTHER: THE CANADIAN MOSAIC HITS A ROADBLOCK?

Canada is now embroiled in issues facing many other Western countries that are challenging our traditional way of life. For more than a century, Canada has been the destination of many thousands of immigrants that have been mostly welcomed more or less with open arms as they meld into Canadian society. However, in recent times, some female immigrants have chosen to continue wearing hijabs or other head scarves. Some Canadians find this disturbing. The chapter discusses this particular situation, along with the concept of the "Other," which suggests "we" (who presume not to be different in some way) are the dominant and thus real inhabitants or citizens, while the "Others" are deemed inferior or lesser or inappropriate citizens. The challenge for us is to begin to see that it is not the Other that must change, but Canadians, if Canada is to be an open society.

The chapter also identifies some additional groups that have been marginalized as being the Other—for example, LGBTQ+ individuals, Indigenous peoples (ironically, the first inhabitants of this land), and Black Canadians—and also some ways in which these groups are engaging in activism in order to have the same rights and freedoms as any other Canadians.

CHAPTER 8: INDIGENOUS REPRESENTATION IN THE MEDIA

In 2015, the Truth and Reconciliation Commission recommended in its report that journalists in Canada become informed on the history of Indigenous peoples and the issues that affect their lives. This chapter is in response to this recommendation, and is a first step in the education of future journalists about issues important to Indigenous peoples in particular, and Canadians in general. In this sense it is different in its orientation to all of the other chapters in the book.

It begins by describing the mainstream media's role in fomenting public resistance to the first land treaty in the province of British Columbia during the 1990s. This is followed by two in-depth sections designed to introduce students first to race theory, and second to the history of land treaties and Indigenous title in Canada. Issues over land treaties in British Columbia and on the prairies are discussed at great length, including the unfulfilled promises made by the federal government to the leaders of the prairie First Nations in the 1870s. The racist residential school policy is highlighted for its legacy that affects so many Indigenous people today.

After the race theory and the history sections, the chapter focuses on common stereotypes used in the media to represent Indigenous peoples from earlier times to the present. It concludes with in-depth looks at two important examples of Indigenous activism in contemporary Canada—Idle No More and Missing and Murdered Indigenous Women—and how the media portray them. The chapter ends on a hopeful note, as it appears that some journalists are beginning to understand these issues.

CHAPTER 9: WAR AND TERROR: MILITARIZATION AND THE FEARFUL CITIZEN

Over time, and particularly in the aftermath of the events of 9/11, Canada has left behind much of its traditional role of peacekeeping and instead has joined either UK or US conflicts. Since then, there has been "anti-terror" legislation, and related legislation. The key difference in war legislation and preparation of troops is that no war was actually declared. Canada's post-9/11 military assignment in Afghanistan simply followed behind the United States and its "shock and awe" approach of conducting a war, which included graphic media photos and tape of bombs being dropped from planes and bursting.

The chapter concludes that the risk of terror and other such threats will always be with us; however, and unfortunately, such a focus will divert us from issues that have made Canada what it is—for example, its traditional role of peacekeeping. Western societies are under constant threat: what kind of government and what kind of media do we need to continue to see ourselves as Canadians?

CHAPTER 10: THE ROLE AND FUTURE OF JOURNALISM IN SOCIETY

Good journalism plays a vital role in a democracy by nurturing and strengthening the flow of information to citizens and, in return, bringing the issues and opinions of the citizens to the broader public. This chapter examines the role that journalism plays, its key relationship with democracy, and issues facing today's journalists. Journalism itself has undergone considerable changes, particularly since the dawn of the Internet.

As citizens, we need to have confidence in the information we get from journalists, while journalism has undergone steep and broad differences that can have an impact on democratic communication. This chapter probes the changes that have degraded and marginalized a profession that society has relied on and continues to need.

The chapter also delves more deeply into some of the ideas introduced in Chapter 2. Instead of a profession that brought us "all the news that's fit to print," now the Internet has fostered a sense that "everyone is a journalist." It is not certain how mainstream media can continue or even survive, as journalists struggle to take on many roles, doing more with less time. This chapter asks, if we value the democratic role of journalism, how can we make journalism survive and what will it look like? In addition, what kind of training should journalists have, or can anyone be a journalist?

A FEW WORDS TO COURSE INSTRUCTORS

This book has been designed for courses in media literacy. It is also relevant for courses in communications, journalism, and citizenship education. The book has been written in such a way that each chapter could be used in a stand-alone format, and as a supplement to courses in other disciplines as well. Instructors of courses in political science, social studies, Indigenous studies, peace studies, and science education would likely find at least one chapter that might prove useful.

Each chapter includes at least one text box, some longer than others. Most of these boxes provide information related to the main topic of the chapter but focus on a sub-topic. At the end of each chapter is a set of questions that should help students focus on some of the important issues raised in the chapter, and most chapters include an extended assignment that some students may wish to research. Following Chapter 10 there is also a glossary of terms used in the book that students may be unfamiliar with. It is our intention that, taken as a whole, readers will find this book helpful in understanding the issues involved in developing the media literate Canadian citizen who is inspired to engage in our democracy.

A FEW WORDS TO STUDENTS

This book has been designed for people interested in how media outlets influence the ways in which Canadians perceive the society in which they live. The focus is especially on mainstream print media (i.e., newspapers), although attention is also given to social media and alternative media online sites. Because you are reading this book, it is presumed that you have an interest in the media and how to make sense of it. Chapter 1 addresses political ideology and the current dominant economic paradigm called *neoliberalism*. This chapter lays the groundwork in order to make the following chapters easier to comprehend.

Whether you are studying to be a journalist, to be an educator, or to work in communications, this book will provide a way of looking at the media in terms of *hegemony* and *counter-hegemony*. After the final chapter, there is a glossary that explains some terms you may be unfamiliar with. You might also appreciate that each chapter includes text boxes that address interesting topics related to the chapter's main focus. Each chapter also includes questions for discussion that are designed to help you consider aspects of the chapter topics not particularly addressed in the chapter. Almost all of the chapters include an extended assignment at the end that will allow you to think critically about the main topic on a deeper level.

Please read the book with an open mind. Do your own fact-checking on any claim you come across that you are unsure of. The main objective of this book is to foster an informed and active citizenry so that civil society and democracy in Canada are strengthened. Very few Canadians would disagree with this goal.

We hope that you find reading the book worthwhile.

1 Ideology Critique and the Media in an Era of Neoliberalism

> Don't you see that the whole aim of Newspeak is to narrow the range of thought? In the end we shall make thoughtcrime literally impossible, because there will be no words in which to express it.
> —George Orwell, *Nineteen Eighty-Four*, 1949

As the quote from George Orwell's (1949/1983) *Nineteen Eighty-Four* suggests, the language used by corporate media outlets is specifically chosen by political forces to achieve political ends. Oftentimes, the language chosen has the intention of inhibiting vigorous debate. Orwell was concerned that those in authority would keep vital information away from the public, that the truth would be hidden from us, and that people would not be able to break free of the constraints imposed by these hegemonic discourses. Foreshadowing the insights of **poststructuralism**, Orwell postulated that the elites would use language to create a captive society, even fill it with fear if that is what was warranted. Was Orwell right? It would seem so, given how many people vote against their own best interests (Frank, 2012, 2004; Orlowski, 2011).

Orwell's contemporary, Aldous Huxley, predicted a different future for Western nations. In *Brave New World* (1932/1998), Huxley described a society in which no one would want to read a book, that the truth would be impossible to distinguish from spectacles of illusion, and that people would tend toward irrelevant distraction rather than comprehension of social forces impinging upon their day-to-day lives. In a somewhat prescient manner, Huxley described an irrelevant society, one that would be fixated on entertainment for the sole purpose of being entertained. Herbert Marcuse (1964) furthers Huxley's thesis by arguing that individuals are integrated into the capitalist system of production and consumption through the entertainment industry. Were Huxley and Marcuse onto something? The preponderance of computer game playing and television viewing of reality shows, sporting, and celebrity events suggests so.

Orwell, Huxley, and Marcuse assumed that knowledge is socially constructed, and upon reflection it is not difficult to see the validity in this position, especially as it pertains to the media. The issues the media focus on, the ways in which groups are represented or not represented, the language used to frame debates, and what is omitted from these debates are some of the ways in which knowledge is socially constructed. Further, all knowledge is ideological and, therefore, has political implications. Understanding the importance of this statement is the goal of this chapter. Indeed, an informed citizenry that comprehends the political implications of what constitutes knowledge is the basis of any truly democratic society. Only a media literate citizenry can possibly understand the forces aligned to dismantle hard-won victories like public healthcare, public education, and other components of the commons. Media literacy is necessary to stop **neoliberalism**, which in its most blatant expression is the corporate takeover of society. Before we discuss neoliberalism, however, it is necessary to discuss media literacy.

SOME RELEVANT THEORY ABOUT MEDIA LITERACY AND RELATED CONCEPTS

In general, there are three main categories of media literacy. One common approach emanates from a *cultural* paradigm—it analyzes how various groups are represented in the media, including advertisements. An excellent example of this type of media literacy is shown in the documentary film series *Killing Us Softly* (1979, 1987, 2000, 2010) by feminist educator Jean Kilbourne. These films address the objectification of females in ads in order to sell products, and analyze the subsequent effects on gender construction and gender relations. The second type of media literacy is also common, and is concerned with traditional liberal democratic concerns of diversity and voices of dissent (Cottle, 2003). This type, similar to the previous one that focused on representation, is also part of the cultural paradigm in that it explores "symbolic power" (Cottle, 2003, p. 7) and gives voice to groups that typically do not belong to the elites. The increasing number of representatives of various cultural groups in the mainstream media is one aspect that concerns this type of media literacy.

There is much value in both of these kinds of media literacy, but they will not be discussed here.

The type of media literacy most required for an informed citizenry, and the focus of this chapter, is concerned with understanding the political ideology behind corporate media. In 2003, prominent Canadian journalist Lawrence Martin made the case that corporate media in Canada had shifted significantly to the right. A report from the Canadian Media Concentration Research Project (Tencer, 2015) found that in 2011, 95 percent of Canadian newspapers endorsed the Harper Conservatives, while in 2015, 71 percent of newspaper endorsements went to the same party. In both cases, the percentage of newspaper endorsements for the Conservatives was almost three times that of the popular vote. This is ironic given that conservative politicians in Canada (and the US) claim that mainstream media is biased against them.

This type of media literacy also aims to illuminate the machinations of power by demonstrating how powerful interests use the media to strive for a "definitional advantage" in public discourse on important social, political, and economic issues (Cottle, 2003, p. 7). It assumes the social construction of knowledge and the media's relationship to "wider structures and systems of power" (Cottle, 2003, p. 3). One example of definitional advantage is the mainstream media's frequent use of the term *tax relief* in place of *tax cuts*. Tax cuts benefit the economic elites, and with subsequent cuts to social programs and the commons, do significant damage to the well-being of the working and middle classes. It is important for citizens to understand the power inherent in these word plays. Without critical reflection and comprehension by citizens, definitional advantage results in perspectives that strengthen the power of political and economic elites, perspectives that become accepted as common sense. This is a form of what critical theorists call **hegemony**.

Hegemony refers to the ideal representation of the interests of the most privileged groups as universal interests, which are then accepted by the masses as the natural economic, political, and social order. This conception of hegemony explains how social hierarchies and order are maintained within capitalist societies. Force is not required to maintain these hierarchies if citizens willingly give their consent to accept them (Gramsci, 1971). The general acceptance of tax cuts for the richest Americans is an example of this (Frank, 2012).

The effects of hegemony are so difficult to combat because hegemonic discourses shape how people view life itself through a set of social relations that enables meaning to be made. Unfortunately for those people not belonging to economically privileged groups, which is the majority of Americans and

Canadians, this meaning often results paradoxically in an unfair distribution of wealth and power. In other words, resisting hegemonic discourses becomes more difficult as these discourses colonize the minds of citizens. The effects of these discourses in the corporate media are what Orwell captured in the excerpt at the beginning of this chapter: "the whole aim of Newspeak is to narrow the range of thought." Newspeak refers to a way of speaking by certain politicians and bureaucrats that is intentionally ambiguous and misleading. Journalists of similar ideological perspectives may adopt these manipulative terms. A contemporary example of Newspeak is the so-called "war on terror" that resulted in Bill C-51. Also known as the anti-terror bill, this legislation "provides excessive powers to federal agencies to monitor and profile ordinary Canadians" (LeBlanc, 2015).

Another important aspect of hegemony that must be considered is *false political consciousness*. This term features prominently in critical theory, and refers to the purpose served by thought itself in the collective life of humanity. It attempts to explain why some people (for instance, the working classes) consider themselves to be politically conscious and yet vote against their own best interests. In *What's the Matter with Kansas?* (2004), Thomas Frank contends that the backlash against progressive politics in many parts of 21st-century America is about a corporate elite that has managed to manipulate "cultural anger … to achieve economic ends" (p. 5). He posits that the corporate elites obtain support from the working classes by having politicians and journalists supportive of their agenda champion conservative positions on cultural issues such as gay rights and abortion. Frank further extrapolates that there is a "primary contradiction of the backlash: it is a working-class movement that has done incalculable harm to working-class people" (p. 6). Public support for tax cuts for the country's most wealthy citizens during the presidencies of George W. Bush and Donald Trump attests to this, and exemplifies how hegemonic processes work to further entrench the interests of the elite. Deconstructing false political consciousness is an important goal of critical media literacy. In order to do so, an understanding of political ideology is necessary.

POLITICAL IDEOLOGY: A VERY SHORT PRIMER

Ideology is about the "thought-production of human beings" (Giroux, 1981, p. 19). A political ideology contains "a specific set of assumptions and social practices" that leads to various "beliefs, expectations and biases" (p. 7). In other words, a political ideology socially constructs its own knowledge. Further, political ideology is at the root of most important debates in our society on matters of social, economic, and political relations. Ironically, there is a lack of awareness and general knowledge of political ideology and how it organizes our lives. A media literate citizenry would change this.

In order for citizens to become media literate, it is crucial for them to have a comprehension of the major political ideologies in Canada and the US. This is the first step in understanding the hegemonic and counter-hegemonic discourses that they are bombarded with. We are arguing for citizens to be educated in political ideology at a more analytic level (see Orlowski, 2011). It is helpful to briefly describe the core characteristics of the three major political ideologies in Canada and the United States: liberalism, social democracy—or what in the American context Rorty (1998) refers to as the *reformist left*—and conservatism.

The first ideology to articulate a new way of perceiving the world and organizing society through human reason, **liberalism**, arose during the **Enlightenment**. *Emancipation of the masses* and *democracy* are the progeny of classical liberalism. Initially, liberals were quite happy to engage in the pursuit of wealth through laissez-faire economic policy and the conquest of nature. By the early 1900s, however, classical liberalism in many western European nations had evolved into progressive or reform liberalism in which a more state-interventionist approach developed (partially to appease growing working-class discontent). Reform liberalism, based upon **Keynesian economics**, also included a tempered individualism, which developed out of the inevitable tension between an ideal of liberty and an ideal of equality. In North America, only during and after the Great Depression and World War II did classical liberalism give way to the more progressive version of liberalism. (Beginning in the 1980s, Keynesian economics has been replaced by a model of unfettered capitalism called neoliberalism.) Liberalism has become associated with human rights that emphasize inclusivity around social issues.

Socialism can be seen as a spin-off ideology from liberalism, another attempt to realize the goal of emancipation. For Karl Marx, liberalism's major flaw was its emphasis on the individual as the most important unit in society. Because of grotesque disparities in wealth in 19th-century Europe, Marx and other socialists considered social class to be the crucial aspect of a person's identity. As the capitalist system demonstrated its resilience by surviving the Great Depression of the 1930s, and knowledge of the atrocities of the Stalin-led Soviet Union became known to people in Western nations, the popularity of socialism began to wane. Toward the mid-20th century, a new leftist political ideology popular in parts of Europe gained currency in Canada and to some extent in the US, a hybrid of socialism and liberalism merging together to form **social democracy** (Orlowski, 2011). The basic tenets of social democracy include an acceptance of a regulated capitalism with the intention of helping those social groups that have little chance of improving their economic standard of living. It also shares with liberalism a respect for *the rights of the individual*, something that most forms of socialism do not value to the same extent. (See Box 1.1 on individual rights versus individualism.)

BOX 1.1: INDIVIDUAL RIGHTS VERSUS INDIVIDUALISM

There appears to be some confusion around two concepts that are vastly different in important ways. These two concepts are *individual rights* and *individualism*. Yes, they do sound similar, but from an ideological standpoint they are light years apart. In the current era of neoliberalism and corporate power, the first discourse seems to be in retreat, while the other thrives.

Individual rights was one of the major victories for citizens in Western nations and is an important component of civil society. *Individualism*, on the other hand, especially the rugged individualism symbolized in American pop and consumer cultural representation, has very little civility in it at all. It is a strategy promoted by American propagandists. Individual rights refers to basic human rights around economic and especially social issues, while individualism is an Orwellian word play that promotes a pull-yourself-up-by-the-bootstraps philosophy. The former is about increasing inclusivity, while the latter means that significant numbers of people are to be economically excluded. This translates into a dismantling of the social welfare state.

Despite two world wars and examples of extreme genocide, the 20th century is considered to be the Century of Human Rights. This dynamic reached its zenith in 1948 with the UN's Universal Declaration of Human Rights. Discrimination against an individual based on identity markers such as race, culture, class, gender, religion, and nationality was strongly discouraged. Many Western nations followed the UN's lead by getting rid of racist legislation (aka, institutionalized racism). For example, in 1951 the Canadian federal government amended the Indian Act to allow First Nations people to once again practice their traditional cultural ceremonies such as the powwow, the Sun Dance, the sweat lodge, and the potlatch. (They had been outlawed in 1881, although many First Nations still practiced them.) In spite of this amendment, Indigenous peoples in Canada have struggled to maintain their traditions.

Racism still existed after the removal of these laws, of course, mostly in the form of racist attitudes or systemic racism. But at least getting rid of racist laws was a major first step. And yes, today many Western nations are in the process of including the rights of gays and lesbians into their body politic. These are *human* rights, not special rights as many conservatives would have us believe. Individual rights are an important aspect of a socially just and civil society. For the most part, they are attempts to make society more inclusive, especially regarding social issues.

So what does *individualism* refer to? In the context of the United States, the *rugged individual discourse* hints at the self-made man (or woman), one who has been able to pull themselves up by the bootstraps and make their own way. In the past few decades, individualism has been framed within Ayn Rand's economic philosophy, called *objectivism*, which is a version of *libertarianism*. In simple terms, **libertarians** believe that no one should expect help from them, and in turn, they should not expect any help from others. It should not be too difficult to see that such a philosophy supports tax cuts for the wealthy (and for everyone else), as well as the end of social programs and the entire social welfare state. Advocates of Keynesian economics know that libertarianism is the antithesis of civil society. Similarly, the economic paradigm known as neoliberalism (aka, the corporate agenda) relies to a large extent on the acceptance of the rugged individual discourse for its own success.

The acceptance of individualism as an underpinning of American society is enabling the neoliberal agenda to become even more entrenched than it already is. Of course, all people are individuals, but they are also members of social groups. These social groups have unequal status in our society, as well as unequal access to resources. A civil society comprising media literate citizens who understand the power of the collective would work toward rectifying these social injustices.

In sum, a civil society supports the expansion of individual rights. At the same time, it discourages rugged individualism as an ethos for its citizens to live by. Citizens can enact agency on this front by voting in governments committed to a set of individual rights that includes, among laudable progressive positions on social issues, the right to a life of dignity from an economic standpoint. A media literate citizenry is able to combat neoliberal forces and strive to once again build strong and healthy communities, including a vibrant commons.

Source: Adapted from Orlowski, P. (2013). "The Universal Declaration of Human Rights versus the Marlboro Man." *Rabble.ca.*

Conservatism as an ideology arose as an alternative to the rapid changes occurring in Europe because of liberalism and new-found wealth (Schwarzmantel, 1998). A central tenet of conservatism is that society should be led by a stable group of people who, through past experience, would have the ability to do so wisely. For them, human nature is flawed. For conservatives, tradition gains strength from the long-held views inherent in the common sense of the community. Authority should be respected. The idea of each person accepting their place in society at least partially explains why there has been a vociferous conservative backlash against feminism, multiculturalism, and trade unions in recent years. Today conservatism has evolved into an ideology that promotes traditional hierarchical social values with aggressive support for the interests of the economic super-elite. The US-based Tea Party movement is a striking example of this evolution.

These three political ideologies—liberalism, social democracy, and conservatism—are the major ones vying for power in Canada. In the US, the political struggle is primarily between the ideological binary of conservatism and liberalism. Yet, as Rorty (1998) explains, social democracy, or the reformist left, has also made many contributions to American society. Moreover, recently Vermont senator Bernie Sanders promoted a social democratic agenda in his bid to win the Democratic presidential nomination in 2016. It is noteworthy for the focus on neoliberalism in this chapter that Sanders is particularly adamant about the need to regulate Wall Street and the Big Banks. This could at least partially explain why the corporate media ignored Sanders' campaign for the first part of the Democratic primaries (Byers, 2016).

How does this relate to media literacy? Counter-hegemonic perspectives in corporate media outlets are either marginalized or ignored altogether. There will never be a front-page headline, for instance, that touts the benefits of raising taxes on corporations. In short, corporate media have corporate interests. Citizens need to understand this in order to become media literate and therefore better informed. (See Box 1.2 on teaching about political ideology.)

Ideologies change over time as social and economic conditions change. In recent years, the corporate agenda has gained political traction in both the United States and Canada. Academics and some journalists call this agenda neoliberalism, and many will recognize its traits from knowledge of our collective past.

NEOLIBERALISM: LAISSEZ-FAIRE ECONOMICS REVISITED

Neoliberalism can be a confusing term for students to comprehend. After all, progressive Americans and Canadians accept the basic tenets of liberalism in

BOX 1.2: TEACHING FOR COMPREHENSION OF POLITICAL IDEOLOGY

Left-wing ideas in Western democracies are rooted in a sense of freedom, equality, egalitarianism, human rights, and social justice. In the main, these ideas champion a strong social welfare state and the rights of any oppressed group, such as women, gays, the elderly, the disabled, religious minorities, and non-White peoples. The ideas of the right wing, on the other hand, have evolved to include policies that encourage the individual to advance economically and socially on their own accord, without help from the state. As well, the right wing is dismissive of claims by various minorities that the system is inherently unfair. Conservatives and right-wing liberals have co-opted the notion of meritocracy in order to maintain privilege in current-day social, political, and economic hierarchies.

An effective way to have students understand what is meant by the left and the right in political terms is to *consider all issues as either economic or social*. Economic issues are those that represent significant amounts of money, while social issues do not. For example, tax reform is an economic issue, while capital punishment is a social issue. Some issues, such as healthcare, are both social and economic, yet, to save on getting mired in semantics, the basic economic/social distinction is useful (see Figure 1.1).

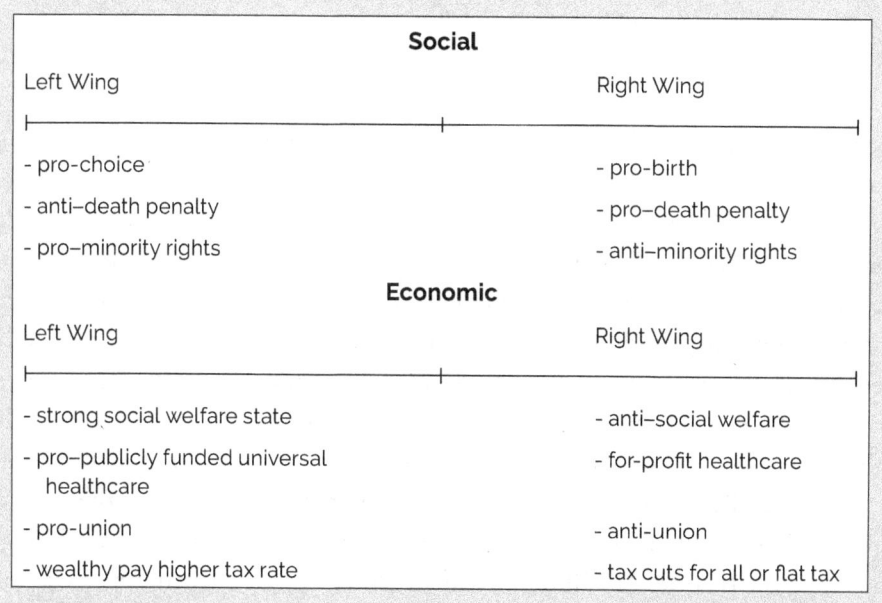

Social	
Left Wing	Right Wing
- pro-choice	- pro-birth
- anti–death penalty	- pro–death penalty
- pro–minority rights	- anti–minority rights
Economic	
Left Wing	Right Wing
- strong social welfare state	- anti–social welfare
- pro–publicly funded universal healthcare	- for-profit healthcare
- pro-union	- anti-union
- wealthy pay higher tax rate	- tax cuts for all or flat tax

Figure 1.1: Left and Right on the Social and Economic Spectra

(continued)

> With political ideologies and political issues divided into the economic and the social, students are able to make headway around why certain media are called left wing by some, and the very same media outlets are called right wing or right-leaning by others. For example, during the past few federal elections in Canada, leaders of the federal Liberal Party have appealed to social democrats (that is, supporters of the New Democratic Party) by espousing values that have appeared to be out of the same concerns for justice, and insisting that NDP votes should therefore switch to the Liberals. The truth of the matter is that on social issues, these Liberal leaders are correct. On economic issues, however, the two parties diverge significantly—the Liberals are to the right of centre, closer to where the Conservatives are positioned, while the NDP are to the left of centre. And yet, this distinction of the Liberal Party being left wing on social issues and right wing on economic issues is rarely mentioned in the corporate media.
>
> In the United States, the media usually refer to the Democrats as left wing, and on social issues they do champion the rights of minorities. Yet, on economic issues, both parties develop policy supported by the corporate sector and most wealthy individuals. In other words, neither of the two major American parties would be considered left wing on economic issues.
>
> *Source:* Adapted from Orlowski, P. (2014). "Critical Media Literacy and Social Studies: Paying Heed to Orwell and Huxley." In E. W. Ross (Ed.), *The Social Studies Curriculum* (4th ed.) (pp. 335–352). Albany, NY: State University of New York Press.

terms of individual rights. Neoliberalism, however, refers only to economic issues, not social issues. The "liberal" part of neoliberalism refers to its association with classical liberalism that was discussed above in terms of liberalizing the movement of money. Adding to the confusion, both liberal and conservative governments in the US and Canada have passed neoliberal legislation. Many social democratic governments in Western nations have also been influenced by neoliberal economic orthodoxy. This kind of legislation has first and foremost the goal of increasing corporate shareholders' profits over all other concerns. The following discussion will help clarify this focus on corporate power and profits.

Neoliberalism's comeback as an economic paradigm began with the work of Fredrick Hayek (1944) and gained more popularity in the United States through the economic theories of Milton Friedman (2002). It has elicited various definitions from academics since the 1970s when the first attempt at its implementation into a nation's economic policy took place in Chile (Boas & Gans-Moore,

2009). Since then, neoliberal policy has become the norm in most capitalist nations today, replacing the more centrist Keynesian economic paradigm that was dominant in Western nations from the late 1940s until the early 1980s (Harvey, 2005). There are four main tenets to neoliberalism on the domestic front: the deregulation of private industry, tax cuts (primarily for corporations and the wealthy), privatization of the commons, and the weakening of collective bargaining rights for workers (Orlowski, 2011, 2015). On the international front, neoliberal politicians push for trade arrangements that are euphemistically called "free" trade deals, all of which give more power to corporations (Klein, 2014).

In short, neoliberalism refers to economic and public policy based on a powerful discursive formation that aims to entrench the corporate agenda throughout society. Recent calls for austerity, attacks on public sector workers, and the threat to seniors' pensions are all part of the neoliberal agenda (Caplan, 2012; Kennedy & Press, 2012). Citizens in many countries have been inundated with a "permanent campaign of persuasion" in the mainstream media to garner support for economic policies favoured by neoliberals and politicians willing to implement them (Kozolanka, 2007, p. 7). Of course, social values are also affected, but economic and political policy is the main focus of neoliberalism (Albo & Fanelli, 2014).

In high school social studies and history courses, students learn that income inequality, inhumane conditions for workers, and the lack of social safety nets were features of *laissez-faire economics*. Government-imposed regulations on industry were seen as impediments to financial profit for the capitalist class, and consequently, were unacceptable. Supporters of this doctrine in the 18th, 19th, and early 20th centuries preferred the *invisible hand* of the market to influence economic arrangements, to use the term proffered by the Scottish economist and philosopher Adam Smith (1776/2003) in *The Wealth of Nations*. They were hostile to the state intervening in economic affairs, especially around the regulation of industry.

It is clear that similar support for the deregulation of industry has permeated the thinking of many of the economic and political elites today. The economic crisis that befell most Western economies in 2008 resulted from the deregulation of industry in general, and the financial industry in particular (Frank, 2012). Paradoxically, this near collapse has resulted in calls for even greater austerity measures against the downtrodden and more economic opportunity for those who were doing well in the first place. With a streak of false consciousness, some middle- and working-class people support these policies that are clearly not in their best interests. An understanding of a powerful contemporary hegemonic discursive formation trumpeted in the corporate media offers a partial explanation.

One particularly effective discourse emanating from corporate propagandists in the mainstream media is the frequently heard *trickle-down* theory stating that neoliberalism will help everyone no matter their social and economic standing—the deregulated economy will create a rising tide and all of the boats, big and small, will rise with it (Harvey, 2005). The evidence shows otherwise, however. The burgeoning gap in income inequality is dramatically widening to proportions not seen since the 1930s (Frank, 2012; Albo, Gindin, & Panitch, 2010). Related to the trickle-down discourse is the *corporations as job-creators* discourse. This discourse suggests that by cutting corporate taxes, more jobs would be created, and by corollary, there would be more workers paying taxes that would be used to strengthen the commons, including public healthcare and public education. Yet research in Canada and the United States demonstrates that large corporations do not use the money gained from tax cuts to create jobs, but instead hoard the money or pay dividends to shareholders (Hungerford, 2012; Stanford, 2011). In fact, the International Monetary Fund (IMF) recently released a report called "Neoliberalism: Oversold?" in which the authors conclude that cutbacks in social spending and privatization of the commons have resulted in more problems than with Keynesian economics (Ostry, Loungani, & Furceri, 2016).

Despite this rather late admission by the IMF, hegemonic neoliberal discourses are extremely powerful and difficult to challenge. Neoliberalism has thus affected almost all aspects of civic life in Canada and beyond (Orlowski, 2015). Under the banner of fiscal responsibility, neoliberal supporters in government, in the private sector, and in the media want opportunities for the few to profit from privatizing the commons. They want funding cuts to public education at the same time that government funding for private schools is increasing (Willcocks, 2016)—neoliberalism's assault on public schools will be discussed in a subsequent section. In Canada, entrepreneurial forces are pushing for the creation of a two-tiered healthcare system to replace the country's treasured universal public healthcare system and tacking on "Medical Services Plan" fees to erode the notion of a free, public service. It is ironic that the province where Medicare was born, Saskatchewan, currently has a provincial government that is incrementally privatizing its once coveted healthcare system (CBC News, 2016). Government-run pension plans in both countries are also vulnerable.

Perhaps somewhat surprisingly, much of the public does not seem too disturbed to hear these discourses during a period in which the gap between the rich and the poor is increasing to grotesque proportions in both countries. The mainstream media's focus on Huxley's spectacle and its ubiquitous usage of Orwell's Newspeak partially account for this passivity. Yet the massive Occupy

Wall Street movement demonstrated that a significant segment of people are beginning to make some powerful connections and new coalitions. The support among young American voters for Bernie Sanders' bid to become the president in 2016 was also a testament to a growing political consciousness. A media literate citizenry will make these movements even stronger.

For several decades, the economic elites of the United States and Canada have dismissed any notion that *they* have been implicated in any kind of class warfare. Indeed, the elites and the media pundits working on their behalf often use the term *class war* whenever they detect "public contempt for investment bankers" (Frank, 2012, p. 37). Yet, despite the media's attempt at obfuscation, when one considers increasingly massive gaps in wealth, there can be little doubt that neoliberalism is indeed "a project aimed at the restoration of class power" (Anijar & Gabbard, 2009, pp. 45–46). Harvey (2005) states that "if it looks like class struggle and acts like class war then we have to name it unashamedly for what it is" (p. 202). From this perspective, policies that support austerity are considered to be instruments of class warfare. Consumers of mainstream media, however, would not hear it described as such.

Neoliberalism provides the basis for a new class war, one that is attempting to replace the Fordist arrangement between capital and labour, and end the influence of Keynesian economics. Evidence suggests that there has been a class war enacted by the economic and political elites for over 30 years—first, the victims were working-class families, and in recent years the middle class has been targeted (Monsebraaten, 2011; OECD, 2011; Yalnizyan, 2011). A false political consciousness is leading many working- and middle-class people to support neoliberal policies for deregulation, privatization of the commons, union-busting, and tax cuts for corporations and the wealthiest citizens (Frank, 2012). Neoliberalism emphasizes that the role of the state must include creating markets in areas such as education, healthcare, social security, and environmental pollution (Harvey, 2005). Put more succinctly, "[n]eoliberalism attacks human dignity" (Kumar, 2015). If more citizens understood this, it is unlikely that citizens would support the neoliberal project.

CORPORATE MEDIA AS A HEGEMONIC DEVICE

In *Media Think* (2002), James Winter argues that the concentration of Canadian media ownership to a shrinking group of powerful corporations has resulted in media championing the interests of the elite by a consistent and constant repetition of hegemonic discourses. The concentration of media ownership makes it easier to marginalize counter-hegemonic discourses. Winter developed his notion of "media think" on what George Orwell, writing in the 1940s, referred to as "the prevailing orthodoxy":

> At any given moment there is an orthodoxy, a body of ideas which it is assumed that all right-thinking people will accept without question.... Anyone who challenges the prevailing orthodoxy finds himself silenced with surprising effectiveness. A genuinely unfashionable opinion is almost never given a fair hearing, either in the popular press or in the highbrow periodicals. (cited in Winter, 2002, p. xxvi)

The prevailing orthodoxy represents the set of values and positions associated with a particular political ideology that is accepted and promoted by the majority of mainstream media outlets. Karl Marx referred to this as "the dominant ideology." For the past few decades, virtually every mainstream media outlet has supported the neoliberal economic doctrine. In other words, neoliberalism is a major component of the current prevailing orthodoxy.

A profound example of silencing any challenge to the prevailing orthodoxy is the almost total invisibility of Noam Chomsky in mainstream American media. Chomsky is a linguist and longtime professor at the Massachusetts Institute of Technology (MIT) and is perhaps the world's foremost scholar on the role of corporate media as a propagandist instrument in the service of the elites. The social activist and media critic, who has been politically active since the 1960s, has written over 100 books and is considered by many to be one of the preeminent political intellectual giants of the 20th century and into the 21st century. He is perhaps best known for his insightful critique of American foreign policy and the ways in which American hegemony manifests domestically and in the global context. Edward Herman and Chomsky (1988) have added the term *manufacturing consent* to the political lexicon to point out the propagandistic function of the mainstream media in the service of the elites. Remarkably, Chomsky has not been invited to appear in *any* major American media outlet for many years (Rosenmann, 2016). His unwavering commitment to speaking truth to power is likely the reason that he has not been invited to speak in the mainstream media in recent decades. There is no other credible explanation as to why an American intellectual of such international stature would be blocked from sharing his views with a mainstream audience in the United States. The silencing of Chomsky demonstrates the validity of Orwell's premise. This is a classic case of the corporate media intentionally employing omission as a hegemonic strategy.

Winter (2002) claims that the corporate media have applied Orwell's theory of prevailing orthodoxy to a massive list of topics pertaining to economics in Canada and the United States. Perspectives that challenge the prevailing hegemony are marginalized, distorted, or, as with Chomsky himself, completely ignored. Some of these topics include strikes versus lockouts, royalty rates in North America versus royalty rates in Europe, the weakening of pension plans across Western nations at the same time, corporate tax rates today compared to the 1960s, industrial catastrophes and deregulation, worker wages today versus the 1960s, the true costs of private healthcare compared to public healthcare, and the true costs of using fossil fuels compared to alternative energy sources. Corporate media may allow the token op-ed column that challenges hegemonic economic thinking. But for the main, they have been instrumental in pushing the neoliberal agenda into policy as the social welfare state built by Keynesian economics and progressive tax reform is being incrementally dismantled. In other words, corporate media has demonstrated its effectiveness as a hegemonic device.

The situation suggests that mainstream media have become an important influence on the ways in which citizens view the world. Media expert David Buckingham (2003) concurs—he argues that the media have overcome the family, the church, and the school to become the dominant socializing force in Western nations. It is important to examine why corporate media's influence has increased to the extent that it has.

THE MEDIA IN AN ERA OF MEGA-SPIN

Spin has long been one of the most effective and mystifying strategies used by governments and other political operatives to gain the "definitional advantage" mentioned earlier. In terms of media manipulation, *spin* is understood to be the power of persuasion used in tandem with rhetoric and propaganda. It is an important concept for the general public to understand.

> The term "spin" is conventionally used to refer to the process and products of purposively managing information in order to present institutions, individuals, policies, practices and/or ideas in a favourable light and thereby mobilize support for them. Attempts to manage news and political communications are not new. (Gewirtz, Dickson, & Power, 2004, p. 321)

Despite the fact that spin and propaganda have been used for centuries, they are still extremely effective means of swaying significant numbers of people to accept a perspective that may not be in their best interests. The support for across-the-board tax cuts among working and middle classes is a case in point. Why does spin remain so influential in the minds of citizens?

Part of the reason is the increasingly sophisticated art of propaganda. There are legions of propagandists, also known as *spin doctors*, working for government, industry, and other organizations. Spin doctors are "political advisors responsible for policy presentation and information management" (Gewirtz, Dickson, & Power, 2004, p. 324). Public relations spin doctoring has been a developing profession since the early 20th century, yet since the 1970s there has been an exponential growth in the numbers of professional spin doctors (Council of Public Relations Firms, 2005).

We are living in a time in which spin in its commonly understood form has been hyperbolized to obscene proportions. Linguist George Lakoff (2004) points to examples of legislation passed by the George W. Bush administration. These include The Clear Skies Act, which enabled polluting corporations to increase the amount of toxins they admit into the atmosphere, and The Healthy Forests Act, which allowed forests in federal parks to be clear cut. An example in the Canadian context is the former Conservative government's legislation called The Clean Air Act that would force corporate polluters to clean up their act—50 years down the road! Moreover, some politicians and journalists use Orwellian Doublespeak terms to conceal the truth from the public. Examples that you may have heard include *intensity targets*, which pertains to acceptable toxin levels, and *enhanced interrogation* in place of *torture*.

In sum, spin doctors are able to utilize mega-spin to meet their neoliberal objectives because of several factors. These include the economic stress that almost all working-class and most middle-class families are experiencing, the general public's fascination with spectacle, and most important of all, the development of a sophisticated use of language to deceive. Spin doctors understand that the manipulation of words can be effective in manipulating reality for media illiterate people. Moreover, whoever controls the meaning of words influences the hegemonic discourses that work to control what the people understand of their situation. As a case study, neoliberalism's effect on public education will make this point clear.

NEOLIBERALISM'S ASSAULT ON PUBLIC EDUCATION

> The media's coverage of education plays a pivotal role in shaping, reinforcing, and normalizing contemporary discourses of education policy, particularly around school reform and teacher quality, including merit pay and what accounts for teaching and learning.
>
> —Garcia, 2015

A strong public education system has been one of the hallmarks of civil society since the late 19th century (Dewey, 1916). Before the advent of public schools, only the children of the elite developed strong skills in literacy and numeracy, and by extension, thinking. Public schooling changed all that. It has enabled some members of marginalized groups to become educated so that they become professionals in various occupations (Orlowski, 2011). A significant number of people from non-elite groups have long considered *public* education as the best vehicle for "redressing social inequalities through the equalization of educational opportunity" (Apple, 2004, p. 18). If this is the case, why has the public allowed their cherished school system to be systematically de-funded and weakened over the past few decades?

Once again, the answer lies in the numerous strategies employed by neoliberal politicians and mainstream media outlets (Ford, Porfilio, & Goldstein, 2015). Most of this effort supports the privatization of schools, and this includes the push for teacher accountability and the bashing of teacher unions. Charter schools and voucher schools continue to be in vogue in the United States. Charter schools receive government funding but are privately owned, a clear example of the neoliberal tenet of privatizing the commons. The school voucher system is like a lottery in which a few students from lower socioeconomic school districts are allowed to go to well-funded schools. Carr and Porfilio (2011) contend that these initiatives are "linked to further eradicating public education, promoting corporate interests over the needs of children and the U.S. at large, and pressuring the public to accept the notion that corporate involvement will improve all elements in the social world" (p. 7). These hegemonic neoliberal discourses are especially prevalent in the media (Faltin Osborn & Sierk, 2015). The supportive ways that the "edupreneurial" Teach For America has been cast provide an example of how the media encourages corporate involvement in schools. The Canadian version, called Teach For Canada, has been having more difficulty in gaining acceptance, most likely because neoliberalism has not been as readily accepted here as south of the border, especially around privatization of the commons.

Neoliberal proponents for corporate intrusion into public schools have also relied on other forms of media for support. They have utilized the American journal *Education Week* to promote the virtues of Teach For America and the importance of standardized testing to measure teacher quality (Gautreaux, 2015). Hollywood films like *Bad Teacher* imply that the neoliberal agenda for education is the norm and an "inescapable reality that students, teachers, administrators, and parents encounter in their everyday experiences in the school" (Garcia, 2015). Interestingly, popular television shows like *The Simpsons* employ subtle techniques to critique the neoliberal model of privatization and performativity (Garcia, 2015; Kiedrowski, 2013). For example, Kiedrowski (2013) describes a scene in which the pressures put upon students to perform well on high-stakes standardized testing led an unprepared Lisa Simpson to cheat on a test by buying the answer key beforehand from one of the ne'er-do-well boys.

On the other hand, some forms of media create space for counter-hegemonic discourses. For example, political cartoons are often utilized to open up a discursive space that "questions the benefits of charter school reform and stands in opposition to the neoliberal discourses now influencing educational policy" (Feuerstein, 2015). Some teachers have taken to social media to reframe teaching from a non-neoliberal perspective. Through blogs, Twitter, and Facebook, teachers are able to "speak back to dominant discourses" and challenge neoliberalism on education policy issues (Shiller, 2015, p. 2). Chapter 3 of this book addresses the ways in which social media forms challenge hegemonic discourses in mainstream media.

The neoliberal influence on educational reform, however, is strongly promoted in the corporate media. Current trends in education reform in both the United States and Canada have promoted teacher accountability through mandatory standardized testing, increased funding for private schools, and the denigration of the teaching profession and teacher unions.

A MEDIA LITERATE CITIZEN REQUIRES AN UNDERSTANDING OF POLITICAL IDEOLOGY

This chapter explained that the first step in becoming media literate is to develop an understanding of political ideology. There are difficulties in attaining a politically conscious citizenry, such as Huxley's contention that people are more interested in entertainment and spectacle than they are in learning about the economic forces that shape and define their lives. The chapter included a discussion of the importance of Orwell's insight around language used to deceive and manipulate. The promotion of spectacle and the use of Orwellian Newspeak are common hegemonic strategies used by the corporate media.

All citizens should understand where the three major political ideologies in Canada and the United States today—liberalism, social democracy, and conservatism—stand on social and especially economic issues. It is the lack of a politically conscious citizenry that allows hegemonic discourses to resonate to the point that many people vote against their own best interests. The role of the corporate media is paramount in this dynamic. All citizens need to understand that in the role of hegemonic device, corporate media have corporate interests.

We are currently living in a perilous time in which corporate power is unprecedented. The economic paradigm known as neoliberalism has replaced Keynesian economics, and the standard of living for working- and middle-class people has decreased because of this. In particular, the gains made over the second half of the 20th century for the commons and a collectivist view of society have been thoroughly weakened because of a steady bombardment of hegemonic discourses in the corporate media. The chapter concluded with a case study of how neoliberal discourses have attacked the public school system. A media literate citizenry would make these processes much more difficult, and in turn make it much more difficult for the economic elites to succeed in this neoliberal project.

QUESTIONS FOR DISCUSSION

1. When progressive politicians discuss wealth inequality, the mainstream media and right-wing politicians accuse them of engaging in class warfare. Is this a valid criticism? Discuss.
2. *Newspeak* is a term that refers to language used by politicians and journalists that is highly deceptive and manipulative. It was first used in George Orwell's famous novel *Nineteen Eighty-Four*. Discuss the intention of each example of Newspeak in the suggested contexts:
    - *collateral damage* in the context of war
    - *freedom fighter* versus *terrorist* in the context of resistance movements
    - *tax relief* in the context of privatizing the commons
    - *freedom of speech* in the context of expressing hate toward a particular group
    - *ethnic cleansing* in the context of war
    - *extremist* in the context of growing the commons (e.g., Bernie Sanders' electoral platform)

- *the gay rights agenda* in the context of what conservative Christians are calling for
- *friendly fire* in the context of war
- *War on Terror* in the context of human rights
- *political correctness* in the context of using offensive language about social groups

3. What are some other examples of Orwellian Doublespeak that you come into contact with in the mainstream media?

ASSIGNMENT

Research Keynesian economics and its perspectives on the commons. Research neoliberal economics and its perspective on the commons. Which economic paradigm is more supportive of civil society? Explain.

WORKS CITED

Albo, G., & Fanelli, C. (2014). *Austerity against democracy: An authoritarian phase of neoliberalism?* Toronto, ON: Centre for Social Justice.

Albo, G., Gindin, S., & Panitch, L. (2010). *In and out of crisis: The global financial meltdown and left alternatives.* Oakland, CA: PM Press.

Anijar, K., & Gabbard, D. (2009). Vouchers, charters, educational management organizations, and the money behind them. In D. Hill (Ed.), *The rich world and the impoverishment of education: Diminishing democracy, equity and workers' rights* (pp. 21–50). New York, NY: Routledge.

Apple, M. (2004). *Ideology and curriculum* (3rd ed.). New York, NY: Routledge-Falmer.

Boas, T., & Gans-Morse, J. (2009). Neoliberalism: From new liberal philosophy to anti-liberal slogan. *Studies in Comparative International Development, 44*(2), 137–161.

Buckingham, D. (2003). *Media education: Literacy, learning and contemporary culture.* Malden, MA: Blackwell Publishing.

Byers, D. (2016, January 18). How the media missed Bernie Sanders. *CNN.* Retrieved from www.cnn.com/2016/01/18/politics/bernie-sanders-media/index.html [June 30, 2016].

Caplan, G. (2012, February 24). Don't tell us it's not class war. *The Globe and Mail.* Retrieved from www.theglobeandmail.com/news/politics/second-reading/gerald-caplan/dont-tell-us-its-not-a-class-war/article2349194/ [March 2, 2012].

Carr, P., & Porfilio, B. (2011). The Obama education files: Is there hope to stop the neoliberal agenda in education? *Journal of Inquiry and Action in Education, 4*(1), 1–30. Retrieved from digitalcommons.buffalostate.edu/cgi/viewcontent.cgi?article=1031&context=jiae [August 9, 2013].

CBC News. (2016, June 9). Law to allow private purchase of CT scans is "troubling": Opposition. Retrieved from www.cbc.ca/news/canada/saskatchewan/saskatchewan-private-health-procedures-1.3625315 [June 10, 2016].

Cottle, S. (2003). *News, public relations & power.* London, UK: Sage.

Council of Public Relations Firms. (2005). *2002 public relations industry revenue and performance data fact sheet.* Retrieved from www.prfirms.org/docs/2002rankings/factsheetFINAL.doc [June 30, 2016].

Dewey, J. (1916). *Democracy and education.* New York, NY: MacMillan.

Faltin Osborn, S., & Sierk, J. L. (2015). Teach For America in the media: A multimodal semiotic analysis. *Critical Education, 6*(16). Retrieved from ojs.library.ubc.ca/index.php/criticaled/article/view/184961 [June 21, 2016].

Feuerstein, A. (2015). Political cartoons and the framing of charter school reform. *Critical Education, 6*(10). Retrieved from ojs.library.ubc.ca/index.php/criticaled/article/view/184931 [June 21, 2016].

Ford, D. R., Porfilio, B., & Goldstein, R. A. (2015). The news media, education and the subversion of the neoliberal social imaginary. *Critical Education, 6*(7), 1–24. Retrieved from ojs.library.ubc.ca/index.php/criticaled/article/view/186119 [June 21, 2016].

Frank, T. (2004). *What's the matter with Kansas?* New York, NY: Henry Holt & Co.

Frank, T. (2012). *Pity the billionaire: The hard-times swindle and the unlikely comeback of the right.* New York, NY: Henry Holt & Co.

Friedman, M. (2002). *Capitalism and freedom* (2nd ed.). Chicago, IL: University of Chicago Press.

Garcia, J. (2015). Learning from bad teachers: The neoliberal agenda for education in popular media. *Critical Education, 6*(13). Retrieved from ices.library.ubc.ca/index.php/criticaled/article/view/184935 [June 30, 2016].

Gautreaux, M. (2015). Neoliberal education reform's mouthpiece: Education Week's discourse on Teach For America. *Critical Education, 6*(11). Retrieved from ojs.library.ubc.ca/index.php/criticaled/article/view/185228 [June 21, 2016].

Gewirtz, S., Dickson, M., & Power, S. (2004). Unravelling a "spun" policy: A case study of the constitutive role of "spin" in the education policy process. *Journal of Education Policy, 19*(3), 321–342.

Giroux, H. A. (1981). *Ideology, culture, and the process of schooling.* Philadelphia, PA: Temple University Press.

Gramsci, A. (1971). *Selections from the prison notebooks of Antonio Gramsci*. New York, NY: International.

Harvey, D. (2005). *A brief history of neoliberalism*. Oxford, UK: Oxford University Press.

Hayek, F. A. (1944). *The road to serfdom*. Chicago, IL: University of Chicago Press.

Herman, E., & Chomsky, N. (1988). *Manufacturing consent: The political economy of the mass media*. New York, NY: Pantheon Books.

Hungerford, T. (2012, September 14). Taxes and the economy: An economic analysis of the top tax rates since 1945. *Congressional Research Service for Congress*. Retrieved from graphics8.nytimes.com/news/business/0915taxesandeconomy.pdf [May 12, 2016].

Huxley, A. (1998). *Brave new world* (First Perennial Classics ed.). New York, NY: HarperCollins Publishers. (Original work published 1932).

Kennedy, M., & Press, J. (2012, January 26). "Major transformations" coming to Canada's pension plan, Harper tells Davos. *National Post*. Retrieved from news.nationalpost.com/2012/01/26/major-changes-coming-to-canadas-pension-system-harper-says-in-davos-speech/

Kiedrowski, J. (2013). *The Simpsons* as a satirical portrayal of neoliberal influence on public education. *Pedagogy, Culture, and Society, 21*(2), 195–215.

Kilbourne, J. (1979, 1987, 2000, 2010). *Killing us softly* [Documentary film series]. Northampton, MA: Media Education Foundation.

Klein, N. (2014). *This changes everything: Capitalism versus the climate*. Toronto, ON: Alfred A. Knopf Canada.

Kozolanka, K. (2007). *The power of persuasion: The politics of the new right in Ontario*. Montreal, QC: Black Rose Books.

Kumar, R. (2015). Education, the state, and market: Anatomy of neoliberal impact. *Critical Education, 6*(21). Retrieved from ices.library.ubc.ca/index.php/criticaled/article/view/185901 [June 30, 2016].

Lakoff, G. (2004). *Don't think of an elephant! Know your values and frame the debate*. White River Junction, Vermont: Chelsea Green Publishing.

LeBlanc, D. (2015, March 6). Anti-terror bill powers "excessive," Canada's Privacy Commissioner says. *The Globe and Mail*. Retrieved from beta.theglobeandmail.com/news/politics/anti-terror-bill-powers-excessive-canadas-privacy-commissioner-says/article23325129/ [July 14, 2016].

Marcuse, H. (1964). *One-dimensional man*. New York, NY: Beacon Press.

Martin, L. (2003, January 23). It's not Canadians who've gone to the right, just their media. *The Globe and Mail*, p. A8.

Monsebraaten, L. (2011, July 13). Canada's income gap growing. *Toronto Star*. Retrieved from www.thestar.com/news/article/1024027--canada-s-income-gap-growing [March 21, 2014].

OECD. (2011). *Divided we stand: Why inequality keeps rising.* Paris, France: Organization for Economic Co-operation and Development. Retrieved from www.oecd.org/documentprint/0,3455,en_21571361_4431 [August 12, 2012].

Orlowski, P. (2011). *Teaching about hegemony: Race, class & democracy in the 21st century.* New York, NY: Springer.

Orlowski, P. (2015). Neoliberalism, its effects on Saskatchewan, and a teacher educator's response. *Alternate Routes: A Journal of Critical Social Research, 26*(1), 223–250.

Orwell, G. (1983). *Nineteen eighty-four.* New York, NY: Penguin Group. (Original work published 1949).

Ostry, J., Loungani, P., & Furceri, D. (2016, June). Neoliberalism: Oversold? *International Monetary Fund—Finance & Development, 53*(2). Retrieved from www.imf.org/external/pubs/ft/fandd/2016/06/ostry.htm [July 4, 2016].

Rorty, R. (1998). *Achieving our country: Leftist thought in 20th-century America.* Cambridge, MA: Harvard University Press.

Rosenmann, A. (2016, October 12). Noam Chomsky unravels political mechanics behind his gradual expulsion from mainstream media. *Alternet.* Retrieved from www.alternet.org/media/noam-chomsky-unravels-political-mechanics-behind-his-gradual-expulsion-mainstream-media [October 13, 2016].

Schwarzmantel, J. (1998). *The age of ideology: Political ideologies from the American revolution to postmodern times.* New York, NY: New York University Press.

Shiller, J. (2015). Speaking back to the neoliberal discourse on teaching: How U.S. teachers use social media to redefine teaching. *Critical Education, 6*(9). Retrieved from ojs.library.ubc.ca/index.php/criticaled/article/view/184931 [June 24, 2016].

Smith, A. (2003). *The wealth of nations.* New York, NY: Bantam Classics. (Original work published 1776).

Stanford, J. (2011). *Having their cake and eating it too: Business profits, taxes, and investment in Canada—1961 through 2010.* Ottawa, ON: Canadian Centre for Policy Alternatives.

Tencer, D. (2015, November 10). Canada's newspapers were in the tank for Harper, media analysis finds. *Huffington Post.* Retrieved from www.huffingtonpost.ca/2015/11/10/newspaper-endorsements-harper-study_n_8523676.html [August 9, 2016].

Willcocks, P. (2016, June 20). To tackle inequality, start with BC's two-tier education. *The Tyee.* Retrieved from thetyee.ca/Opinion/2016/06/20/BC-Two-Tier-Education/ [June 25, 2016].

Winter, J. (2002). *Media think.* Montreal, QC: Black Rose Books.

Yalnizyan, A. (2011, April 7). Middle class in decline is the electoral elephant in the room. *The Globe and Mail.* Retrieved from www.theglobeandmail.com/report-on-business/economy/economy-lab/the-economists/middle-class-in-decline-is-the-electoral-elephant-in-the-room/article1974539/ [April 2, 2014].

2 Building an Inclusive Society: The Role of Alternative Media

We can all agree that "information is an essential element in a democratic public sphere" (Fletcher, 2014, p. 27). However, information is only useful if it is meaningful to those who receive it. Moreover, whose information prevails and what can be seen as essential in a staggeringly huge global world of information? As Hackett and Carroll (2004) have noted, "democracy has never been a gift handed down from elites" (p. 14). Instead, democracy needs to be fought for to keep the democratic values and benefits that we have achieved over time. To keep moving forward, democracy also needs to adapt society's norms and values to include new "ways of seeing" (Berger, 1972). Importantly, this requires broadening, adapting, and representing society fully and equally. In reality, however, history shows that mainstream society doesn't easily let go of its power in order to welcome new voices or ideas. Keep in mind that power—and staying in power—is a dazzling prospect for politicians and elites (including owners of large media corporations) who govern or have influence on countries or cities. This isn't because mainstream politics is corrupt; instead, even in a democratic political environment, we may ignore, reject, or never even consider what lies beyond our own personal understandings and mental borders.

This chapter will examine the role of alternative media and social movements in society, first by laying out how mainstream media work in Canada, then by examining the systems that divide and define the roles of different media, and finally by articulating the role of alternative media and social movements that can produce more equitable and inclusive views, as well as bring more democratic change to society.

MAINSTREAM MEDIA IN CANADA

In order to understand why alternative media exist, we need to have a broad understanding of mainstream media. When we talk about "the media," we are usually referring to the mainstream media in society, that is, the media corporations that dominate most of our media environment. We also refer to the mainstream media as the dominant media. They are dominant because they are part of a set of broader institutions that dominate society. Some of those other institutions are: Parliament and the public service, schools and universities, business and industry, non-governmental organizations, and health and hospital services.

Mainstream media and other institutions of society reflect and incorporate our values and beliefs. These values and beliefs guide us in what we do and how we behave. They form our dominant or mainstream system of meaning and values. What is important for citizens is that the mainstream media play a key role in incorporating the dominant ideas and beliefs of society and circulating them as part of the dominant ideology.

This mainstream system is never fixed or stagnant. Instead, it actively negotiates and interprets values and beliefs in our daily lives. This is an ongoing and active process; that is how it stays dominant. It is continually and actively renewed, recreated, defended, modified, and reinforced. But there is another side to this system: it means that the mainstream media can also play a role in rejecting or trivializing or ignoring ideas and beliefs that they think do not fit in with how society thinks—or that mainstream journalists may not be comfortable with.

Table 2.1: Media Giants in Canada

Market Share	Media Corporation	Type of Holdings
26.7%	Bell Media	Cable, TV, internet, satellite, radio
15.6%	Rogers	Cable, TV, internet, satellite, radio, press
14.6%	Telus	Cable, TV, internet, satellite, radio, press
6.1%	Shaw	Cable, TV, internet, satellite, press
5.0%	QMI	TV, radio
68.0%	**Total**	

Source: Winseck 2015, www.cmcrp.org.

Note: The next corporations (in order from large to small) are: Canwest, CTVglobemedia, MTS, CBC, and COGECO for a total of 12.4% of market share. For a poster of Canada's top media and updates on media giants, check out http://www.cmcrp.org/wp-content/uploads/2016/11/Canadas_Top_Media_Concentration_Canada_2015.pdf.

The dominant or mainstream media disseminate mainly mainstream views—the ones that are acceptable to the mainstream of society. They don't do this because they do not want to uphold the ideals of democratic communication or are lazy or haven't been trained properly or any number of other reasons that we could come up with. Instead, the mainstream media can be unsuccessful in fulfilling these democratic roles because they are faced with practical issues that prevent them from doing so.

There has been a great deal of media analysis conducted over a great many years on how the media do their work. Some of the analysis has to do with how the media are organized and owned. Other analysis focuses on how journalists go about their daily work.

In 1996, Blumler and Gurevitch wrote that there are three main categories of issues—*political*, *economic*, and *cultural*—faced by the mainstream media in how they are organized and how they go about their daily work, and little has changed over time.

Regarding the first category, *political* issues, Blumler and Gurevitch pointed out how official and elite sources predominate in the media. Most sources in mainstream media coverage come from official or elite sources of different kinds, such as politicians, royalty, business leaders, and even celebrities. With so much of media content tied up in what elites do, there is little room for unofficial sources or local or community sources. Often these unofficial or local or community sources are unknown names, which means they do not have personal legitimacy, or they are from unknown groups or organizations or smaller political parties, so journalists are not familiar with them. These groups stand less of a chance of seeing their views in the media. Communication laws and policies in Canada are very explicit about how the media need to uphold the public interest, but governments change, and priorities and visions of how media and society should work change as well.

For example, the Conservative government of 2006–2015 was not seen as friendly to public media (like the CBC), which explicitly have the mandate to uphold the public interest. Instead, it bypassed CBC and selected private-sector media for interviews. Also, that government did not give the CBC the funding it needed to fulfill its mandate, and that was a political constraint that our public media faced. The Liberal government that followed in 2015 did not fully redress that loss of funding.

Second, Blumler and Gurevitch said the mainstream media also have to deal with *economic* issues. Most media run on the market imperative; they are for-profit media. They serve their boards of directors, their shareholders, and their advertisers; in fact, they can be seen to be selling their audiences, as Smythe

(1981) once pointed out. They do not necessarily put citizens and democratic citizenship first. It was often said that stories in hard-copy newspapers filled what is called "the news hole" that is left after the advertising has been placed!

Within the media, newsroom staffs are smaller than they used to be, and there is not enough time or money for journalists to undertake lengthy, in-depth investigative pieces. Instead, journalists may write the quick and easier stories that they have time for. This may mean they have no time for reflection or for going beyond their usual sources. It is easy to see how this feeds back into the political issue of using mostly official sources that they know already—for example, mayors, lawyers, and executives.

Third, Blumler and Gurevitch indicated that there are *cultural* issues to resolve. A multilingual, multi-ethnic country like Canada can have its challenges in including multiple points of view. Given the other issues facing the media, it is hard to expect that journalists will be able to work "outside the box" of their own cultural understandings when they have to produce news stories on a quick deadline. Mainstream journalists have the same values and beliefs as the rest of mainstream society. When a story arises that may involve other cultures or religions, it takes time and effort to be able to understand why a situation or an event could be significant to some people, or to have the cultural knowledge to be able to write the story appropriately, and journalists cannot always seek out what they do not know is there.

The different constraints under which journalists do their jobs are reflected in how they go about their work, that is, in the practices they use to produce news (for example, interviewing sources). It is also reflected in the content of their work itself: what you read and see in the resulting media product.

Overall in the mainstream media, *non*-mainstream or *non*-dominant views are unlikely to appear, and when they do, they have less prominence and less favourable coverage. This is not unusual as, given the values and beliefs that are common to mainstream society, it is clear that the media are part of that society and bring those same values and beliefs to their work. In other words, usually the journalist and the citizen have values in common and can relate to each other, so a mainstream journalist's stories will tend to be comprehensible to the average citizen or reader. This also extends to how long it takes for citizens to answer the questions of journalists; there is little room or time for complex explanations.

Importantly, the views that we see in mainstream media also have a lot to do with who owns the media. While it is common to say that the media are fair and impartial—that's how journalists have been taught to think about their work—in reality, the media are large corporations that exist to accumulate profit for owners and shareholders, just like any other corporations. They also have their own ideas and ideals on how to run their corporations and what society should be like—and they want to see that in the media that they own. Big media have an advantage over the much smaller media of the local newspaper of the past. For example, during elections, media corporations usually endorse candidates and political parties for readers and viewers to consider those candidates favourably when they vote. Additionally, over time, the loss of local media and the rise of 24-hour television and Internet news has had an impact on the information and communication that communities receive, leaving a vacuum in local and community information.

Whether deliberately or as consequence of how the media do their work, views and perspectives that are different from the mainstream are often sidelined or marginalized. Instead, much mainstream media activity produces news that is comfortable and that makes common sense to those who are involved in producing it (editors, journalists, official sources, readers/audiences, etc.). These are the main people and organized groups that are involved in the selection process and/or appear in media stories. However, this narrow selection excludes many other unknown sources and many stories that are less comfortable to deal with, or that are more complex or unfamiliar, on issues that mainstream media know little or nothing about. This has an impact on the democratic role the media are supposed to play and on democratic communication, which, as we know, should be inclusive of different views. We need to ask ourselves: where is the diversity and multiplicity of views that we saw supported in Canadian communication laws, regulations, and public policies in the past?

The focus so far has been on the constraints on journalism from the point of view of how the mainstream media do their jobs and what their stories look like. But we haven't yet talked about citizens in their role as the audience that receives the stories that the media print or broadcast (Blumler and Gurevitch, 1996, p. 33). In a democratic media system and society, the needs of the audience should play an important role, and that is what the social responsibility approach to the media tells us. However, in reality, audiences are the least powerful and the least organized—until they decide to go somewhere else for news and information. Audiences are usually important to the mainstream mass media as numbers of viewers or readers. Basically, they are statistics for the purpose of establishing ratings so a media outlet can solicit advertising. That's what an audience—which we need to see as a commercial term—is for.

However, if we want to think of audiences instead as citizens, information that is useful to audiences must be sensitive to their wants and needs. If audiences are known only by their numbers, that is, if they are seen by their consumer profile, they will be open to stereotyping. In other words, they will be reduced to a category. Also, if audiences are treated as if they are capable of absorbing only what their consumer profile suggests they want, and nothing more, they will be seen only as they are and not as they could be if they were supplied with different media content.

A commercialized media environment is thus very cautious and conservative in a way that tends not to upset the **status quo**. If it does, it will lose advertisers, and it will not be able to stay afloat. Thus, by its very nature, commercialized media might not create an environment that is open to non-mainstream, diverse, or new perspectives.

In Canada, there is a strong corrective to mainstream commercial media. The Canadian Broadcasting Corporation (CBC) was founded to provide media in the public interest (see Chapter 5). It was intended to be informative, educational, non-commercial, and Canadian-made. Over time it has lost some of its original mandate, due mostly to inadequate funding, but also to governments that believed that such media shouldn't be funded by governments or just that they didn't need a public channel. The CBC faces challenges from for-profit media. It has fragmented audiences, because it serves everyone, not just one audience, and is underfunded and therefore forced to take advertising. We could ask: Is this in the public interest? Either the CBC exists to be public and be for the public, or it doesn't. Right now, it does both.

These are some of the important issues and problems faced by mainstream media, as well as the possibilities that mainstream society hasn't addressed over time. Yet there are other ways to see society that are not focused on mainstream views. Notably, Raymond Williams has laid out a way of understanding the differences found in society.

RAYMOND WILLIAMS AND MEANING SYSTEMS

Raymond Williams was a Welsh academic who was seen as one of the founders of **cultural studies**. He had an interesting way of looking at society through the lens of communication, and looking at communication through the lens of society. His ideas on society and communication can be very useful in understanding alternative media.

Williams (1977) said that society was a complex interaction of political, social, and economic forces (p. 108). He didn't favour one over the other; instead, he believed that these forces worked together in society. By "society," he meant political institutions such as Parliament and government apparatus, educational institutions and actors, cultural values, social processes and religious affiliations, and so on. Altogether, these different forces could be organized into ideological systems, that is, they are not neutral, but have their own ideas. Using Williams' work as a base for understanding society, these processes and forces can be categorized into three social systems to define society: a *dominant* or mainstream system, an *alternative* system, and an *oppositional* system. Each of the three systems has its own meaning and values. The dominant or mainstream system of meaning and values consists of a social process that is unconscious (seemingly natural to us so that we don't even think about it), and a political process that is conscious (aware of practices and expectations). Together, the social unconscious process and the political conscious process form the hegemonic worldview, or the system of being in which we live. Williams' concept of "meaning systems" is used here as a base for understanding ideology and applying this concept to situate the media into three ideological systems: *mainstream*, *alternative*, and *oppositional*.

The *mainstream* society in which most of us live can be seen as hegemonic, that is, it is ongoing, and it renews, recreates, defends, and modifies itself. It is never static, but is continually resisted, limited, altered, and challenged by outside pressures. This emphasizes that the **hegemony**, although always dominant, is never total or exclusive. In fact, there are two different and ongoing challenges from two areas beyond the hegemonic or dominant meaning system. Williams called them *alternative* and *oppositional* meaning systems.

The *alternative* meaning system includes views and beliefs that challenge the dominant system, but that do not threaten its existence or its hegemony. This alternative kind of view can be as simple as an opposition party putting out a different point of view than the government, or a pressure group advocating for a change in policy.

Williams calls *oppositional* the views that are considered not acceptable to society and that challenge the hegemony. Examples of this could be: separatist movements within countries, as in Canada some years ago in Quebec (**Péquistes**), in Spain (**Basques**), or in Mexico (**Zapatistas**). A group that calls for outright revolution, rather than making simple changes to society, would be considered oppositional to the state's hegemony.

But remember that hegemony is never static or unchangeable. Issues that were once thought incompatible with mainstream or dominant society have now become incorporated into the mainstream. Examples of this could be the relaxation of divorce laws in 1968 and, much more recently, the equal or same-sex marriage decision from our Supreme Court in 2015.

Over time, it is possible for an oppositional position to move into the alternative meaning system (where it still challenges, but is more acceptable to society) and even enter into the mainstream meaning system. Williams' meaning systems are very useful for examining alternative media because they describe how society is organized and how it changes, and also provide us with a way of organizing and studying different media. We should remember that the mainstream media—which are dominant and hegemonic in society—play a central role in either incorporating dominant ideas or depoliticizing or delegitimizing them (Gitlin, 1980, pp. 254–259).

ALTERNATIVE MEDIA

Not everyone in society thinks the same way, just as not all media are the same. The mainstream or dominant system in which we live is also continually resisted, altered, and challenged. These challenges take place in our social and political system all the time, so the dominant or mainstream media are often challenged quite legitimately. This happens as simply as through a letter to the editor. Or, it could be a campaign against a media outlet's way of characterizing a particular issue. Or, sometimes, when people feel strongly that their views and perspectives are not being represented in the mainstream media, they might be moved to create their own media.

At this point, it is useful to remind ourselves about the roles that the media are supposed to play in a democracy. One way of seeing the media is through the lens of what is called **libertarian** theory, which is also often called the "free press" approach. This approach to the media was conceived in England in the 17th to 19th centuries and spread to North America. It was based on the free will of individuals (at the time, that meant men only) to express themselves as they wished and that carried over into the newspapers of the time. Under this approach, the press had full freedom of expression. The ideal was that the press would give citizens information and that citizens would decide rationally and freely what to believe or do. To an extent, many American media still defend these libertarian ideals.

A later and more advanced understanding of the role of the press that developed early in the 20th century (and that is still with us today) is that the media have evolved to become socially responsible, using their privileged position in society to be a watchdog for abuses of power in society. In Canada, the social responsibility approach also takes place within a mixed system, with public media in the public interest such as the CBC alongside private, for-profit media. Basically, this comes down to the ideal that media play an important role in renewing democracy. There are democratic values that lie at the foundation for our media system, and they can be summed up as participation (that everyone should have a right to speak and be heard), debate (that everyone's opinion matters), and respect (that they not only can speak, but will also be heard). These values are the basis for democratic communication. If the communication doesn't involve participation, debate, and respect, it is not democratic.

However, it is difficult to define precisely what the "alternative" in alternative media means, because alternative media take many different forms. We have already established that alternative media are not mainstream media, but this does not mean that anything can be alternative. It is not sufficient to be merely "different." If that were the case, then any new example of the media could be considered alternative simply because it is new. For instance, the free daily newspapers like *Metro* are (fairly) new and different, but those newspapers are not alternative. It is also not sufficient that something is digital or that it appears on the World Wide Web. The form of the media (for example, online) does not make it alternative either. They can vary considerably. It is not necessarily a case of a clearly alternative media product or a clearly mainstream media product.

Instead, there is a continuum, a range of different alternative media. For instance, some are more radical than others, some are not radical at all, and some are examples of radical social movements that want to break away from and establish their own sovereign nations. If we wanted to be concrete on a definition, we would say that truly pure alternative media have their own special attributes or characteristics. It is clear from these attributes that "being alternative" isn't just being different; instead, alternative media are organized and conceptualized differently.

In *Alternative Media in Canada* (2012), Kozolanka, Mazepa, and Skinner identified three key attributes of alternative media. The first is that alternative media are *participatory*. They subvert the way mainstream society is organized and create their own non-hierarchical structure, such as organizing as a collective. They may even rotate roles and functions. In contrast, mainstream media are hierarchical, from the owner and publisher at the top to the student interns at the bottom.

Second, alternative media are different *structurally*. They are usually non-profit-oriented. There is little expectation amongst alternative media practitioners that they will make a profit from their work. They are almost always non-commercial. They mostly exist outside the market and thus are not likely to be seen in stores that sell mainstream magazines. They do not accept corporate advertising, although they can exchange ads with like-minded media that advertise their own work. They also often sell their own products, such as back issues, T-shirts, and books. Some alternative media actually give away their work for free or for a small donation. In contrast, the mainstream media are profit-oriented and rely on advertising, without which they would not survive.

Third, alternative media are also *activist* in some way. They see their work as part of a larger project of reorganization of society: it is political and it is hegemonic, in the sense that they want a different society, somewhat like a social movement, only about media. At the very least, even if they do not want to change all of society, they are committed to social change of some kind and to some degree. For example, think of media that promote one issue, such as environmental issues or gender equality; *AdBusters*, for example, focuses on consumerism. In contrast, the mainstream media reflect the status quo, or mainstream society generally.

Alternative media that have all three of these characteristics—participation, structure, activism—are rare, but not as rare as one might think. Often we don't know enough about them and how they work because they are operating at the grassroots or community level. There is very often no mass distribution as there is for mainstream media, or they have their own following and are not on our radar unless we go looking for them.

BOX 2.1: DEFINING ALTERNATIVE MEDIA

In his book *Alternative Media* (2002), Chris Atton attempts to nail down the different and elusive ways to describe alternative media through those who have tried to define it. One composite definition from this discussion is that alternative media are *oppositional, distinctive and independent, with their own media processes and formations* (p. 158). In addition, Stephen Duncombe, author of the *Cultural Resistance Reader* (1997), sees alternative media as a *model of participatory cultural production and organization that are acted on and enable social change* (in Atton, 2002). These two different but complementary definitions cover most of the terrain and scope of alternative media. Some other ways to describe alternative media include *reformist, radical,* and *counter-hegemonic* (Atton, 2002, p. 18). One further way of defining alternative media recognizes that how these media are actually produced—perhaps as a cooperative group working together—gives them their authenticity and alternativeness (p. 18).

WHY DO WE NEED ALTERNATIVE MEDIA?

Alternative media play an important role in a democratic society. They provide an alternative voice or perspective, one that is often missing from mainstream media. Thus, alternative media can be said to counter mainstream news accounts, because they are *different*, as well as improve mainstream news accounts, by adding *perspective*. In terms of their significance, they are key to build community and animate social change. Clearly, alternative media see themselves as taking on the democratic functions of participation and dialogue that the mainstream media may not have been fulfilling. In addition, alternative media do this because they firmly believe that the mainstream media have not been representing the views of all society.

In fact, the idea that news is "missing" from our media came from analysis by Hackett and Gruneau (2000), whose research pointed out that most mainstream media and news are about the "famous," "infamous," and "powerful." In addition, their analysis showed that what was missing in the news showed a "systematic pattern" (p. 165), that is, the same issues were never or almost never seen in the media, while others received plenty of coverage. They called the missing news "blindspots," because no one seemed to see them. Some of the blindspots they noted included news and information about labour, corporate power, and social inequality. The year 2000 was a long time ago, and perhaps we might think that things have changed. However, as it turns out, the School of Communication at Simon Fraser University has updated the research over the years since 2000, and many of the same blindspots recur. The overall impact of missing news cannot be counted or understood, and it is fair to wonder why news stories are tilted away from other important spheres in our society.

This does not happen only in Canadian mainstream media. The *New Internationalist*, an alternative global magazine that began publishing in 1973, prints an annual story on what it calls the "unreported year." These are stories from around the world that we never hear about, mostly because the media in the Western hemisphere either don't believe that their readers are interested in such stories or they don't have the space or time to properly report them. Here are some examples from the 2016 report of issues in the world you likely never knew about:

- The European Court of Human Rights ordered Bulgaria to protect the rights of citizens to religious freedom, after police raided the home of a member of the World of Life church;
- In Japan, 5.5 million black sacks of radiation-contaminated soil from the nuclear disaster in 2011 have nowhere to go, and it was expected that at the end of 2017 the number of sacks would have reached 20 million;

- In Peru, the world's fifth-largest producer and exporter of gold, illegal mining (about 10 percent of Peru's mining) has destroyed more than 50,000 hectares of rainforest; and
- A new constitution in Nepal in 2016 denied women the ability to pass on their citizenship to their children, which can mean that children of a single mother and unknown father do not get Nepali citizenship.

In addition, in the United States, Project Censored released an annual list of the top underreported stories of the year. When we do not see or hear about issues outside our own territorial boundaries, we tend only to think about our own personal issues and our country's issues, and our world becomes smaller.

At the same time, the media do bring to our attention other issues that are happening here and around the world. In 2017, many media stories focused on the famine in Africa that had spread to other countries on that continent—yet the famine in South Sudan was underreported in the mainstream media. But unless there is an emergency or war, we usually know little beyond our own borders. Certainly, we don't know about such famines until they have hit a dire point, such as a huge number of deaths, unless alternative magazines like the *New Internationalist* bring them to our attention.

With this in mind, if we think back to alternative media's three key attributes—participation, structure, and activism—we can clearly see the purpose of alternative media: they are looking for transformational change in society, here in Canada and elsewhere in the world. Specifically, however, they also take on another area that the mainstream media have not shown themselves to be effective at reaching, and that is that they want to mobilize audiences to become involved in the issues facing us. A lot of their work takes place at the community and grassroots levels, where they stimulate dialogue and include ordinary citizens. This takes us back to the democratic role of media in terms of participation, dialogue, and respect. To some extent, alternative media are trying to foster the traditional democratic ideal of media.

SOCIAL MOVEMENTS AND ACTIVISM

Alternative media are also closely connected to social movements. Many people who are concerned about some issue in society that they want to change for the better, often through joining with others to lobby a government or work together to make something happen, organize themselves for the specific purpose of changing something that they believe is amiss or wrong in society. For instance, it could be

BOX 2.2: SOME ALTERNATIVE MEDIA IN CANADA

Briarpatch is an independent, award-winning magazine out of Regina that focuses on politics and culture. Its key features are that it is "proudly polemical" and reports from a grassroots perspective. It is committed to both reporting on and building social movements (https://briarpatchmagazine.com).

Canadaland is a news site that focuses on the media, using the growing podcast network in Canada as its preferred medium. Canadaland podcasts range from issues such as queer media to covering Omar Khadr to newspaper bailouts. It also has been the first media to break news before mainstream media. These stories include that CBC was publishing advertorials and that no one knows how diverse Canada's private broadcasters are (www.canadalandshow.com).

Daily Xtra is a digital newspaper in Toronto, Vancouver, and Ottawa that gives in-depth coverage to issues important to gay and lesbian Canadians. It is published by Pink Triangle Press and was founded in 1971 to advance the struggle for sexual liberation. It is a not-for-profit corporation, and it appears to be self-sustaining (www.dailyxtra.com).

Georgia Straight is a Vancouver tabloid founded in Vancouver in May 1967 as "an anti-establishment alternative" newspaper, but now calls itself simply an "independent newspaper." Early on, it was raided by police for publishing what the police called "obscene material, but the charges did not hold up" (www.straight.com).

Herizons is a national magazine that has focused on "women's news + feminist views" since 1979. It publishes four times a year from its base in Winnipeg and its articles run the gamut from women's accomplishments to its special focus on arts and culture, alternative health, political affairs, and legal issues facing women (www.herizons.ca).

National Campus and Community Radio Association (NCRA) is the umbrella group for community and campus radio in Canada (http://ncra.ca).

National Observer (Canada) is a daily online newspaper founded in 2015 with a focus on politics, the environment, and energy issues. It has won several Canada's Online Publishing Awards for best news coverage, column, and digital solution. In several stories in 2017, it reported on animal abuse at an Ottawa-area zoo and the fast-melting Arctic as a sign of bad global warning (www.nationalobserver.com).

Rabble.ca is a rarity in alternative media for having survived and prospered since its beginnings in 2001. It is deliberately online to reach larger audiences, "blurring the line between readers and contributors" (http://rabble.ca).

Ricochet produces "independent journalism and ideas in the public interest." Instead of subscriptions, Ricochet has members and works by crowdfunding— accumulating as many members as possible who donate small amounts. Crowdfunding is seen as an alternative way of financing and is a growing practice (https://ricochet.media/).

Shameless magazine is based in Toronto. It was started in 2004 and calls itself a proudly independent grassroots magazine. It says it is an "independent voice for smart, strong, sassy young women." Its mandate is "for teen girls and trans youth." The magazine's team of volunteer staff members is guided by a teen editorial collective. It has been nominated for many independent media awards (http://shamelessmag.com).

Straight Goods was an independent, online newsmagazine; it is no longer publishing separately and has been rolled into Rabble.ca as "SGNews."

The Real News Network was a news site that was an offshoot of the American network of the same name. It had a studio in Toronto as well as Washington. There were high hopes that it would survive as an unusual television alternative in Canada, but that did not happen, although it is still publishing through its American site (http://therealnews.com/tag/canada).

The Tyee is a very well-known online newspaper. It is based in Vancouver and is one of the best alternative media news websites in Canada today. It has a Mediacheck column and is strong on excellent opinion (https://thetyee.ca).

This Magazine has been around for so long that it is almost an honorary mainstream magazine. Its roots were in social change in Toronto back in 1966, when a group of education activists started a journal called *This Magazine is About Schools*. Now simply called *This Magazine* or even just *This*, it self-describes as "subversive, edgy and smart" and is about politics and culture as well as education. It has won many awards for its work (https://this.org).

that they are concerned about the deleterious impact the tar sands in Alberta might have on the environment. Or they might be worried about the injustice for someone who has been wrongly imprisoned, or perhaps they come together to lobby the government to alleviate child poverty. While these groups know a lot about the problem or issue that turned their beliefs and work into a social movement, they may not understand how to communicate with the public to further their cause.

One example of a social movement with good communication is the Black Lives Matter (BLM) movement, which has brought to the attention of the public the shocking numbers of Black persons being killed by police. While it started in the United States, the movement has broadened to Canada as well. BLM used a hashtag (#blacklivesmatter) as a simple, inexpensive, and quick medium to pass on information and, when needed, to bring out its followers to protest quickly when something relevant to its issues was happening, and a crowd was needed to bring it to the media's attention. However, a drawback to movements and activism online, as well as other new media, could be the lack of face-to-face engagement. "Clicktivism"—clicking to agree or disagree with an issue on a website or through one's smartphone (White, 2010)—can rack up the numbers of those who agree with your issue or movement, but it is not the same as a meeting or a rally where people can ask questions and invigorate their beliefs within a crowd of like-minded people.

A very successful social movement took place in Quebec in 2012. It, too, used communication tactically to get across its message and build the movement. Traditionally, Quebec's university and college tuition fees were much lower than in other provinces, but a new government decided to increase university tuition fees by 75 percent. The students formed a movement that saw 300,000 students leave their classrooms and go on strike. In the months that followed, the students engaged in demonstrations and daily direct actions to keep the movement strong, as well as to have continued prominence in the media. Two communication tactics worked well for the strike. First, the emblem of the strike was a small square of red felt (*carré rouge*) that the students wore as their badge to support the movement. Before long, many Canadians across the country, especially university and college students, started wearing the *carré rouge*. Second, YouTube became a site for uploading videos of the many and varied demonstrations held by the students, some of them with themes. The themes of the marches ranged from riding bicycles instead of walking, to dressing in costumes, to wearing only underwear.

The Quebec government then passed a law against preventing any student from being allowed to receive an education, as well as strict limitations on the right to assemble. The law was seen as a violation of freedom of assembly and other freedoms, and four days later, the citizens of Quebec showed their anger in a march that drew 400,000 people, which Rabble.ca called "the largest protest in Canadian history" (Annis, 2012). In the provincial election in Quebec that fall, the government that wouldn't budge on its high tuition fees lost its majority and, in an election 18 months later, was defeated. The new government reversed the tuition hike.

In recent years, some contemporary social movements have been grounded in issues regarding Indigenous peoples. In late 2012, a grassroots social movement called Idle No More sprang up. Led by Indigenous women, the movement is "a grass-roots advocacy group, opposing unilateral and colonial legislation and supporting empowerment" for Indigenous peoples (Idle No More, 2012). Idle No More is known for its use of social media, which allow its followers and potential followers to quickly and easily know what it is doing and to join in. The movement quickly amassed 45,000 members and support from Amnesty International, Black Lives Matter, unions, and many leading Indigenous people, as well as Canadians across the country. Idle No More was very clear in its mission statement that it called on "all people to join in a revolution" that "honours and fulfills indigenous sovereignty, which protects the land and water" (CBC News, 2013).

While the movement had many issues, it focused on lobbying against one piece of legislation (C-45) introduced by the federal government of former prime minister Stephen Harper. The legislation would have made changes to the Indian Act, along with two federal acts that would have an impact on Indigenous people, including giving a cabinet minister the power to "surrender" (sell) territory on First Nations land. Idle No More believes that individual First Nations should continue to hold the right to their land. The movement called for a National Day of Action, putting out the call through various social media. The Day of Action brought 3,000 to Parliament Hill on December 12, 2012, with many other demonstrations across the country. Since then, it continues to raise awareness of issues facing First Nations peoples. With 45,000 members behind it, it is likely to keep on "support[ing] and encourag[ing] grassroots to create their own forums to learn more about indigenous rights and … responsibilities to our Nationhood via teach-ins, rallies and social media" (CBC News, 2013). Other examples of social movement activism started by Indigenous people include the resistance to the Dakota Access Pipeline (from Canada into the US) in 2016–2017 and the Standing Rock Indian Reservation anti-pipeline protest in 2017.

CHALLENGES FOR ALTERNATIVE MEDIA

There will always be people, organizations, and governments that see alternative media as disturbing to their own way of life, while others see it as an important part of a democratic society. But sometimes alternative media fail, regardless of criticism. Sometimes in order to stay afloat and continue to be effective, alternative media take on the attributes or values of mainstream society. For example, they could take on advertising. But if they start to take on ads, it is just one step further to also take on marketing. Before long, they can lose their alternative focus and become part of the mainstream (an example could be the *Georgia Straight* newspaper, which is now more mainstream than it was when it was first published in the late 1960s). For social movements, the need is to communicate and publicize their alternative views, but to do that, they have to become media-friendly. They may then start to develop actions and policies that make them more interesting to the mainstream media. Yet, if they play by the rules of the mainstream media, they can become assimilated or co-opted. It becomes an agonizing choice between staying true to your aims and principles, but perhaps not meeting your goals, or making changes to soften your views and aims in order to have a presence in society.

An example of this was written about in the 1960s by activist Todd Gitlin, who was part of a radical social movement called the Students for a Democratic Society (SDS). Later on, as an American professor, he wrote about social movements, with the SDS as an example. Gitlin (1980) identified the specific stages that the mainstream media use to destabilize a movement, as they did with the SDS. First, the media ignored the SDS. Secondly, it reported on it, but in a way that trivialized it. In the third stage, the media sensationalized the activities of the movement. In the fourth and final stage, the media then incorporated the movement's values into its own values, so there was no reason for an SDS to exist. To some extent, it sounds like a victory that some of SDS's principles became part of the mainstream, but it meant the collapse of the stronger democratic aims of the SDS movement.

Hackett and Carroll (2004), who have written extensively on social movements and media reform, agree that the key to success is for such groups to have access to public communication. In 1993, Gamson and Wolfsfeld noted that social movements need access to communication to succeed, as that will give them visibility in the public, validation within mainstream media, and a vehicle to broaden and balance their movements.

While the alternative media sector plays a strong role in democratic communication, it doesn't have the resources it needs to be on the same footing as mainstream media. There are many structural barriers that prevent this from happening. Most importantly, in an era when many heritage newspapers and new media ventures have gone under, there are few resources available to finance this kind of enterprise, especially distribution. Many print media have already switched to online; others just close down. With alternative media in particular, they don't have the professional or legal protections that mainstream journalists have. For example, there are no lawyers on retainers in case of a lawsuit and no pension to look forward to, due to low or no wages. Also, alternative media are known for their precarious labour, as the alternative media they are working for may not survive. Sadly for most of our historical alternative media, there are very few archives that have these many small broadsheets or spools of tapes. Unfortunately, this means that our alternative media heritage has not been documented fully. The only hope for preserving current and future alternative media lies with the Internet—provided their work can be stored properly and updated easily when needed.

Inclusive media such as alternative media can also be in danger from a media environment that requires very little from its viewers. Over time, citizens have become used to being viewers rather than producers of media. It is much easier to choose from the plethora of media channels and always find something to entertain oneself. This "clicktivism," as viewers keep changing channels or webpages until they find something else to watch, is not only a danger to the survival of activism generally and alternative media specifically, but to one's well-being as well (White, 2010).

A key issue for alternative media is the lack of its own history. If such media cannot be preserved, then there is no evidence that there are different ways of seeing or being, and only mainstream histories will prevail. There are two ways to preserve this history. First, the Canadian government has partially funded small magazines—many of them alternative, community, and ethnic magazines—and could increase the funding. Second, another way to ensure that we remember all the different aspects of our past is through archiving alternative media and artifacts. Again, there is a blockage, as the National Library and Archives is curtailed in the space available for collections, and alternative media artifacts are not one of its priorities. However, alternative media archiving and public funding—or even just a stronger government publication program—would allow for a broader understanding of Canada's alternative media. Without that, we will not have a complete history, and without understanding our past, we won't be able to have a more inclusive future.

QUESTIONS FOR DISCUSSION

1. What is the democratic role of alternative media?
2. What is the reason for having alternative media, when everyone and anyone can now make and consume their own media?
3. How can we help alternative media to survive?
4. Should alternative media be subsidized by the federal government? Why or why not?

ASSIGNMENTS

1. Divide into groups and research a contemporary or recent Indigenous social movement in North America. Research how the movement began (what was its issue and its purpose?), how members built their movement (online; by word-of-mouth; through social media, demonstrations, an existing organization, etc.), and what their goals were. How did the movement keep moving forward? What role did mainstream media play and what role did social media play? Was the movement "successful"? (Note that there are many ways a movement can be considered successful.)
2. Create a fictitious example of alternative media or a social movement and, using the attributes in this chapter, build its profile using what you have learned about their purpose and their attributes.
3. For a long time, the Canadian government has provided assistance to help small and alternative media to survive. Research the history of this subsidy, who got a subsidy, who still gets one, and how much they get. Make a case as to why or why not some of these media should get a government subsidy.

WORKS CITED

Annis, R. (2012, 15 June). Quebec students keep up pressure, Charest ponders election options. *Rabble.ca*. Retrieved from www.rabble.ca/news/2012/06/quebec-students-keep-pressure-charest-ponders-electoral-options [November 21, 2012].

Atton, C. (2002). *Alternative media*. London, UK: Sage.

Berger, J. (1972). *Ways of seeing*. London, UK: Penguin Books.

Blumler, J. G., & Gurevitch, M. (1996). Media change and social change: Linkages and junctures. In J. Curran & M. Gurevitch (Eds.), *Mass media and society* (pp. 120–137). London, UK: Arnold.

CBC News. (2013, January 5). 9 questions about Idle No More. Retrieved from www.cbc.ca/news/canada/9-questions-about-idle-no-more-1.1301843 [April 14, 2017].

Fletcher, F. J. (2014). Journalism, corporate media, and democracy in the digital age. In K. Kozolanka (Ed.), *Publicity and the Canadian state: Critical communication perspectives* (pp. 27–48). Toronto, ON: University of Toronto Press.

Gamson, W. A., & Wolfsfeld, G. (1993). Movements and media as interlocking systems. *Annals of the American academy of political and social science, 528*, 114–125.

Gitlin, T. (1980). *The whole world is watching: Mass media in the making and the unmaking of the New Left*. Berkeley, CA: University of California Press.

Hackett, R. A., & Carroll, W. (2004). Critical social movements and media reform. *Media Development, 51*, 14–19.

Hackett, R. A., & Gruneau, R. (2000). *The missing news: Filters and blind spots in Canada's press*. With R. Gruneau, D. Gutstein, & T. A. Gibson. Toronto, ON: University of Toronto Press.

Idle No More. (2012). Idle No More. @IdleNoMore4, #idlenomore. Retrieved from www.twitter.com/IdleNoMore4?ref_src=twsrc%5Egoogle%7Ctwcamp%5Eserp%7Ctwgr%5Eauthor [April 15, 2017].

Kozolanka, K., Mazepa, P., & Skinner, D. (Eds.). (2012). *Alternative Media in Canada*. Vancouver, BC: UBC Press.

New Internationalist. (2016). The unreported year. January. Compiled by Jo Lateu. Retrieved from https://newint.org/features/2016/01/01/the-unreported-year/ [January 1, 2017].

Smythe, D. (1981). *Dependency road: Communications, capitalism, consciousness and Canada*. Norwood, NJ: Ablex Publishing.

White, M. (2010, August 12). Clicktivism is ruining leftist activism. *The Guardian*. Retrieved from www.theguardian.com/commentisfree/2010/aug/12/clicktivism-ruining-leftist-activism [December 31, 2016].

Williams, R. (1977). *Marxism and literature*. London, UK, and New York, NY: Oxford University Press.

Winseck, D. (2015). CMCRP: Canadian Media Concentration Research Project. Retrieved from www.cmcrp.org [March 31, 2017].

3 Democracy in a Changing Landscape of Media Sources

> Either the Internet has freed us from the stifling grip of the old, top-down mass media model, transforming consumers into producers and putting citizens on par with the powerful, or we have stumbled into a new trap, a social media hall of mirrors made up of personalized feeds, "filter bubbles," narcissistic chatter, and half-truths.
>
> —Taylor, 2014, p. 69

Most citizens today are aware that in recent years traditional newspapers are having a difficult time surviving financially at the same time that they must compete with social media sites such as Twitter and Facebook. Social media advocates claim that new media offer different news to the public, often providing a plethora of topics intentionally or unintentionally omitted in the mainstream media. Indeed, for many people, the mainstream corporate media is a hegemonic device that supports the status quo, especially on issues related to the economy. According to this line of reasoning, the corporate media is *not* offering the public the important news stories they need to become informed citizens. Many consider social media venues capable of filling the void created by the omission of vital topics in the mainstream media. Moreover, social media outlets are also able to provide multiple perspectives on almost every issue imaginable. Hence, the reasoning goes, democracy is strengthened by Twitter, Facebook, and other media formats found on the Internet. But is this actually true?

Very few would dispute the notion that social media have been a major factor in the seismic shift the journalism world has undergone in recent years. There also appears to be a gargantuan change occurring within democracy in many

Western nations today—populist sentiments are often no longer in line with the corporate agenda of the mainstream media. The 2016 results of the Brexit vote in the United Kingdom and the US presidential election victory of Donald Trump attest to this. This chapter explores the quickly changing dynamics in contemporary journalism and its evolving effects on citizenship and democracy.

JOURNALISM—THE CURRENT LANDSCAPE IS SHIFTING SAND

Journalism has experienced a drastic decrease in public trust in recent years, some of it its own doing. For example, one historic blunder on the part of the mainstream media was the loud and incessant reporting on non-existent weapons of mass destruction in Iraq shortly after the September 11th attack on the World Trade Center. The media-fuelled hysteria culminated in the US-led invasion of Iraq in March 2003. Claims by the American and British governments that the Iraqi government was stockpiling chemical and biological weapons in order to cause mass carnage among innocent people across Western nations resulted in over half a million innocent Iraqis being killed (Sheridan, 2013). This infamous usage of incendiary words predates the current explosion of fake news by about 15 years.

A more recent omission of massive proportions on the part of mainstream media pertains to the deregulation of the American financial sector that led to the subprime mortgage scandal. This deregulation resulted in colossal corruption that, in turn, led to the catastrophic economic crash across much of the globe in 2007–2008. To say that this was a miss on the part of mainstream media would be a serious understatement. It is no wonder that in 2013 the US-based Pew Research Center for the People and the Press found that 63 percent of poll respondents believe that news in the mainstream media is often inaccurate (cited in Taylor, 2014). Moreover, the percentage of American citizens who believe that journalists contribute a lot to society decreased by 10 percentage points, from 38 percent in 2009 to 28 percent in 2013. A 2016 Gallup poll asked a related but different question. It found that the trust placed in the mainstream media by Americans had dropped to its lowest level since Gallup began polling this question in 1972: only 38 percent claim to have a "great deal or fair amount of trust in the media" (Swift, 2016).

The trust that Canadians put in their mainstream media is not much better. According to the 2017 Edelman Trust Barometer, the trust level among

Canadians dropped from 55 percent to 45 percent between 2015 and 2016 (cited in English, 2017). When considering an informed citizenry for a stronger democracy, these numbers are disconcerting. The frequently heard claims of fake news by certain American politicians such as President Trump will undoubtedly exacerbate this situation. (The topic of fake news will be addressed in Chapter 4.) This lack of trust is a factor in fewer readers of traditional newspapers in both countries, which has hurt their revenues.

Not all of the factors causing decreased readership in mainstream print media have been self-inflicted, of course. One factor related to social media that has greatly altered the economic conditions for the traditional newspaper has to do with *bundling*. Social media have taken apart the different sections that comprise the newspaper. The total readership for newspapers used to be an amalgamation of people interested in local, national, and international current events, crossword puzzles, sports, celebrity gossip, and business news. This model created a large enough readership for corporate advertisers to offer significant dollars for space to help sell their products. Important endeavours like investigative journalism, never popular with the masses to the same extent as sports or entertainment, existed because newspapers had enough revenue from advertisers and readers to pay journalists for their long and arduous hours working on a story.

The Internet has in effect unbundled this winning combination of packaged functions. Readers can now find the specific things they are interested in without paying for the entire package by going to multiple websites for alternative media, political blogs, online sports and entertainment sites, Facebook or Twitter. Indeed, it looks like things could get much worse for newspapers. Facebook founder and CEO Mark Zuckerberg recently posted a memo to Facebook in which he describes a future vision of Facebook "for keeping us safe, for informing us, for civic engagement, and for inclusion for all" (cited in LaFrance, 2017, p. 2). Each one of these points happens to be a major function of the mainstream media, especially newspapers.

The aforementioned economic calamity caused by deregulation of the financial sector has also resulted in smaller advertising revenues for newspapers because many corporations simply can no longer afford to advertise to the same extent (Taylor, 2014). Moreover, the dollars that corporations still have for advertising have been going elsewhere, mostly to the Internet giants. As a case in point, "85 percent of all online advertising revenue is funneled to either Facebook or Google—leaving a paltry 15 percent for news organizations to fight over" (LaFrance, 2017, p. 1). The technological changes resulting in a vast and burgeoning abundance of numerous media sources offering countless perspectives on infinite topics to the public have been particularly damaging to newspapers.

Declining readership numbers and shrinking advertising revenues for newspapers have put extraordinary financial pressure on newspapers to survive, and some of them have not. Active citizenship is more likely to decrease after major newspapers close their doors for good. This is exactly what occurred in Denver and Seattle when the *Rocky Mountain News* and the *Seattle Post-Intelligencer* stopped publishing. A 2014 study found that in the year following the closure of each newspaper (2008–2009), civic engagement in Denver and Seattle dropped significantly (Shaker, 2014). This decline in active citizenship was not replicated in other large American cities during the same period, suggesting that the newspaper closures were factors in a situation of weakened local democracy.

Newspapers still in operation have also been greatly affected by the new economic reality. Revenues are not the only aspect of the mainstream newspapers that are shrinking—there has been a significant decrease in the number of paid working journalists. According to the Pew Research Center, there were fewer full-time positions for journalists in American newsrooms in 2013 than in 1978, when the population of the US was 30 percent less than it is today, a very telling statistic (cited in Taylor, 2014). In this scenario, the first casualties of cutbacks are the investigative journalists and those working in foreign affairs. In other words, political journalism has taken a serious hit.[1] For major news stories, most newspapers have been forced to increasingly rely on wire services such as Reuters, the Associated Press, or the Canadian Press. Some papers rely on major international news outlets such as the *Washington Post* and the *Guardian* for foreign affairs articles. Their own journalists are often relegated to cover more superficial topics, more often than not dictated by what they perceive the readers *want*, rather than what they *need* in order to become informed citizens (McChesney, 2007). Further, many larger media sources cannot even afford to dedicate journalists to cover *local* politics, a scenario that often leads to increased political corruption. Further, a relatively unknown but massive American broadcast company called the Sinclair Media Group owns almost 200 television stations. Called a "conservative giant" by the *New York Times*, "Sinclair forces its local stations to run pro-Trump 'news' stations" (Graves, 2017). Local news is becoming a hegemonic device, yet very few people realize it.

The landscape may improve, of course, but the trend is worrying for citizens desiring a stronger democracy. Before the advent of social media, the mainstream media had overcome the family, church, and school to become the dominant socializing influence in society, and the major analytical source of important events (Buckingham, 2003). A brief discussion of some of the very important contributions the mainstream media have traditionally offered and continue to offer in terms of fostering an informed citizenry is next.

MAINSTREAM MEDIA'S CONTRIBUTIONS TO A SOPHISTICATED CITIZENRY

> [T]he revolutionary idea of professional journalism—the formal separation of the owner from the editorial function—emerged.... Citizens no longer needed to worry about private monopoly control over the news; trained professionals serving the public interest were in charge and had the power.
> —McChesney, 2007, p. 26

In the early decades of the 20th century, popular resistance to the control of American media outlets by the economic elites grew increasingly stronger. Upton Sinclair's (1920/2003) 440-page opus *The Brass Check: A Study of American Journalism* was a top-selling book that decried the moneyed interests in the media (McChesney, 2007). It contributed to a growing citizen resistance to economic power controlling American mainstream news.

At about the same time, another source of the resistance was coming from the people who were responsible for the content of the newspapers:

> As owners began trumpeting editorial independence in their marketing, journalists seized on it to upgrade their professionalism. A generation of early press critics emerged, such as Will Irwin, a former newspaper reporter and editor of *McClure's Magazine*, who in 1911 published a bracing fifteen-part series in Collier's chronicling in bold detail the abuses of the press.... Newspaper editors in turn reacted to the rhetoric of their bosses and the rebukes of the critics, and they tried to professionalize as a group. (Kovach & Rosenstiel, 2014, p. 14)

The opposition created by both engaged citizens and newspaper editors and journalists eventually led to the notion of the *professional journalist* who was unencumbered by the perspectives of wealthy owners of the media. It also led to the creation of journalism schools across the United States and Canada.

The entire idea of the professional journalist evolved into many genres, and the one that arguably influenced a nation's values and ethics the most was and still is the *investigative* journalist. This kind of journalist explores single issues involving political corruption or corporate wrongdoing in an in-depth analysis, sometimes spending months or even years to do so while overcoming many obstacles. Investigative journalism was and to a large extent still is usually exclusive to one media outlet—the public learns about an issue that otherwise would not have been in the open. Investigative journalists almost by definition take a *critical* approach to their work as they seek to illuminate the hidden and nefarious workings of power.

The most famous, or rather infamous, example of investigative journalism in North America involved the Watergate Scandal of the early 1970s. The *Washington Post* assigned two young reporters, Carl Bernstein and Bob Woodward (1974), to investigate corruption in the White House. They used informants inside the government to eventually force the sitting Republican president of the United States, Richard Nixon, to resign from office in 1974.[2] **Watergate** has since come to represent a warning to all incumbents in political office that it is wise to play by the rules. (For some elected officials it likely means that they should be more careful if they do not want to play by the rules.) Watergate has also become synonymous with political or corporate corruption: the suffix "gate" is often attached to a signifier word representing a case of nefarious behind-the-scenes political activity. Since Watergate, some of the more infamous examples are Climategate, Bridgegate, Panamagate, and Canada's own Robogate.

Panamagate refers to a more recent example of impressive investigative journalism involving perhaps the biggest data leak anywhere, and is more well known by the moniker the **Panama Papers** (Harding, 2016). The Panama Papers is the result of a massive collaborative effort spearheaded by the International Consortium of Investigative Journalists. The contributors to this undertaking comprised 107 mainstream media sources, including the BBC, the CBC, and large newspapers such as the *Guardian* and the *Toronto Star*. The investigation lasted for over a year and revealed that many of the world's wealthiest people have been refusing to pay taxes by hiding their fortunes in offshore tax havens. It is estimated that this amounts to trillions of US dollars, and critics point to this as one of the reasons many governments can no longer afford to adequately fund public education, public healthcare, and other components of the social welfare state.

As a result of this collaborative investigation, governments worldwide have launched numerous investigations into these tax havens for economic elites who refuse to pay taxes (Oved, 2016). It is noteworthy that the investigative journalists who worked on this project have received 22 awards for their efforts, many of them from the most prestigious journalism organizations in the world. Indeed, the judges for the British Journalism Award praised the investigation because it "shone a light in some of the darkest corners of international finance" (cited in Oved, 2017).

These are but two of countless successful investigations by committed journalists whose efforts reveal unethical and otherwise hidden behaviour pertaining to major political and economic activity. When the public is informed of illegal behaviour and corruption, democracy is strengthened as citizens can and do lobby their elected representatives for change. The point to be made here is that for a variety of reasons it is impossible for the citizen journalists using social media platforms like Facebook and Twitter to engage in investigative journalism. This is one of the many areas where social media cannot compete with mainstream media on important matters related to democracy and civil society. There are many others.

Take cultural analysis, for example. Since 1998, *Toronto Star* journalist Haroon Siddiqui has used his weekly column to explore Canada's relatively recent demographic transformation into a global village. For over 17 years, Siddiqui has explored topics omitted in other mainstream media sources from the point of view of the "new cosmopolitan Canada" (Siddiqui, 2015). He theorizes that multiculturalism in Canada conjoined with the Charter of Rights to create a "rights revolution" that influenced issues such as "employment equity, access to professions, fair policing, balanced media portrayal of minorities, etc." (Siddiqui, 2015). This is an example in which mainstream media is producing important work in the development of a progressive national identity and a more civil society in a changing Canada. Social media and individual political blogs cannot compete at this level, and people who get their news solely from these sites are simply missing out. They become less informed in comparison with regular readers of respected newspapers such as the *Toronto Star*. Cultural insight and analysis found in the work of Siddiqui and others is impossible to replicate in social media. There are many other areas where this is the case, too many to mention here. Certain aspects of mainstream media, however, are not at all helpful in fostering an informed citizenry.

MAINSTREAM MEDIA AND OBSTACLES TO AN INFORMED CITIZENRY

> The mass media serve as a system for communicating messages and symbols to the general populace. It is their function to amuse, entertain, and inform, and to inculcate individuals with the values, beliefs, and codes of behavior that will integrate them into the institutional structures of the larger society. In a world of concentrated wealth and major conflicts of class interest, to fulfil this role requires systematic propaganda.
> —Herman & Chomsky, 1988, p. 1

In 1988, *Manufacturing Consent: The Political Economy of the Mass Media* was published. Written by media critics Edward Herman and Noam Chomsky, the book is still considered by many critical media educators to be a very important contribution to the field of political media literacy. As the title suggests, the authors claim that American corporate media is part of a massive communications system that serves a hegemonic propaganda function to persuade citizens to accept the interests of the elites as universal interests. This perspective is very much in keeping with the theoretical approach known as the political economy of communication. It reflects both the prevailing orthodoxy or dominant ideology as well as the related concept of false political consciousness.

Since the 1980s, these interests of the elites have been encapsulated in the prevailing orthodoxy of neoliberalism, an economic paradigm focused on strengthening corporate power and profits (see Chapter 1). Herman and Chomsky contend that mainstream media typically promote tax cuts, privatizing of the commons, free trade deals that diminish workers' rights, politicians around the world who support US business interests, and in regions contending with military conflicts, the side best suited to those same business interests. The mainstream media define the acceptable boundaries of political and cultural discourse by modelling what one is allowed to say and how it is to be said or framed. Of course, dissenting voices appear from time to time, but they are in the minority and most often marginalized (Herman & Chomsky, 1988). Although this seminal book was first published 30 years ago, the claims made by Herman and Chomsky still hold significant validity today.

None of this should be surprising to anyone who understands that corporate media have corporate interests. By extension, it collectively functions as a hegemonic device. In a provocative *Belfast Telegraph* column written in 2013, Chomsky contends that if mainstream American newspapers gave *front-page* coverage to a wide range of topics pertaining to economics, civil society in the United States would greatly strengthen. He claims that most progressive initiatives involving social and economic topics are already supported by the majority of American citizens. Chomsky believes that a mainstream media committed to civil society has a major role to play. The initiatives he wants front-page coverage for include increased taxation rates for the wealthiest Americans and corporations, support for the creation of a universal public healthcare system and subsidized public transportation systems, and ending government financial support for the banking industry, especially the major banks (Chomsky, 2013).

In general, the segment of the American population that supports these progressive ideas comprises the bottom 70 percent of the income ladder.[3]

Chomsky makes the case that this rather large segment of American society possesses absolutely no influence in what gets covered in the media, nor on government policy itself. This is where an understanding of political economy enters the discussion. In the US, Canada, and all countries that adhere to a capitalist economic system, *political economy* refers to the distribution of wealth and decision-making power, or capitalism in a democracy. Ever since the time of ancient Greece, there has been political tension between those who own property and wealth and those who do not. It is difficult to fathom how political equality can exist where economic inequality is massive. If the mainstream media refuse to address what the majority of Americans want, and ignore the reasons for the growing wealth gap in the country, it is an obstacle to democracy. Inequality weakens democracy. Consider the following example.

The Democratic Party presidential nomination campaigns for the 2016 election provide further evidence of corporate media functioning as a hegemonic device. The two candidates, secretary of state Hillary Clinton and senator Bernie Sanders, ran on vastly different economic platforms. Most pundits saw Clinton as representing the interests of Wall Street. Sanders, on the other hand, called himself a "democratic socialist" and used the Nordic nation of Denmark as an existing example of what kind of policies he would try to implement in the US (Moody & Rosen, 2016). Corporate interests were at stake, as Sanders wanted to raise corporate taxes to pay for universal healthcare, a better public education system, and free tuition for post-secondary education. As the Vermont senator's campaign gained strength, the mainstream media stepped up their attacks. On one day alone, the *Washington Post* published sixteen anti-Sanders articles, with four of them condemning Sanders' tax plans (Johnson, 2016). One of these articles was titled "Sorry, Bernie fans, his healthcare plan is short by $17 trillion," a number that the news organization Fairness & Accuracy in Reporting (FAIR) claims was pulled out of thin air (Johnson, 2016).

Influential *New York Times* columnist and past recipient of the Nobel prize in economics Paul Krugman (2016), an outspoken supporter of Hillary Clinton, wrote a column called "Sanders over the edge" in which he decried Sanders' suggestion that America's biggest banks should be broken up. The mainstream media's many attacks against Senator Sanders continued unabated until he was finally forced to end his campaign, resulting in Hillary Clinton being declared the Democratic presidential nominee. The relentless and aggressive opposition to Senator Sanders and his agenda to help Americans in need of economic support demonstrates how mainstream corporate media can and do perform their main hegemonic function clearly and effectively.

In case there was any doubt about elements in the corporate media playing a role as a hegemonic device, leaked emails immediately prior to the 2016 presidential election provide some evidence. Internal party documents outline which journalists Hillary Clinton's campaign team considered trustworthy to publish stories the way they wanted (Greenwald & Fang, 2016). The correspondence included lists of journalists they wanted to invite to informal, off-the-record gatherings with Clinton, and which journalists were to be blocked from attending because they were unsure of the perspective they might take in stories about the secretary of state.

This was not a new strategy—the campaign team for John McCain's successful bid to become the Republican candidate in the 2008 election did something very similar (Bailey, 2008). What appears to be an original strategy for American politics, however, is what President Trump did in the weeks following his inauguration in early 2017. After speeches in which the president called the media the "enemy of the people," he banned certain major news organizations from attending a press briefing (Dale, 2017). These organizations included the *New York Times*, the *Los Angeles Times*, CNN, and the BBC, all media sources that had published stories unfavourable to the president immediately prior to the announced ban. It is uncertain how the mainstream media will react to this new strategy of "the exclusion of critical outlets from official presidential briefings [which] is without modern precedent" (Dale, 2017). President Trump's relationship with the media is further addressed in Chapter 4.

Elections often provide obvious examples of corporate media having corporate interests. It would be difficult to find a case where the corporate media in Canada or the United States supported a political party that wanted to raise corporate taxes or royalty rates in order to build a stronger commons. The 2011 and 2015 federal elections that took place in Canada are a case in point: a study proved that "Canadian newspapers overwhelmingly supported Stephen Harper's Conservatives in the past two elections, much more so than they would have if they had reflected public opinion" (Tencer, 2015). This study, done by the Canadian Media Concentration Research Project, found that for the 2011 election an astonishing 95 percent of daily newspapers endorsed the Conservatives, approximately three times their standing in public opinion polls at the time (Tencer, 2015). For the 2015 election, 71 percent, or 17 out of 23 dailies, endorsed the Conservatives, while the rest supported the Liberals. Not one newspaper supported the social democratic NDP. What was even more remarkable in 2015 was that Postmedia's CEO Paul Godfrey commanded all 16 of its newspapers across Canada to support the Conservatives, regardless of local issues or sentiments. Given that the Liberals won a majority government, it was clear that Canada's biggest newspaper chain was out of step with public sentiment. Despite the outcome, the edict to its entire newspaper chain to endorse the Conservatives is a demonstration of the threat to democracy with a highly concentrated media ownership.

Condemnation of Postmedia's edict from their national office was swift and cutting. The chair of the board of Canada's highest-circulation newspaper, the *Toronto Star*, wrote a scathing editorial of how Postmedia had let its readers down, indeed, had let democracy down by neglecting to support the democratic process in each locale (Honderich, 2015). The online alternative media source Rabble.ca published an incisive critique of the two national newspapers, the *National Post* and the *Globe and Mail*, for writing editorials in praise of the Harper Conservatives for managing Canada's economy so well (Dobbin, 2015). Apparently, the two newspapers had ignored a study that found the Conservatives had been the worst federal government since 1945 in 13 of 16 economic indicators (Stanford, cited in Dobbin, 2015). One of the few indicators where they truly did excel, according to investigative journalist Murray Dobbin (2015), was in one particular aspect of the economy, namely, the part that is "for the corporate elite, the 1%—not the economy of ordinary wage and salary earners." Dobbin contends that the *owners* of these national newspapers are "as contemptuous of democracy and society as the [Conservative] party they endorsed." The majority of comments on social media sites like Facebook and Twitter were even more scathing of these newspapers for their support of Harper's Conservatives, a party and a government very much despised, as the final election results demonstrated. The social media reactions to election campaigns will be discussed later in this chapter.

Mainstream corporate media have been trumpeting the virtues of neoliberalism or global capitalism for over 30 years, especially in the Unites States, the United Kingdom, and Canada. The calls for diminished roles for government, particularly around the regulation of industry, have led to a situation in which media ownership is concentrated far beyond what is healthy for democracy. The greatest concentration of media ownership of any Western nation is in Canada, and there does not seem to be a public outcry pushing politicians for reform (Dobbin, 2015). This was not always the case. The federal Liberal governments of Pierre Trudeau established two commissions to study the impacts on Canada from media concentration. The 1970 Davey Report and the 1981 Kent Royal Commission on Newspapers recommended limits to media concentration because of what they perceived to be as not in the best interests of Canadian democracy.[4] Had their recommendations been implemented, "the history of the country may well have been altered" (Dobbin, 2015).

BOX 3.1: CORPORATE MEDIA HAVE CORPORATE INTERESTS: A CASE STUDY

Media critics Edward Herman and Noam Chomsky claim that American corporate media is part of a massive communications system that serves a hegemonic propaganda function to persuade citizens to accept the interests of the elites as universal interests. The example of investigative journalist Gary Webb is a case in point. In the mid-1990s Webb made a determined attempt to expose the CIA's involvement in cocaine smuggling to help fund a nefarious regime-change scheme in Nicaragua. Nicaragua's Sandinista government in the late 1970s and 1980s was decidedly leftist—it had the support of the agrarian working classes for its policies supporting land reform, workers' rights, better schools, and a universal public healthcare system. Seeing their bottom line threatened, American corporations with interests in Central America did not support these reforms, and the CIA was instructed to rectify the situation. Webb went to great lengths to tell readers about the CIA's plan to destabilize the Sandinista government, and mainstream media's complicity in it. As soon as his investigative work was published in the *San Jose Mercury News*, he incurred the wrath of American elites and the mainstream media (Hedges, 2014). His credibility and character were mercilessly attacked.

After the 2014 release of *Kill the Messenger*, the film based on this story, major American newspapers renewed their attacks on Webb almost 20 years after the first round of written and verbal assaults. Former *New York Times* journalist Chris Hedges (2014) contends that major American news outlets, including the *Times* and the *Washington Post*, did all they could to pillory Webb in their quest to protect the integrity of the CIA. According to Hedges, it was "a seedy, disgusting, and shameful chapter in American journalism. But it was hardly unique." Hedges bolsters his argument by invoking C. Wright Mills, the American sociologist of the mid-20th century, who argued that the corporate media are essential in order to influence the masses into conformity. This is another way of saying its role is to manufacture consent. In the case of Gary Webb, rather than supporting a fellow journalist, the mainstream media viciously attacked his credibility and only stopped when Webb took his own life (Hedges, 2014). None of this should be surprising to anyone who understands that corporate media have corporate interests.

There is an irony here, of course. The acute concentration of media ownership, especially with newspapers, has led to a narrowing of acceptable views among columnists and editorials, and often these views are not in step with mainstream Canadian values. The position of the huge Postmedia chain to support the Harper Conservatives for the 2015 election is a case in point. Many Canadians have turned away from corporate newspapers to get their news, ostensibly because they do not see their perspectives reflected in corporate media. Some turn to social media, while others go to progressive alternative online news sites that are gaining popularity, such as the Canada-wide Rabble.ca and the BC-based Tyee.ca. It is conceivable that if the *Globe and Mail* and the *National Post* hired regular columnists with views counter to the prevailing neoliberal orthodoxy, the current trend of shrinking daily readerships for these two national newspapers would reverse. Of course, some people consider the mainstream media outlets to be too liberal. Online news sites that are sometimes referred to as containing alt-right perspectives have also become popular. In Canada, Rebel Media is known to provide incendiary views on race and culture, while in the US Breitbart.com provides pro-Trump and White nationalist perspectives.

The discussion thus far has demonstrated that the mainstream corporate media are heavily influenced by powerful economic and political forces, resulting in a clear bias in favour of the corporate agenda. This partisanship is especially pronounced and overt at election time. Are social media free of political and economic interference? The next two sections will explore this question.

ARE SOCIAL MEDIA A PANACEA FOR AN AILING DEMOCRACY?

> It is a widely held belief that conversations among citizens—and between citizens and politicians—concerning matters of common interest are essential to well-functioning democracies. This has been a key idea in theories of deliberative democracy.
>
> —Sorensen, 2016, p. 664

Social media have vast potential to increase citizen participation in the democratic process and, by corollary, strengthen democracy. The possibilities are particularly intriguing because, by a variety of measures, contemporary democracy is ailing across Canada and the US (P. Orlowski, 2011). The question about the effects of Facebook and Twitter on the distribution of economic, social, and political power is worth exploring. Put differently, do social media venues actually support democracy?

In certain respects, yes they do. For example, political conversations used to occur in town halls and coffee houses, but social media have given hope to reinvigorating the public sphere. A recent study in Denmark examined the "political conversations between Danish Members of Parliament (MPs) and citizens on Facebook" (Sorensen, 2016, p. 665). It found that "the majority of Danish MPs (125 out of 170) do have some kind of dialogue with citizens via their Facebook pages" (p. 667). This usage of social media for dialogue between politicians and citizens may not be as prevalent in Canada and the US, as "Denmark has a high level of political interest combined with a general trust in politics and society" (Jensen, 2011, as cited in Sorensen, 2016, p. 268). One might speculate from observing social media that comments made to politicians from Canadian and especially American citizens would likely not be as respectful as they are from Danish citizens.

Another example that demonstrates the ways in which social media can strengthen democracy pertains to the commons. It is no secret that the public education system throughout the US is chronically underfunded. Media attacks on teachers and especially teacher unions deflect attention from the issues of poverty and underfunding (Orlowski, 2014). Teachers in Detroit have taken to Twitter to help the public understand "the horrendous conditions of their schools" by posting photos of mouldy, rat-infested classrooms where they and their students spend their school days (NationofChange, 2016). Effective Twitter handles such as @BadAssTeachers, which has over 33,000 followers, post daily tweets about poverty, inequality, and schooling in the US. Both Twitter and Facebook are replete with articles and information about the neoliberal dismantling of public education. Teacher-authored blogs have enabled individual teachers to challenge attacks on the quality of the teaching profession, and the neoliberal impulse to reduce teaching to improved test scores (Shiller, 2015). Mainstream media, by comparison, are almost bereft of the many negative effects of neoliberalism upon the commons.

Social media are also effective venues for groups like Black Lives Matter, Idle No More, and Standing Rock to raise awareness of important social, political, and environmental issues. Again, by comparison mainstream corporate media have been extremely slow to give coverage to these social movements and others. From a conservative perspective, these groups are viewed as *radical* and as threats to the status quo. Supporters of these progressive social movements argue that the status quo needs to be challenged in order for social and ecological justice to be realized. Similarly, the massive Occupy Wall Street movement of 2011 was all over social media during the summer of that year, but mainstream media outlets gave it attention "only when protesters began being arrested" in the autumn (K. Orlowski, 2011). Photos and video clips from events organized by all of these groups instantaneously gain viewers the moment they are uploaded onto social media platforms. This is arguably good for an informed citizenry and democracy.

Facebook and Twitter are also invaluable media outlets for marginalized and oppressed groups that are in need of *international* support. The Israeli military incursion into Gaza in the summer of 2014 provides a clear example of the power of social media. Instant access to information and images influenced global reaction to what was happening in Gaza, and challenged the hegemony of Israeli perspectives: "The Israeli narrative dominates the mainstream media outlets but on Twitter, Facebook and other social media avenues, Gaza's story had a Palestinian face to it" (Bazian, 2014, p. 1). During the actual conflict, Palestinian activists utilized social media and in tandem with local and international political bloggers managed to alter the highly controlled political narrative of the Israeli government. Prior to social media, this had not happened before. As the Israeli military moved into Gaza, hashtags began to dominate the Twitterverse: #GazaUnderAttack was used in 4.3 million tweets, while the pro-Israeli #IsraelUnderFire hashtag was used in only 197,000 tweets, almost a reverse ratio of the perspectives dominating the mainstream media (Finighan, 2014). Similarly, Twitter has brought vivid and heart-wrenching images from the conflicts in Yemen and Syria to international audiences.

Earlier in the chapter there was a discussion about the mainstream media's coverage of the two Democratic nominees vying to become the party's candidate in the presidential election of 2016, secretary of state Hillary Clinton and senator Bernie Sanders. For most of the Democratic primaries, Senator Sanders, a self-identified "socialist," received very little coverage in mainstream media outlets. From reading the *New York Times* and the *Washington Post*, it appeared as though Secretary of State Clinton was assured of being the Democratic Party's candidate long before it actually occurred. Yet for people on Twitter, it seemed as though the opposite was true. Although it is very difficult to get the exact numbers from Twitter, pro-Sanders hashtags such as #FeelTheBern appeared to dwarf the number of tweets and retweets for pro-Clinton hashtags like #ImWithHer. Photographs of Sanders delivering speeches to massive crowds across the US were immediately uploaded. The few photos of Clinton events, by comparison, showed small and unenthusiastic audiences. This juxtaposition led many of the interested members of the so-called Twitterverse to think that the US was going to have its first socialist candidate for president since Eugene Debbs in the early

1900s. The Sanders campaign was gaining momentum as pro-Sanders hashtags and tweeters gained popularity. As political watchers learned from both mainstream and social media outlets, however, the Democratic Party establishment conspired to block Sanders in order to give Clinton the nomination (Roberts, Jacobs, & Yuhas, 2016). Had the campaigns been allowed to continue without political interference, the Sanders campaign looked as though it might have prevailed *without* the help of the mainstream media and *with* the help of social media. This is significant.[5]

Clearly there is an argument to be made that social media enhance democracy by increasing the number of perspectives offered in local and global power struggles. The interests of the elites are being challenged in ways that have never before been utilized. Voices that traditionally have been excluded from the mainstream media can and do access social media outlets to reach massive audiences. Progressive movements are also better able to get exposure for their ideas, and to demonstrate how these ideas are resonating with citizens. Yet in terms of citizenship, social media are not without their pitfalls and can also lead to a democratic deficit.

SOCIAL MEDIA SHORTCOMINGS FOR AN INFORMED CITIZENRY

> Facebook and Twitter have recently deleted thousands of posts, pages and accounts in response to demands from the Israeli ministry of justice.
> —*Middle East Monitor*, June 9, 2016

The quote above leads to an important question: how do social media giants like Facebook and Twitter decide what posts, if any, should be deleted? After all, it is unlikely that groups like Hamas or Hezbollah would be able to convince Facebook or Twitter to delete posts that place them in an unfavourable light. Black Lives Matter and Idle No More would also have little political, economic, or social capital to be able to sway popular social media outlets to adhere to their wishes. Indeed, as with mainstream media outlets, this example suggests that hegemony, political ideology, and power are clearly involved in these decisions.

Similar to Noam Chomsky's emphasis on political economy mentioned earlier, media scholar Robert McChesney (2013) contends that *any* analysis of the potential of social media to affect democracy must be grounded in political economy. By this he means that analyzing the effects of social media must be placed within the frame of the relationship of capitalism to democracy. An in-depth discussion of political economy is beyond the intentions of this book, but suffice to say that capitalism dominates social life to the extent that it is often taken for granted. As the profit motive is at the root of capitalism, the development of the Internet in capitalist countries is also subservient to ways in which financial profit can be maximized. McChesney (2013) contends that capitalism "sets the terms for understanding not only the Internet, but most everything else of a social nature, including politics, in our society" (p. 13). It does this through advertising, public relations, and marketing all in the name of profit. Corporate media outlets are obviously not immune from these forces, but neither are social media outlets.

Power is at stake when the machinations of democracy are activated. This explains the constant battles over access to the Internet in general and social media in particular in Canada and elsewhere. Indeed, the Canadian federal government wants to implement Internet taxes that would limit access for less financially able people (Tabish, 2016). However, governments are not the only ones seeing potential income from the Internet. In early 2017, President Trump appointed Ajit Pai (Finley, 2017) to be the director of the Federal Communications Commission (FCC). As a member of the FCC, Pai had opposed all the major reforms that were passed, including the wide-ranging net-neutrality regulations passed in 2015. His stance has been to deregulate the entire Internet in order to allow investment and entrepreneurial opportunities. The appointment of the neoliberal Pai exemplifies the point McChesney makes about the need to ground analyses of social media's potential to strengthen democracy within a political economy frame.

There are myriad examples of social media being delegitimized as a credible news source. In Britain, heated arguments have erupted over whether security forces are using social media to pretend to be supporters of leftist Labour leader Jeremy Corbyn, who, like Bernie Sanders, wants to raise taxes on wealthy individuals and major corporations. In an attempt to stop Corbyn's momentum heading into the next national election, these pretend supporters were thought to be behind the "abuse and intimidation of MPs on social media" (Elgot & Aitkenhead, 2016). The idea that security forces such as MI5, MI6, the FBI, the CIA, the RCMP, or CSIS might utilize social media in less-than-upfront ways to protect the elites or the status quo is not far-fetched. Moreover, this is not the only way that security forces want to involve themselves in citizens' usage of the Internet.

In Canada, the intense public resistance to Bill C-51, originally designed by the Harper Conservatives in 2015, pits the concerns of national security forces against privacy concerns of individual citizens. The Liberal government implemented a public consultation process that critics contend was designed to favour "police and other authorities" (Nuttall, 2016). Advocates call Bill C-51 an anti-terrorism bill, while critics see it as a bill designed to legitimate the act of spying on citizens. In 2013, former CIA analyst Edward Snowden leaked documents from the National Security Agency as evidence that the American government and others spy on their citizens through massive and complex global surveillance programs.

There are other issues related to social media and democracy. Social media outlets such as Twitter use algorithms that tailor the views we see trending to our tastes. This leads to **filter bubbles** in which people tend to connect with perspectives much like their own. When people do come across views they disagree with on Twitter and other social media, however, the discussions are usually polarized, often becoming vitriolic (Pariser, 2011). Online hate speech is difficult for nations to control, as is organized trolling where targets are attacked for their views or even who they are.

Studies indicate that online political polls that frequently make the rounds on Facebook and Twitter reduce many progressive people's inclinations toward activism to what is becoming known as "clicktivism" (Sorensen, 2016). If a strong and well-functioning democracy requires an informed and active citizenry, clicktivism tends to remove the active component, which is very disconcerting. But are citizens becoming more informed from the boom in access to social media? Study after study indicates that young people are "shockingly ignorant of civics, history, geography, science, literature, the works" (McChesney, 2013). This may not be a particularly new phenomenon, but because of the quick access to incredible amounts of information, it is likely exacerbated. We are living in extremely ironic times in which people are being overwhelmed with data, statistics, and stories, but overall know less about important social, economic, and political issues at home and abroad.

This situation could very well be to the liking of those in power. It should not be a surprise that our governments often attempt to block the democratic potential of social media. After all, teaching high school students to foster a political consciousness has not been a priority in Canada or the US (Westheimer, 2015; P. Orlowski, 2011; Apple, 2004). Further, as discussed above, the mandate of corporate media is *not* to create an informed and active citizenry. Indeed, it most often acts as a hegemonic device. For the main, it is no different with social media. We are aware that countries like China block the democratic potential of social media. It would be myopic to believe that Western governments would be willing to promote true democratic initiatives through social media. As a general rule, those with power want to keep it.

Of course, there is also the situation that arises when a leader of a country prefers to speak to citizens through Twitter rather than through the mainstream media. Immediately after becoming president of the United States in January 2017, Donald Trump began to attack mainstream media outlets, calling them the "enemy of the people" in front of a partisan crowd at the Conservative Political Action Conference (Dale, 2017). The American president has a reputation of being a voracious tweeter, and has over 51 million followers on Twitter. He knows he can reach these followers without having his views and statements subjected to scrutiny by journalists.

Is the creation of an informed and active citizenry too much to ask of social media? It would appear so. Yet, as with the other topics in this chapter, this discussion only touches the surface of the ways in which social media affects citizenship and democracy.

ASSESSING THE MEDIA LANDSCAPE AND WHAT IT MEANS FOR DEMOCRACY AND AN INFORMED CITIZENRY

This chapter explored the evolving world of media outlets and how these changes might be affecting democracy and citizenship in Canada and the United States. Several media outlets were briefly mentioned, and many of the citations were from online alternative media outlets. The main forms of media discussed in the chapter, however, were the traditional print newspaper and social media outlets such as Twitter and Facebook.

For a variety of reasons, financial stability is an issue for all newspapers big and small in this era of neoliberalism. Perhaps the biggest factor for this is the appearance of social media outlets and the unbundling of the overall package of news provided by newspapers. Declining readership numbers and advertising revenues have created a situation in which many newspapers have reduced the number of investigative and foreign affairs journalists. This decrease in the number of journalists dedicated to covering politics and corruption in in-depth analyses creates the conditions for a weakened democracy. It also has the potential for a vicious cycle: as staff numbers decrease, the newspaper's value to readers may be diminished, resulting in smaller readership numbers and, therefore, decreased revenue, which in turn may lead to further staff cuts.

In two large American cities where a major newspaper closed its doors, a study demonstrated that there was a significant drop in civic engagement in the following year. This highlights a major concern in the push for fostering a more informed and active citizenry. In order to strengthen democracy, *every* city and town should have its own newspaper, and if possible, more than one. Coverage of local issues is one important reason, of course, but so is what the investigative journalist provides citizens. Online alternative media outlets such as Rabble.ca and TheTyee.ca, both of which provide excellent journalism from progressive perspectives, fill the gaps to some extent, but they operate on small budgets and are also vulnerable to financial instability. Some readers turn to far-right online websites such as Rebel Media. The main point here is to emphasize that without investigative journalism, something vital for a vibrant democracy is lost.

Mainstream media has always had to contend with charges of bias and propaganda, and attempts to become more objective have come up against many obstacles ever since the appearance of the professional journalist almost a century ago. The biggest obstacle, however, may be the popularity of social media outlets such as Twitter and Facebook. Social media outlets must also contend with partisanship and fake news, with the latter likely being more of a problem than in mainstream media. From an epistemological standpoint, the social construction of knowledge itself leads to the impossibility of creating news that is objective and free of bias from *any* media outlet. At the crux of the struggle to develop the media literate citizen is becoming aware of subjectivity and the nature of knowledge itself.

Many aspects of social media have value in terms of strengthening democracy. Offering information on topics omitted in the mainstream media, multiple perspectives that include those of marginalized groups, and up-to-the-minute photographs and video clips from military conflicts and political events are only some of these. As a case in point, Black Lives Matter grew to the size it has across the US and parts of Canada precisely because of the injustices done to young Black youths that found coverage on Facebook and Twitter. As well, social media provide venues for citizens to discuss important issues with each other and with politicians.

Social media, however, are not a panacea for all problems pertaining to our waning democracies. Charges of bias toward social media outlets are also warranted. Advertising and marketing are increasingly finding their way into Facebook and Twitter. More disconcerting, however, is the increasing prevalence of fake news on social media. (This will be explored in Chapter 4.) Further, state surveillance of the Internet in general and social media in particular present an Orwellian chill factor for citizens and for democracy itself.

The situation is indeed grim, but it is not past the point of no return. The sun may once again shine on mainstream media. Media owners and the journalists who work for them must figure out how to navigate these shifting sands. The public deserves strong investigative journalism and cultural analysis that cannot be replicated on social media. In fact, an informed citizenry requires both the benefits of the best of what mainstream media provides, and the networking potential of social media. The ills of *all* forms of media may be diminished by the creation of a media literate citizenry. In this way democracy will indeed be strengthened.

QUESTIONS FOR DISCUSSION

1. What were the recommendations of the 1970 Davey Report and the 1981 Kent Royal Commission on Newspapers? Why were their recommendations not implemented? Speculate on how Canadian politics may be different today had their recommendations been implemented.
2. The dire financial conditions that many Canadian newspapers have faced in recent years led to a well-publicized debate about whether the federal government "should step in to 'save journalism'" (Ballingall, 2017). Read the *Toronto Star* article cited in this question. What are the pros and cons of both sides of this debate? What other issues may arise from government involvement?
3. Research the original mandates of public broadcasters such as the BBC, the CBC, and Australia's ABC. How have these mandates evolved over time? Investigate the rules governing NPR, the largest American public broadcaster, and how its governance differs from other public broadcasters like the BBC and the CBC.
4. Choose a significant political scandal that, in some form or other, has had the suffix "-gate" added to it in the spirit of Watergate. Write a summary that describes both the scandal and the investigative journalism that brought the scandal to the public's attention.
5. Noam Chomsky is one of the world's foremost critics of corporate media and of American foreign policy. He is almost never given space to discuss his ideas in American mainstream media. Investigate the venues Chomsky uses to get his ideas across to vast numbers of people in the US and elsewhere. If the American commitment to free speech is to be believed, analyze why it is that Chomsky is rarely given that chance in the mainstream media.

ASSIGNMENT

Choose a major current event. Examples include federal elections, social movements, and military conflicts. Go to Twitter and find the popular hashtags for the current event from differing perspectives. Do a quantitative analysis of the number of tweets for each perspective.

To extend this activity further, study the ways in which mainstream newspapers cover the same current event. Analyze the level of support for each perspective in the newspapers. (Note: If the current event under study is national or international, the best Canadian newspapers to analyze coverage are the *Globe and Mail*, the *National Post*, and the *Toronto Star*.) Compare how the mainstream newspaper and Twitter differ in their support for each perspective.

NOTES

1. There are other forms of political journalism that are still in operation in most cities, however. Coverage of business and civic affairs are examples of this.
2. Hollywood has taken an interest in the important work done by investigative journalists. In 1976, *All the President's Men* was released, a political thriller about two *Washington Post* journalists and the Watergate scandal. More recently, *Spotlight* won the 2016 Oscar for its depiction of the investigative journalism done by journalists at the *Boston Globe* to uncover the massive scandal of child molestation and cover-up in a Catholic Archdiocese.
3. A percentage of this 70 percent voted for Donald Trump in the 2016 presidential election, suggesting either a false political consciousness or a naive belief in the rhetoric of the businessman and reality television host.
4. Brian Gorman's (2015) book called *Crash to Paywall* addresses the issue of highly concentrated media ownership from a Canadian perspective.
5. It is generally accepted that one of the major reasons why Barack Obama won the Democratic Party nomination and the presidential election in 2008 was his team's mastery of social media.

WORKS CITED

Apple, M. (2004). *Ideology and curriculum* (3rd ed.). New York, NY: Routledge-Falmer.

Bailey, H. (2008, March 2). McCain feeds his "base" BBQ. *Newsweek*. Retrieved from www.newsweek.com/mccain-feeds-his-base-bbq-84405 [December 21, 2016].

Ballingall, A. (2017, June 6). John Honderich, Andrew Coyne debate if government should step in to "save journalism." *Toronto Star*. Retrieved from www.thestar.com/news/canada/2017/06/06/john-honderich-andrew-coyne-debate-if-government-should-step-in-to-save-journalism.html [June 6, 2017].

Bazian, H. (2014, September/October). War on Gaza, social media and efficacy of protest. *Islamic Horizons*. Retrieved from www.academia.edu/8168450/War_on_Gaza_Social_Media_and_Efficacy_of_Protest [June 10, 2017].

Bernstein, C., & Woodward, B. (1974). *All the president's men: The greatest reporting story of all time*. New York, NY: Simon & Schuster.

Buckingham, D. (2003). *Media education: Literacy, learning and contemporary culture*. Malden, MA: Blackwell Publishing.

Chomsky, N. (2013, October 12). Noam Chomsky: What I'd like to see on front pages of newspapers. *Belfast Telegraph*. Retrieved from www.belfasttelegraph.co.uk/opinion/noam-chomsky-what-id-like-to-see-on-front-pages-of-newspapers-29654898.html [June 10, 2017].

Dale, D. (2017, February 24). White House blocks major news organizations from briefing, escalating Trump's war on the press. *Toronto Star*. Retrieved from www.thestar.com/news/world/2017/02/24/the-white-house-has-banned-several-news-organizations-including-the-new-york-times-and-cnn-from-todays-daily-briefing.html [February 24, 2017].

Dobbin, M. (2015, October 30). Want democratic reform? Let's start with newspapers. *Rabble.ca*. Retrieved from rabble.ca/columnists/2015/10/want-democratic-reform-lets-start-newspapers [January 28, 2017].

Elgot, J., & Aitkenhead, D. (2016, July 22). Len McCluskey: Intelligence services using "dark practices" against Corbyn. *The Guardian*. Retrieved from www.theguardian.com/politics/2016/jul/22/intelligence-services-using-dark-practices-against-jeremy-corbyn [July 23, 2016].

English, K. (2017, March 3). Democracy demands media literacy: Public editor. *Toronto Star*. Retrieved from www.thestar.com/opinion/public_editor/2017/03/03/democracy-demands-media-literacy-public-editor.html [March 3, 2017].

Finighan, A. (2014, July 22). Gaza and Israel: War of the hashtags. *Al Jazeera*. Retrieved from www.aljazeera.com/programmes/insidestory/2014/07/who-winning-social-media-war-over-gaza-2014722172425666235.html [January 22, 2017].

Finley, K. (2017, January 23). Trump's FCC pick does not bode well for net neutrality. *Wired*. Retrieved from www.wired.com/2017/01/trumps-fcc-pick-signals-end-net-neutrality-efforts/ [January 26, 2017].

Graves, L. (2017, August 17). This is Sinclair, "the most dangerous US company you've never heard of." *The Guardian*. Retrieved from www.theguardian.com/media/2017/aug/17/sinclair-news-media-fox-trump-white-house-circa-breitbart-news [August 18, 2017].

Greenwald, G., & Fang, L. (2016, October, 9). Exclusive: New email leak reveals Clinton campaign's cozy press relationship. *The Intercept*. Retrieved from theintercept.com/2016/10/09/exclusive-new-email-leak-reveals-clinton-campaigns-cozy-press-relationship/ [October 28, 2016].

Harding, L. (2016, April 5). What are the Panama Papers? A guide to history's biggest data leak. *The Guardian.* Retrieved from www.theguardian.com/news/2016/apr/03/what-you-need-to-know-about-the-panama-papers [April 6, 2016].

Hedges, C. (2014, October 26). The myth of the free press. *Truthdig.* Retrieved from www.truthdig.com/report/item/the_myth_of_the_free_press_20141026 [January 15, 2017].

Herman, E., & Chomsky, N. (1988). *Manufacturing consent: The political economy of the mass media.* New York, NY: Pantheon Books.

Honderich, J. (2015, November 9). Postmedia let down readers by dictating election endorsements. *Toronto Star.* Retrieved from www.thestar.com/opinion/commentary/2015/11/09/postmedia-let-down-readers-by-dictating-election-endorsements-honderich.html [January 29, 2017].

Johnson, A. (2016, May 11). Washington Post squeezes four anti-Sanders stories out of one tax study over seven hours. *FAIR—Fairness & Accuracy In Reporting.* Retrieved from fair.org/home/washington-post-squeezes-four-anti-sanders-stories-out-of-one-tax-study-over-seven-hours/ [August 29, 2016].

Kovach, B., & Rosenstiel, T. (2014). *The elements of journalism.* New York, NY: Penguin Random House.

Krugman. P. (2016, April 8). Sanders over the edge. *The New York Times.* Retrieved from www.nytimes.com/2016/04/08/opinion/sanders-over-the-edge.html [August 29, 2016].

LaFrance, A. (2017, February 17). The Mark Zuckerberg manifesto is a blueprint for destroying journalism. *The Atlantic.* Retrieved from www.theatlantic.com/technology/archive/2017/02/the-mark-zuckerberg-manifesto-is-a-blueprint-for-destroying-journalism/517113/ [February 19, 2017].

McChesney, R. (2007). *Communication revolution: Critical junctures and the future of media.* New York, NY: The New Press.

McChesney, R. (2013). *Digital disconnect: How capitalism is turning the Internet against democracy.* New York, NY: The New Press.

Middle East Monitor (2016, June 9). Under Israeli pressure, Facebook and Twitter delete large amounts of Palestinian content. Retrieved from www.middleeastmonitor.com/20160609-under-israeli-pressure-facebook-and-twitter-delete-large-amounts-of-palestinian-content/ [August 29, 2016].

Moody, C., & Rosen, A. (2016, February 17). Bernie Sanders' American Dream is in Denmark. *CNN Politics.* Retrieved from www.cnn.com/2016/02/17/politics/bernie-sanders-2016-denmark-democratic-socialism/ [August 29, 2016].

NationofChange (2016, January 18). Detroit teachers use Twitter to raise awareness of the conditions of their schools. Retrieved from www.nationofchange.org/2016/01/18/detroit-teachers-use-twitter-to-raise-awareness-of-the-conditions-of-their-schools/ [January 18, 2016].

Nuttall, J. (2016, September 9). Privacy advocates fear Bill C-51 consultations will be skewed. *The Tyee*. Retrieved from thetyee.ca/News/2016/09/09/Bill-C-51-Consultations-Skewed/ [September 16, 2016].

Orlowski, K. (2011, September 26). Big Media afraid to take Wall Street protest seriously. *The Tyee*. Retrieved from thetyee.ca/Mediacheck/2011/09/26/Occupy-Wall-Street-Coverage/ [February 3, 2017].

Orlowski, P. (2011). *Teaching about hegemony: Race, class & democracy in the 21st century*. New York, NY: Springer.

Orlowski, P. (2014). Social studies & civil society: Making the case to take on neoliberalism. *In Education, 20*(1), 3–24.

Oved, M. (2016, April 5). World leaders react to secret dealings revealed by Panama Papers. *Toronto Star*. Retrieved from www.thestar.com/news/world/2016/04/05/world-leaders-react-to-secret-dealings-revealed-by-panama-papers.html [April 7, 2016].

Oved, M. (2017, February 21). Top honours for Panama Papers reporting. *Toronto Star*. Retrieved from www.thestar.com/news/world/2017/02/21/top-honours-for-panama-papers-reporting.html [February 21, 2017].

Pariser, E. (2011). *The filter bubble: How the new personalized web is changing what we read and how we think*. New York, NY: Penguin.

Roberts, D., Jacobs, B., & Yuhas, A. (2016, July 25). Debbie Wasserman Schultz to resign as DNC chair as email scandal rocks Democrats. *The Guardian*. Retrieved from www.theguardian.com/us-news/2016/jul/24/debbie-wasserman-schultz-resigns-dnc-chair-emails-sanders [July 27, 2016].

Shaker, L. (2014). Dead newspapers and citizens' civic engagement. *Communication Faculty Publications and Presentations*. Paper 17. Retrieved from pdxscholar.library.pdx.edu/comm_fac/17 [January 28, 2017].

Sheridan, K. (2013, October 15). Iraq death toll reaches 500,000 since start of US-led invasion, new study says. *Huffington Post*. Retrieved from www.huffingtonpost.com/2013/10/15/iraq-death-toll_n_4102855.html [August 30, 2016].

Shiller, J. (2015). Speaking back to the neoliberal discourse on teaching: How U.S. teachers use social media to redefine teaching. *Critical Education, 6*(9). Retrieved from ojs.library.ubc.ca/index.php/criticaled/article/view/184931 [March 21, 2016].

Siddiqui, H. (2015, March 28). Challenges we've met, and new ones we need to. *Toronto Star*. Retrieved from www.thestar.com/opinion/commentary/2015/03/28/challenges-weve-met-and-new-ones-we-need-to-siddiqui.html [March 29, 2015].

Sinclair, U. (2003). *The brass check: A study of American journalism*. Chicago, IL: University of Illinois Press. (Original work published 1920).

Sorensen, M. (2016). Political conversations on Facebook—the participation of politicians and citizens. *Media, Culture & Society, 38*(5), 664–685.

Swift, A. (2016, September 14). Americans' trust in mass media sinks to new low. *Gallup*. Retrieved from www.gallup.com/poll/195542/americans-trust-mass-media-sinks-new-low.aspx [November 15, 2016].

Tabish, J. (2016, October 3). Stop the federal government before it taxes everything on the Internet. *Financial Post*. Retrieved from http://business.financialpost.com/opinion/stop-the-federal-government-before-it-taxes-everything-on-the-internet [October 9, 2016].

Taylor, A. (2014). *The people's platform: Taking back power and culture in the digital age.* Toronto, ON: Random House Canada.

Tencer, D. (2015, November 10). Canada's newspapers were in the tank for Harper, media analysis finds. *Huffington Post*. Retrieved from www.huffingtonpost.ca/2015/11/10/newspaper-endorsements-harper-study_n_8523676.html [November 15, 2016].

Westheimer, J. (2015). *What kind of citizen? Educating our children for the common good.* New York, NY: Teacher's College Press.

4 Media Literacy in an Era of Fake News and Alternative Facts

> People want to believe that something is the biggest and the greatest and the most spectacular. I call it truthful hyperbole. It's an innocent form of exaggeration—and a very effective form of promotion.
>
> —Donald Trump, 1987, p. 58

The above quote was taken from Donald Trump's (1987) book *The Art of the Deal*, which was published almost 30 years before he entered the world of American politics. As a businessman, what the future politician called "truthful hyperbole" meant little to anyone uninterested in Trump's philosophy of personal finance. It likely did not mean very much to the television audiences that tuned in to his reality show *The Apprentice*, in which he starred from 2004 to 2015. When Trump announced his intentions to become the Republican candidate in the 2016 presidential election, many people were curious, while others were skeptical. It quickly became common knowledge that this man was willing to say just about anything at his rallies. The mainstream media gave his campaign extensive coverage, more than the other Republican nominees combined. After all, here was a candidate more entertaining than anybody had seen on the political circuit for a long time. Trump was viewed as a colourful character who would improve ratings on television news and increase readership numbers in the mainstream newspapers. Mainstream media outlets covered his campaign extensively, focusing on many of the outrageous statements he made often as entertainment.

All of that changed completely on November 8, 2016, when Donald Trump was elected the 45th president of the United States. Citizens in the United States and across much of the world quickly became aware that the new leader of the most powerful nation on Earth repeatedly manipulated and distorted the concept of truth like no other American president before him. Further, he had no qualms whatsoever about displaying disdain and overt hostility toward the mainstream media, especially toward journalists who said anything critical about him or his stated policies.

It was prior to election night, however, that a new term appeared in media coverage of the Republican Party's primaries, one that dwarfs Trump's "truthful hyperbole" in terms of effect: *fake news*. During Trump's successful bid to gain the Republican Party's nomination, political media pundits began to comprehend the fake news strategy of the future president. Once he became the president, it became even clearer. Trump's game plan of manipulating the truth was composed of two basic approaches. The first was his flippant dismissal of facts around particular events or policies that were reported in the mainstream media. "That's just fake news," he would say when someone confronted him with a fact, statistic, or poll he did not agree with or like. The second category of Trump's utilization of fake news, however, was even more disconcerting. This involved the president completely fabricating stories about political opponents such as Hillary Clinton and Barack Obama without any evidence.

Clearly, the strategy to completely concoct false stories and casually toss around the term *fake news* can be very effective in political terms. President Trump has demonstrated this through his foray into politics that led him directly into the White House. Although his ratings were lower than any other American president in the first few months of the presidency, almost 40 percent of voters still supported him after he was caught telling several major falsehoods (Dale, 2017a; Revesz, 2017). Trump's manipulation of the truth is more sinister than what he suggested in his 1987 book about making business deals when he said his words are sometimes an "innocent form of exaggeration." Innocence is not an adjective associated with Trump or his claims of fake news. To be fair, however, over the years many political leaders have been known to bend the truth. The same can even be said of journalists.

BIAS, PROPAGANDA, AND SPIN

Other chapters in this book explain why the social construction of knowledge makes it virtually impossible for any journalist to be truly objective. Indeed, how a story is framed, and the decisions over who and what to include and exclude are just a few of the ways that **bias** is inherent in all journalism. **Partisanship** is also part and parcel of putting the news together. Political partisanship refers to support for a particular person, group, cause, perspective, or ideology. It includes bias but is usually more overt and less subtle in its position than mere bias. Newspapers are filled with bias and partisanship, as are all media sources. (This is understandable, as social science academics, including us, have a bias, albeit most have a progressive bias.) Indeed, shortly before a federal election every major newspaper in Canada will publish editorials endorsing the political party that they trust to implement more of the neoliberal agenda, that is, either the Liberals or the Conservatives.[1] At times, newspapers in Canada and the United States will carry counter-hegemonic perspectives, although for the main they promote hegemonic discourses. (The Trump administration has altered this traditional arrangement. More on this later in the chapter.)

Partisanship seems to be evolving toward more intensely personal stances in the social fabric of American society. In 2009, Sean Westwood, an American political scientist, found that "partisanship [is] one of the most powerful forces in American life" (Taub, 2017). Beginning in the 1980s, according to Westwood, Americans began to despise people who did not support the same political party they did, part of a national trend that has resulted in the political becoming personal. Westwood explains this phenomenon by pointing to the 24-hour news cycle that began on cable television in the 1980s, rose to prominence in the 1990s, and still influences how citizens think about politicians. Non-stop political coverage has in turn led to permanent election campaigning by politicians in the US. Westwood describes a sort of tribalism forming in which people feel the need to support their political party no matter what. One frightening aspect of this tribalism is the growing urge to do whatever it takes to help their party win and, by corollary, help the other party lose. As Westwood explains: "You want to show that you're a good member of your tribe" (cited in Taub, 2017). Social media is a quick and easy way to demonstrate one's allegiance to a political party or ideology. (The impulse to help one's party win at any cost is likely to be a factor in the prevalence of fake news now on social media. This will be briefly discussed later.) It appears that a similar dynamic around political partisanship is rising in Canada.

As mentioned above, the mainstream media is not immune from political partisanship. Critics of the mainstream media such as MIT professor Noam Chomsky consider media outlets to be instruments of **propaganda**. If the ideal of objectivity is at one end of a continuum, propaganda is further away than either bias or partisanship. Propaganda is especially effective when the vast majority of media outlets parrot the same discourses, which is sometimes referred to as *pack journalism* or the *prevailing orthodoxy* (see Chapter 1 for a discussion of this, George Orwell's term for media groupthink). The prevailing orthodoxy encompasses both media bias and its hegemonic function as an instrument for propaganda.

The aforementioned continuum includes yet another term even further away from the objective ideal than propaganda, one that is frequently associated with the mainstream media—this term is *spin* (see Figure 4.1). In media jargon, spin is the power of persuasion coupled with some combination of rhetoric and propaganda. The people hired to produce this sophisticated propaganda are called *spin doctors*. (See Chapter 1 for a discussion on spin and spin doctors.)

```
Objective Ideal    Bias        Partisanship    Propaganda    Spin
|——————————————+———————————————+———————————+—————————+————▶
```

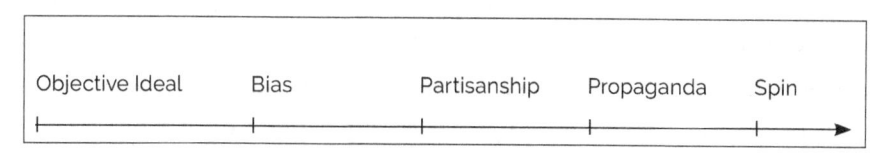

Figure 4.1: Objectivity, Perspectives, and the Manipulation of Facts

One may think that spin would be at the furthest point along the continuum from the objective ideal. One would be wrong, however. The advent of the Trump presidency that officially began on January 20, 2017, immediately enacted a brand new political term to add to the media literacy lexicon: *alternative facts*.

THERE ARE FACTS ... AND THEN THERE ARE ALTERNATIVE FACTS?

> This was the largest audience ever to witness an inauguration, period. These attempts to lessen the enthusiasm of the inauguration are shameful and wrong.
> —White House press secretary Sean Spicer, January 21, 2017

Friday, January 20, 2017, was Inauguration Day for President Donald Trump. During the day, media reports described the relatively small numbers of people attending the opening ceremony of the Trump presidency. The *New York Times* estimated that Trump's inauguration crowd was about one-third that of the turnout for Obama's 2009 inauguration (Wallace, Yourish, & Griggs, 2017). Over that weekend, however, President Trump and his team tweeted that it was the "biggest" turnout for a president's inauguration in the history of the United States. Photographs comparing the crowds at the inauguration ceremonies of

Trump and Obama provided evidence to the contrary; it was clearly not even close. Videos and public transit figures verified the mainstream media's position and contradicted what Trump and his team were saying (Hunt, 2017). The crowds for the Women's March on Washington the next day at the very same National Mall site also dwarfed the number of attendees at the new president's inauguration. Despite this, Sean Spicer used his debut in his new role as White House press secretary to accuse the mainstream media of "deliberately false reporting" and to shout at them that the Trump administration would "hold the press accountable" (D. Smith, 2017a).

Immediately after Spicer's false claims regarding his boss's inaugural ceremony, senior White House aide and presidential advisor Kellyanne Conway went on NBC's *Meet the Press* and defended her colleague by saying that he had merely given "alternative facts" about the number of attendees (Abramson, 2017). Not surprisingly, journalists were upset over this flagrant display of Orwellian Newspeak. The general consensus was that the new administration invented the term *alternative facts* merely to have a creative way of referring to outright lies. Merriam-Webster Dictionary took to Twitter to challenge Conway by stating "a fact is a piece of information presented as having objective reality" (Osborne, 2017). No apology was forthcoming from the Trump team for its failed attempt to alter the definition of the word *fact*, nor for the controversy it caused over the size of the inauguration crowds.

This initial struggle over something as trivial as the number of attendees at a ceremony suggests that much more important battles over facts versus falsehoods await the American public, indeed, the entire world. If the media challenges the president's claims on matters pertaining to budgets, jobs, the environment, or clandestine meetings with top-ranking Russian officials, should citizens expect Trump and his team to simply lie? The short answer is yes (Dale, 2017b). Will usage of the now silly term *alternative facts* keep the media and the public at bay? Here the short answer is no. The reaction of the mainstream media to the Trump team's first usage of this new term for knowingly stating falsehoods was swift and filled with mockery and outrage. This is understandable, of course, because one of the fundamental rules of good journalism is "Thou shalt not lie."

Donald Trump is not the first president to bend the truth. Nor is he the first president to lie to the American people. Recall President Richard Nixon and the Watergate Scandal of the early 1970s before he was forced to resign. Trump is, however, the first president to have his media relations people invoke the term *alternative facts* when telling lies to journalists in the mainstream media. A conservative columnist for the *Wall Street Journal*, former Pulitzer Prize recipient Bret

Stephens, gave a lecture in early 2017 in which he explained Trump's view of facts, truth, and the nature of reality: "He's saying that as far as he is concerned facts, as most people understand the term, don't matter. That they are indistinguishable from, and interchangeable with, opinion.... [In] the Trumpian view of the world.... *Truth is what you can get away with*" (cited in *Toronto Star* Editorial Board, 2017, emphasis added). Clearly, the president's understanding of what constitutes truth is an affront to democracy and an obstacle to an informed citizenry.

Trump has other strategies that are going to make it even more difficult to insist on the integrity of facts. One of these is his habit of changing his position on important issues from week to week. Another is his constant use of the term *fake news*. Deconstructing this complex phrase is very difficult. This strategy is clearly intended to neutralize the mainstream media in its prime function of informing the public. Under the conditions of having a federal government aggressively manipulate public opinion by outright lying, it is not difficult to comprehend the growing problems associated with fostering an informed citizenry to strengthen democracy.

DEMOCRACY IN AN ERA OF FAKE NEWS

> [Trump] can say virtually anything, however false or outrageous, without suffering any political consequences with his base. He can call a female journalist a "bimbo," insult a political opponent's wife, make bogus accusations of widespread voter fraud, say Obama founded ISIS, claim he won a bigger majority in the Electoral College than any President since Reagan—and none of it alienates his core supporters. Arguably, *these outbursts make them like him more*.
> —John Cassidy, *The New Yorker*, March 6, 2017, emphasis added

The very idea that the president of the United States can say whatever he feels like without any regard for the truth and not suffer very much in terms of political consequences for doing so is astounding. It is little wonder, then, that President Trump and his team have utilized fake news as a "go-to" strategy whenever they feel the need to create a diversion or a distraction for the mainstream media. In the introduction to this chapter, Trump was described as adept at utilizing two variations of the fake news strategy—one was to dismiss negative stories about him by investigative journalists as "fake news," and the other was to completely fabricate stories about his political opponents as a distraction for the media and especially the public to ponder.

Both of Trump's approaches to employing fake news appeared in one egregious example within the first two months of the Trump presidency. After being repeatedly asked by journalists about his administration's ties to Russia, the newly elected president employed his first type of usage by dismissing all of these stories as "fake news." Despite Trump's flippant dismissal, his choice for national security advisor and head of the Defense Intelligence Agency, Michael Flynn, was forced to resign when evidence surfaced of a cover-up of his connections to Russian political figures (Bump, 2017). When media stories continued to probe into Russian connections to the Trump administration, the president successfully managed to deflect attention away from this issue by utilizing the second fake news approach—he completely concocted an unrelated story based on no evidence whatsoever. Through a series of tweets Trump alleged that President Obama had wiretapped his communication lines prior to the 2016 election. This claim appeared to catch everyone off guard, including members of his own party, the media, and the American public. The *Washington Post* did not mince words in its coverage of the president's declarations: "Trump did not merely allege that former president Barack Obama ordered surveillance on Trump Tower, of course. He asserted it as fact, and then reasserted it, and then insisted that forthcoming evidence would prove him right" (Rucker & Parker, 2017).

The president, however, was wrong. After investigating his claims, the director of the FBI, James Comey, testified under oath to the House Permanent Select Committee on Intelligence that "Trump had *falsely accused* his predecessor of wiretapping his headquarters during last year's campaign" (Rucker & Parker, 2017, emphasis added). Many in the media, indeed, many American citizens thought that the new president had gone too far. The Trump team, however, was not going to let this challenge to his unsubstantiated story be any kind of serious blow to his authority. Two days after the FBI report that debunked Trump's wiretapping claims was released, Republican Devin Nunes, the chairman of the House Intelligence Committee and a staunch ally of the president, announced to the media that he had seen intelligence reports that made references to Trump campaign officials, and possibly even to Trump himself.[2] Despite the dubious timing and unorthodox context of Nunes' claim, Trump said he "regarded Nunes's disclosures as validation of his ... claim that he was the illegal target of a wiretapping operation last fall ordered by President Barack Obama" (Miller, Demirjian, & Barrett, 2017). Trump supporters quickly took to social media. One tweet claimed: "This is a sad day for America in which the FBI, CIA, and the NSA can no longer be trusted to work in the interests of the country." The tweeter's point was that Trump was telling the truth, and the FBI director was lying. Moreover, two polls found that 60 percent of Republicans thought Trump's wiretapping claims were accurate even after the FBI director went public to say they were not true (Dale, 2017a). For people who want democracy to work, what are we to make of all of this?

The Trump wiretapping lie demonstrated an even more serious problem: many of his supporters apparently knew he had fabricated the entire story, but they simply did not care (Dale, 2017a). Daniel Dale, a Canadian investigative journalist working in the Washington bureau of the *Toronto Star*, did a series of interviews with 25 Trump supporters in "hardscrabble Ohio" a few days after the FBI director had completely debunked the president's claims. Almost all of them supported Trump and the strategy of outright lying. As one "unemployed construction worker" put it, "He's ruffling every feather in Washington that he can ruffle. These guys are scrambling. So yeah! I like it. I think it's a good thing. I want to see them jump around a little bit." Only one person out of the 25 interviewees criticized the president for lying to the public (Dale, 2017a). It would appear that significant numbers of American citizens are not concerned about what constitutes the truth, let alone ways to strengthen democracy.

To have a serious but false accusation levied at a former president by his successor is unprecedented in American history. To then have the FBI director conclude that the current president's allegations were completely baseless brought the American federal government into completely uncharted and dangerous territory. For the FBI director's claims to be almost immediately refuted by the Republican chair of the House Intelligence committee does even further damage to the stability of the democratic system itself. Canadians should ask if a similar dynamic could occur in Canada.

What do these events do to the level of trust American citizens have in their government institutions? There is much more to President Trump's ubiquitous use of the fake news strategy. Before exploring that, however, it is prudent to have a brief discussion about what constitutes fake news.

What Are the Facts about Fake News?

> While real fake news is a matter of legitimate concern, the distinction about what is and is not fake news matters much in this troubling time when we face an assault on truth and daily debate about facts and "alternative facts" in what is increasingly coming to be regarded as a "post-truth world."
>
> —Kathy English, *Toronto Star* Public Editor, February 17, 2017

The phrase *real fake news* sounds like an oxymoron. Yet the term does have meaning and therefore needs to be deconstructed. Recently journalists in Canada and the United States have been receiving increasing numbers of emails from partisan critics containing charges of creating fake news as an all-encompassing statement of ridicule (English, 2017). This often happens whenever the subject of an article concerns President Trump's actions, but it is also hurled at columnists offering opinions on completely unrelated local issues. This is not what fake news is about. Fake news does not necessarily refer to a point of view that is disagreeable to certain readers, but recently it seems to have morphed into this.

There was a time not very long ago when the term *fake news* simply referred to trashy tabloids or those funny mock newscasts such as *Saturday Night Live* and *The Daily Show* in the US, and *This Hour Has 22 Minutes* in Canada. Similarly, the American satirical newspaper *The Onion* was considered to be fake news in print format. Satire, however, is not fake news. Satire is not malicious. These shows and *The Onion* are not expressly out to deceive the public. The meaning of the term *fake news* changed during the 2016 American presidential election campaign.

Shortly after the election in November 2016, Craig Silverman, the Canadian media editor at Buzzfeed, became the first journalist to offer a serious explanation of what constitutes fake news. Silverman contends that three considerations must be met for something to be *real* fake news. First, it must be 100 percent false and not merely a biased piece with a few incorrect statements in it. Second, it must be created with the conscious intention to be false. And third, it must be created with a financial motive (Brown, 2017). Silverman's groundbreaking work is important, but his third point is not a necessary condition for something to be real fake news. As mentioned earlier, political partisanship has become deeply personal and an important part of a person's identity in a similar manner to how tribalism sometimes works. People will say things to denigrate the other team or group or political party, even if it is false. Yes, an economic motive might be there, but it might not. Some people are motivated simply to show others they are doing their part to help their side win. Fake news is total fabrication and is intended to be so, as Silverman correctly surmises. When it is posted on the Internet it often goes viral to large numbers of people who further disseminate it, creating so-called *echo chambers*. In this way, fake news is one of the most effective threats to a healthy democracy.

A study was conducted out of Stanford University's Graduate School of Education that should concern all responsible citizens. The motivation for the study was the dire threat to democracy the authors perceived is posed by fake news. Beginning in early 2015, the responses of almost 8,000 middle school, high school, and college-level students in 12 states to online news stories were evaluated to determine their civic online reasoning. The study revealed some disturbing findings to the authors: "In every case and at every level, we were taken aback by students' lack of preparation" to assess fake news from real news (Donald, 2016). Middle school students had difficulty determining real news from ads. Over 30 percent of high school students considered fake news stories that contained a lot of graphics to be more real than text-based real news stories. Similarly, many college students were swayed by fake news stories that had a "polished" website. The authors of this study plan to use these findings to help educators assess student understanding and adjust pedagogy accordingly. The overall purpose of the research was to demonstrate the connections between digital literacy and informed citizenship in order to counter "the ease at which disinformation about civic issues is allowed to spread and flourish" (Donald, 2016).

A separate study conducted by three researchers at Yale University found that fake news stories are more likely to be believed if the person has already seen it or a similar headline a few days prior (Trilling, 2017). This was the case regardless of a person's political ideology, although the researchers also found that a fake news story is less likely to be believed if it is inconsistent with the person's political beliefs. They concluded that a politician who repeatedly makes the same false statements will be more successful in convincing citizens that they are true statements. It is clear that the ideologically polarized echo chambers created by social media make these findings even more of a threat to democracy.

These studies also demonstrate the vulnerability of American civil society to fake news (and they point to a serious vulnerability for Canadian civil society, as well). Further, the research indicates the ease with which good investigative journalism can be dismissed. Trump, his administrative team, and his supporters have worked to discredit the press, in effect making it extraordinarily difficult for investigative journalists to do their job of informing the public, indeed, to perform their responsibilities in a democracy. This has not been the first time, however, that anti-democratic forces have used the fake news strategy to denigrate the mainstream media.

CLAIMS OF THE "LÜGENPRESSE" AND THE WEAKENING OF DEMOCRACY

> When a video of two Donald Trump supporters shouting "Lügenpresse" started to circulate Sunday, viewers from Germany soon noted its explosive nature.

The defamatory word was most frequently used in Nazi Germany. Today, it is a common slogan among those branded as representing the "ugly Germany": members of xenophobic, right-wing groups.

—Rick Noack, *Washington Post*, October 24, 2016

"Lügenpresse" is a German term that translates to "lying press." It originally appeared in print form in Germany in 1914 to refer to "enemy propaganda" in the context of anti-Semitism. Two decades later, Adolf Hitler and the Nazis used the term to foster hatred of journalists and anyone who opposed the "will of the people" (Noack, 2016). "Lügenpresse" was part of the rhetoric used by Hitler's minister of propaganda, Joseph Goebbels, to gain support for the Holocaust. The term has a horrifying history, and it still has an exceedingly ugly meaning in contemporary Germany. It has been appearing frequently at anti-Muslim rallies organized by far-right groups such as Pegida.

When the word was heard at the Trump rally it understandably raised concerns. The president himself has not uttered it, at least in public. But on many occasions he has said things in English that are very close to the German translation.[3] On February 17, 2017, just four weeks after his inauguration ceremony, the president tweeted: "The FAKE NEWS media (failing @nytimes, @NBCNews, @ABC, @CBS, @CNN) is not my enemy, it is the enemy of the American People!" (cited in Grynbaum, 2017b). A few days later, Trump spoke before a large conservative convention, turning his speech into a "full-throated attack on journalism" as he repeated his attack on journalists who create "fake news" as being "the enemy of the people" (Jackson, 2017). Predictably, the mostly young crowd roared its approval. Shortly afterward, in an unprecedented move, the White House banned many major media outlets from a press briefing with Trump's press secretary, Sean Spicer, including the *New York Times*, the *Los Angeles Times*, and CNN (Bierman, 2017). The invitees included conservative media outlets that always supported Trump's campaign, such as the *Washington Times* and Breitbart News.

Perhaps the clearest indication that President Trump has disdain for the mainstream media is his use of social media. To get his message out to his supporters he most often uses Twitter. At the time of this writing in late May 2018, Trump had over 51 million followers and had tweeted over 37,000 times. Using Twitter as his main conduit for communication with his supporters, the president can bypass the mainstream media and get each message across (in 280 characters or less) the way he wants without a journalist's interpretation. Of course, journalists in the mainstream media also read his tweets and spend much time and effort commenting on them. It is likely, however, that many Trump supporters, possibly the vast majority of them, do not get their news from the mainstream newspapers. Most would receive the president's tweets and perhaps watch the Trump-supporting Fox News on television. Indeed, the president is very well aware of what Twitter can do for him. Less than two months after his inauguration ceremony, Trump told a sympathetic interviewer on Fox News: "I think that maybe I wouldn't be here if it wasn't for Twitter" (Thrush & Haberman, 2017). Twitter has become a very useful instrument of propaganda for President Donald Trump.

Critics contend that *all* of these moves are Trump's attempts to quash dissent in America, or at least curtail criticism of himself and his policies. It quickly became clear to Americans that they had elected a president with an authoritarian streak and no interest in the role of a free press. Indeed, immediately after Trump's inauguration the White House chief strategist, Steve Bannon, who had been on the job for only a few days, said, "The media should be embarrassed and humiliated and keep its mouth shut and just listen for a while" (Grynbaum, 2017a). It became apparent to many observers that under the Trump administration, American democracy could very well be under siege. After all, it is a common feature of authoritarian regimes, including China, Russia, and Iran, to control the media and turn it into an instrument of propaganda. The preponderance of fake news emanating out of the White House and beyond is one very clear indication of this.

MORE EXAMPLES OF FAKE NEWS

> Donald Trump is, frankly, very unique because of the amount of totally false things that he says. And so when you have a major candidate who will consistently say things that are not true, it sort of lays the groundwork and opens the area for lots of other crazy things that are not true to be said as well.
> —Craig Silverman, Buzzfeed media editor, cited in Brown, February 22, 2017

Shortly before the presidential election in November 2016, a story appeared online under a man's name writing for ABC News in which a headline screamed out: "Donald Trump Protester Speaks Out: I Was Paid $3,500 to Protest Trump's Rally" (cited in Blackwell, 2016). The story immediately went viral, helped by a tweet by Eric Trump, the Republican candidate's son: "Finally the truth comes out." The story's author claimed that Hillary Clinton's team had paid him $3,500 to pretend to protest at a Trump rally. Trump's campaign manager, Kellyanne Conway, called the practice "deplorable" as public perceptions of Clinton's ethics began to plummet. And the entire story was a lie. Even though the story's byline said it was ABC News, it was really a fake website called AbcNews.com.co. Around the same time, another story appeared online alleging that Michelle Obama had deleted her pro-Hillary tweets because of an FBI probe. Despite the story being covered by Sean Hannity of Fox News, it was also completely false (Blackwell, 2016). Yet enough damage to Hillary Clinton's public image had been accomplished—she was being increasingly perceived as untrustworthy. Her support decreased and Donald Trump won the election.

It should not surprise anyone that in an era in which a presidential candidate brazenly lies that others would do the same. This is especially true on social media. A study of Facebook carried out over two weeks during the election campaign found that "the fabricated posts were shared by readers far more than the legitimate ones, or than stories on mainstream news sites" (Blackwell, 2016). This practice of outright lying was first noticed in 2008 with attacks on Barack Obama. Although Trump's supporters have far surpassed anything seen before in terms of posting falsehoods, supporters for Clinton also began to engage in this abhorrent practice in 2016, albeit to a far lesser degree (Blackwell, 2016). A major problem is that even when a fake news story has been debunked in the mainstream media, the damage has already occurred. Social media enables fabricated stories to rapidly spread to massive numbers of people. Unfortunately, the subsequent fact-checking to debunk them does not travel as quickly or as effectively.

Another example of fake news will perhaps provide some insight into why President Trump, his staff, and his supporters use this strategy so often. Trump had been president for about a month when he used a rally in Florida to drum up support for his now infamous policy to ban citizens from a select group of predominantly Muslim countries from entering the United States. To back up his common refrain of the need to "keep our country safe," the president said, "You look at what's happening last night in Sweden. Sweden, who would believe this? Sweden! They took in large numbers [of refugees]" (Buncombe, 2017). The problem with this statement was that nothing had happened in Sweden to warrant this attention. The next day the bewildered Swedes asked the president for an explanation, which they received when Trump tweeted that he had learned of a violent attack involving refugees in Sweden on a Fox News report the night before (Bengtsson & Scruton, 2017). Apparently, Fox News had aired part of a documentary made by a filmmaker associated with the far-right media outlet Breitbart News (Buncombe, 2017). The documentary also claimed that crime and rapes had increased in Sweden after the country had accepted many refugees in 2015. Swedish officials quickly set the record straight, and they provided data to prove that Trump had been informed by bogus information (Bengtsson & Scruton, 2017).

Trump's team continued to produce fake news stories to garner support for what became known as the Muslim travel ban. For example, Kellyanne Conway gave three interviews to defend Trump's travel ban policy by claiming that two Iraqis "were the mastermind behind the Bowling Green massacre" (D. Smith, 2017b). Mainstream media outlets were quick to point out that this supposed "massacre" had never taken place. In yet another example of Muslim-bashing, Trump tweeted on March 7, 2016, that "122 vicious prisoners, released by the Obama Administration from Gitmo, have returned to the battlefield. Just another terrible decision." Data from the US government's Directorate of National Intelligence corrected the president—113 prisoners were released from the Guantanamo Bay prison by fellow Republican president George W. Bush, while Obama released only 9 prisoners (Dale, 2017b). At the time, the administration was having trouble getting the courts and the public to accept the racist travel ban, so they worked the fear-inducing fake news strategy as best they could. One can only imagine the psychological effect these baseless stories were having on Muslim Americans and Muslims worldwide.

Readers familiar with the popular Fox News are likely already aware that this major news outlet also uses the fake news strategy. For many years all of the media outlets owned by Rupert Murdoch have exhibited extreme partisanship toward conservative initiatives by instilling fear in American and British citizens (Orlowski, 2011). Airing a documentary that cites non-existent outbursts in Sweden arising from that country's liberal refugee policy or Iraqi-spawned acts of terrorism in Kentucky that never occurred are clear examples of how Trump and Fox News are using fake news to create divisiveness and foment trouble for Muslim people living in the US and elsewhere.

There have been myriad examples of President Trump and his supporters using fake news for nefarious ends, far too many to document here. A few other notable ones that have been completely debunked include the following preposterous claims by Trump supporters: "Pope Francis Shocks World, Endorses Donald Trump for President," and "ISIS Leader Calls for American Muslim Voters to Support Hillary Clinton" (Trilling, 2017). Trump himself claimed that the only reason he lost the popular vote to Hillary Clinton in the presidential election was because millions of people illegally voted for her (Pace, 2017). Trump advisor Kellyanne Conway's claim that the Affordable Healthcare Act created by the Obama administration resulted in millions of Americans losing their doctors and health insurance was also a lie (Abramson, 2017). Trump also claimed that President Obama's Affordable Healthcare Act "covers very few people" when it actually enabled over 30 million Americans to get healthcare insurance who could not afford to do so before (Dale, 2017b). It would seem that Trump has had an obsession with denigrating his Democratic predecessor, Barack Obama, and the Democratic presidential contender, Hillary Clinton, through his fake news approach.

This chapter has mainly focused on fake news and alternative facts in the United States, especially during the short political career of Donald Trump. Although the American president and his supporters are perhaps the world's most prolific creators of fake news, the phenomenon is not restricted only to the United States. In fact, non-Western countries such as India have been dealing with the effects of fake news in their political arenas for years (Goswami, 2017). It is also appearing more frequently in Canada (see Box 4.1).

Thus far this chapter has made a clear case that the rising phenomenon of fake news and alternative facts is proving to be a major threat to civil society and democracy in the United States, and to a lesser extent, in Canada and other countries. The question is what can be done about this. Powerful and effective

BOX 4.1: AN EXAMPLE OF FAKE NEWS IN CANADIAN POLITICS

Canadians need to be aware of the fake news trend, as it is appearing more frequently in Canadian mainstream media and especially on social media sites. One of the most prolific practitioners of the fake news strategy is Nick Kouvalis, a conservative operative who has been the campaign manager for some of Canada's most right-wing conservative politicians. In this role for federal Conservative leadership candidate Kellie Leitch in 2017, Kouvalis tweeted that Liberal prime minister Justin Trudeau was giving "Billions to other countries while Canadians stand in line at Food banks." His actual tweet also claimed that Trudeau had given "Hamas 351 [million dollars] (Designated terrorist organization)." When people challenged him on this, he admitted to tweeting this fake news to "make the left go nuts" (Dickson, 2017). The fact that this man was gloating over the trouble he caused through tweets which he admitted were completely false is a strong indicator that citizens in Canada must be vigilant about the political news they are reading as well.

forces to counter this scourge on progressive values and liberal democracy are required. Resistance to these anti-truth forces will not be easy. But what options do we really have? Few would choose to live in a post-truth era if given a choice. Most of us would prefer to live in a vibrant liberal democracy that values the truth more than any alternatives being offered.

RESISTING FAKE NEWS IS NECESSARY FOR CIVIL SOCIETY AND DEMOCRACY

> The muddling of fact and fiction is a tried-and-true tactic of totalitarian regimes. What's more, when the two are confused for long enough ... it will likely be harder and more tiresome to untangle them and remember a time when a firm line was drawn between the true and the false as a matter of course. If amnesia breeds normalization, fatigue has always served as the authoritarian's great accomplice.
>
> —Jiayang Fan, *The New Yorker*, 2017

Donald Trump had been the president of the United States for less than eight months when already well over 500 of his lies had been documented since his inauguration day (Dale, 2017b). Challenging so many falsehoods is wearisome. The quote above highlights the danger for the American populace. If fatigue sets in, and defiance to his lies diminishes, Trump will be victorious. The authoritarian streak that he and some of his senior advisors clearly possess will only get stronger if the militant will of the people weakens. The 45th president of the most powerful nation on Earth has shown no qualms about manipulating facts to solidify his support with his base and perhaps assuage his ego.

Trump declared war on the mainstream media within days of taking over the White House. As mentioned above, the rules regarding media access to White House press briefings have changed. Trump has indicated that if a media outlet wants to be treated like they have for almost all of the country's history, they will have to acquiesce to his demands. If they do not behave in ways he approves of, they will be branded as "fake news" outlets and "the enemy of the people." Already, "the *New York Times*, the broadcast networks, and CNN, among others" have been labelled as such (Gertz, 2017). The message is out that if a media outlet agrees to be a cheerleader for the White House, they will receive special favour. Fox News and the alt-right news outlet Breitbart.com are in that camp.

Taking criticism from the media, however, must be accepted as simply part of the job of being the president of the United States. To demonstrate how far away the Trump administration had strayed from this maxim, the *Boston Globe* published an article of President John F. Kennedy speaking about the role of the press in 1961, shortly after he had been heavily criticized for the infamous Bay of Pigs invasion of Cuba (DeCosta-Klipa, 2017). Kennedy stated that although it is not pleasurable to read criticism of his actions, the media "is an invaluable arm of the presidency as a check on what is going on in the administration." The president of this bygone era said it is probably easier for Soviet leaders to govern in secrecy because of the control of the media in totalitarian societies. He further opined that "there isn't any doubt that we could not do the job at all in a free society without a very, very active press." The *Boston Globe* published this article, which included a link to a one-minute clip of Kennedy praising the role of critical journalists, a few days after President Trump called the media "the enemy of the American people." The perspectives on the role of the media by these two presidents over 50 years apart highlight the dynamics in American society around challenges to power and hegemony.

Every totalitarian regime in the history of state societies moves to control the media, to control the message, to use the media as an instrument of propaganda. The United States, however, is a difficult nation to control in this way. The resistance to the Trump administration's authoritarian streak from the media outlets that the president has branded as the "enemy of the people" is strong and unlikely to abate. CEOs of mainstream media outlets realized they had been foolish during the election campaigns by giving him so much free prime-time coverage, only to see him turn on them as soon as he became president. They had been duped by the age-old capitalist promise of increased revenue—coverage of Trump increased ratings, which increased advertising dollars.

Civil society and the democratic system, however, are also important. The American Constitution is vital as a guiding light for the United States to realize the promise it offers the world, where individual dignity and freedoms are upheld and even cherished. Trump represents a threat to this American potential. The media appear to have realized their mistake during the presidential election campaign of 2015–2016. These media outlets likely will not acquiesce to what Trump has been calling for simply to be invited to presidential press briefings. The First Amendment appears to be too firmly entrenched in the collective American psyche to be ignored by committed journalists and informed citizens.

This is where social media outlets such as Twitter and Facebook enter the contemporary political scene. President Trump is famously partial to Twitter. His supporters post countless fake news stories on Facebook and on various blogs, and the echo chamber effect helps many of them go viral. Social media enables the producer to micro-target their audience and send the message to intended recipients. As has been discussed earlier in this chapter, Trump can tweet his messages out to his millions of followers without journalist mediators.

There is another aspect of social media that is even more frightening than micro-targeting and echo chambers. In the 21st century authoritarian regimes require new technologies that enable sophisticated surveillance on citizens. These technologies, including social media outlets, aid in the dismantling of civil rights, which taken collectively create some sort of techno-tyranny. It is not overstating the case that the current conditions for democracy and civil society are extremely unstable.

Further, the ubiquitous fake news stories emanating from the White House and its supporters on social media are likely having a psychological effect on American citizens. To be bombarded with fake news stories during election campaigns and afterward must foster attitudes of alienation from the political system and cynicism toward political candidates. Indeed, the head of Apple, Tim Cook, recently called for governments and technology companies to figure out ways to stop the scourge of fake news and misinformation in public discourse (Rawlinson, 2017). According to Cook, fake news is "killing people's minds." He is optimistic, however, stating that fake news is a "short-term thing." Advocates for democracy and civil society must have hope that he is right. After all, the alternatives are seriously bleak. The good news is that many organizations are developing ways to counter fake news and the existential problems associated with it.

STRATEGIES TO RESIST THE FAKE NEWS JUGGERNAUT

> There is nothing new about "fake news." What is different today are the vast social media networks that allow all information—minor or major—to zip around the internet in nanoseconds without regard to truth or importance.
> —Shepard, 2016

It is true that fake news is not a completely brand new phenomenon. History is replete with examples, with most of them emanating from political and military leaders. As recently as 2003, members of the George W. Bush administration went to various media outlets and the United Nations to make the case to bomb Iraq in a preemptive strike on the apparent basis that this country was planning attacks on the US with weapons of mass destruction. As you likely know, American bombs were dropped, hundreds of thousands of innocent Iraqi people died, and there were no such weapons. At the time social media was in its infancy. As this chapter has emphasized, things are different now, mainly because of the Internet, and social media in particular.

Several universities in the US teach journalism students how to "understand the fundamentals of truth," emphasizing Western philosophy to help develop media literacy (C. Smith, 2017).[4] The Observatory on Social Media at Indiana University has created a powerful instrument to fight the explosion of fake news. Called Hoaxy, this website "visualizes how claims in the news—and fact checks of those claims—spread online through social networks" (Indiana University Bloomington, 2016). A user simply enters a claim into the website and will be able to see "incidents of the claim in the media and attempts to fact-check it by independent organizations." These interesting ideas have great potential.

There are a plethora of strategies to help journalists challenge the fake news now proliferating on the Internet. For example, journalists could consider collaborating with universities and specific professors with expertise in certain fields to help sift through the mounds of data to determine its validity. Perhaps these experts can be relied upon to explain complex ideas to the public by way of the mainstream media. Perhaps journalists can work in partnership with citizens' groups to fact-check and provide valuable information (Wallace, 2017). American television news anchor Keith Olbermann offers specific suggestions for journalists covering President Trump and his penchant for fake news. "Stop covering his speeches live. Use a delay. Employ a team of fact-checkers. Play his rants. Each time he lies, stop the tape, state the facts" (cited in Short, 2017). Had the mainstream media employed these suggestions on a consistent basis during the actual election campaign, perhaps the outcome would have been different.

Major Internet companies like Google, Facebook, and Twitter are beginning to take the fake news threat to democracy seriously. They are putting in the effort to vet what gets posted without infringing on the First Amendment of the American Constitution (Shepard, 2016). Twitter and Facebook are attempting to distinguish the accounts of public figures and journalists from those of imposters by placing a blue-and-white checkmark next to the verified, real person's profile name. Facebook and Google have also blocked their advertising services from appearing on any website that posts fake news. Additionally, Facebook has set up a system for users to flag suspicious stories, which are then sent to independent fact-checkers (Indiana University Bloomington, 2016). These are welcome developments as these corporations have a responsibility to figure out solutions to this serious affront to democracy and civil society.

A host of fact-checking sites have been created to help people determine what stories are fake and what sources are trustworthy. Questions at the end of this chapter will take readers to these sites. Briefly, Snopes.com and MediaBiasFactCheck.com analyze stories with a global focus. PolitiFact.com and FactCheck.org analyze the degree of truth in what American politicians and lobbyists are saying. The main focus of MediaMatters.org is to provide its readers with stories containing falsehoods the Trump administration and its allies in the media are disseminating to the American public.

It is possible to create a citizenry capable of not being duped by fake news. The Nordic country of Finland is a shining example of this. Finland has been able to withstand the onslaught of Russian propaganda and disinformation better than most countries (Standish, 2017). The main reason for their success is a strong and well-funded public education system that focuses on critical thinking and ethics (see Box 4.2).

BOX 4.2: WHY ARE THE FINNS ABLE TO DISMISS FAKE NEWS FROM RUSSIA?

In recent years, western Europe has had to contend with fake news stories coming out of Russia. The country that has best been able to fend off this false information onslaught has been one of Russia's nearest neighbours, Finland. According to Finnish government officials, they have been able to deflect Russian propaganda and disinformation because of their "strong public education system, long history of balancing Russia, and a comprehensive government strategy" (Standish, 2017). Finland is world renowned for its excellent school system and highly educated teachers, which are major components of the country's strong commons built through progressive taxation schemes (Orlowski, 2016). In 2015, the Finnish president Sauli Niinistö said it was "the duty of every citizen to combat [fake news]" (Standish, 2017). To that end, the Finnish school system emphasizes critical thinking, cooperation, ethics, and the importance of the commons in its curriculum.

Given the current state of American public education, the treatment of its teachers, and a general disdain for increased taxes in that country (and to a lesser extent in Canada), a different approach must be fostered. It is imperative that students are taught how to fact-check the news they are reading online. Teachers must be taught media literacy and fact-checking skills in order to design pedagogy to teach their students how to not be duped by fake news and alternative facts.

The explosion of information containing varying degrees of truth, courtesy of the Internet, makes it imperative that citizens in Canada and the United States have the skills to determine what is fake news and what sources are trustworthy. They must learn how to distinguish reliable information and credible sources from the unreliable and the purveyors of lies (see Box 4.3). Citizens have a responsibility not to be duped by fake news stories. After all, the truth matters. Facts should be supported. Lies should not.

BOX 4.3: TIPS FOR EXPOSING FAKE NEWS

Several organizations have created suggestions on how journalists and citizens can detect fake news. Here are 10 suggestions that were on all of the lists, plus a few unique ones that hold great potential.

- Use fact-checking websites such as the ones discussed in this chapter and in the Assignments section below.
- Try to think critically about the information being presented. Some fake news stories are too far-fetched to be believed, yet they are shared on social media.
- Check who wrote the article and that person's qualifications.
- If the article is on a website, check the "About Us" section to see if it is credible.
- Check the sources cited in the article to see if they are reputable.
- When was the article originally published? Research on topics such as environmental issues is changing quickly. Studies can be too dated to be useful.
- Academic research is one of the best reporting tools. Researchers are usually accessible and willing to discuss their work. Journalists would be wise to contact them.
- Be wary of research from think tanks, private consulting firms, and special interest groups. Some of these organizations do excellent work, so do not outright dismiss them. (Examples of well-respected think tanks are the Council of Canadians and the Canadian Centre for Policy Alternatives.)
- Know the research methods that were used in conducting the research. This is a good approach for analysis.
- Do not get confused with satire. Not all fakery is to be taken seriously.

CONCLUDING THOUGHTS ABOUT FAKE NEWS AND ITS CORROSIVE EFFECTS ON DEMOCRACY

> In his farewell address as president Tuesday, Barack Obama warned of the dangers of uncontrolled partisanship. American democracy, he said, is weakened "when we allow our political dialogue to become so corrosive that people of good character are turned off from public service, so coarse with rancor that Americans with whom we disagree are not just misguided, but somehow malevolent."
>
> —Taub, January 11, 2017

President Obama's dire warning is well founded. Uncontrolled partisanship appears to be at the root of the fake news explosion. It is not only on social media where it abounds—indeed, even President Trump and his White House team seem to revel in producing it. For Trump, non-partisanship is a non-starter. Each American is either with him and his juggernaut team of inexperienced advisors, or against them. There seems to be no in-between.

Americans are unable to discern whether their president is intentionally conflating fact and fiction to deflect criticism or to confuse them. Whatever the motivation for undermining facts, for demeaning the very idea of objective truth, one thing is certain: if this post-truth era we are heading into lasts for very long, then an existential bleakness among vast swaths of the public awaits. We cannot allow fake news and alternative facts to become normalized. We must challenge Trump and the forces that reject facts, that dismiss climate science, that denigrate Muslims and Latinos and women, and that attack mainstream media. This ugly strategy will inevitably lead to differences of hyper-partisanship that will prove exceedingly difficult to bridge.

Yet despite the bleak prognosis of fake news in this entire chapter, there is plenty of room for optimism. Earlier chapters in this book made a strong case that mainstream corporate media are a hegemonic device in the service of the elites. Indeed, even this chapter makes the case that journalists can never reach the objective ideal. Media outlets have been described in this book as purveyors of bias, partisanship, propaganda, and even spin. The advance of something more sinister than all of these degrees of subjectivity can only lead to one conclusion, namely, that the scourge of fake news and alternative facts must be resisted at all costs. Mainstream media resistance to Trump is already happening.

Mainstream media can change from its hegemonic role that for over 30 years has supported neoliberalism (Orlowski, 2014). Media outlets now might strive to reach their potential as sources of vital information and analysis required to maintain and even strengthen democracy. Mainstream media may once again focus resources on investigative journalism, and in doing so relegate social media outlets that peddle fake news stories to the margins of public discourse. President Trump and his advisors have repeatedly claimed that investigative journalists who write critical pieces on his administration are "enemies of the American people." Nothing can be further from the truth. Investigative journalism is arguably civil society's best weapon against the threat of an authoritarian tyranny that the Trump administration represents.

Citizens must fight back against these manipulations of the truth. They must not allow these forces bent on manipulating fact and truth, on outright lying, from winning. The journalists working for mainstream media outlets are not the enemy of the people, and citizens must support them and their work. In the 1930s, Hitler's administration pushed discourses of the "Lügenpresse" into the consciousness of the German people. This was to discredit journalists and render them impotent against Nazi campaigns of terror and hatred. Despite the threat that the Trump administration poses for civil society in the United States and elsewhere, we must never allow this to happen again.

Media literacy in this era of Trump must necessarily evolve. No longer must the focus be on ideology critique, on determining a journalist's bias as leaning toward conservatism, liberalism, socialism, or even anarchism. That is still a major part of political media literacy to be sure. In contemporary society, however, media literacy must also teach the skills so citizens are capable of determining what is real news based on fact and what is fake news based on lies. Citizens must be equipped to deconstruct and discredit attacks on science, on groups of people, and on truth itself. Media literacy has an important role to play here. Indeed, democracy and civil society depend on it.

QUESTIONS FOR DISCUSSION

1. State the First Amendment of the American Constitution. In what ways has the Trump administration indicated that it is willing to ignore the provisions in this Amendment? Give three examples.
2. Facebook is trying to vet fake news stories from its site without compromising the First Amendment rights of citizens. Explain how attempting to remove fake news may lead to an infringement of the First Amendment of the American Constitution.

ASSIGNMENTS

Many excellent fact-checking websites have appeared on the Internet to help people contend with the proliferation of fake news.

1. One of the most popular fact-checking websites is Snopes.com. Its focus is global, and for every story its staff analyzes in the mainstream media and social media, they give a verdict on how true or false it is. Go to the site and choose any three stories. Summarize the issue and explain why the website staff gave the verdict they did.
2. Another popular fact-checking website is Politifact.com. Its focus is on the United States, particularly claims made by politicians and popular bloggers. For every story its staff analyzes, they give a verdict on how true or false it is. Go to the site and choose any three stories. Summarize the issue and explain why the website staff gave the verdict they did.
3. Similar to Politifact.com, another website that analyzes the degree to which claims of American politicians are true is FactCheck.org. Go to the site and choose any three stories. Summarize the issue and explain why the website staff gave the verdict they did.
4. A fact-checking website that takes a different approach can be found at MediaBiasFactCheck.com. As its name implies, this site checks hundreds of media sources, including the mainstream media, for ideological bias. It assumes that objectivity in journalism is impossible, and therefore analyzes stories in terms of the degree of bias, either to the left or the right on the ideological spectrum (see Chapter 1 for details on the ideological spectrum). This website also explains its methodology in very clear terms compared to the other sites. Go to MediaBiasFactCheck.com and choose any three stories. Summarize the issue and explain why the website staff gave the verdict they did.
5. What are your thoughts on the veracity of the fact-checking websites you studied in questions 1–4? Which one would you say is the best for detecting fake news? Why?
6. Media Matters for America is a website dedicated to analyzing the stories emanating out of the White House (including tweets). It can be found at MediaMatters.org. This website also employs staff to write articles about fake news stories created by Trump, his staff, and his supporters, and how they react to charges that they are doing so. Go to the site and choose any three stories. Summarize the issue(s) in each story and explain why *you* think the stories either are fake or point to an issue that is problematic for democracy.

NOTES

1. The lone exception occurred during the 2011 federal election campaign. Almost every major media outlet endorsed the governing Conservatives to be re-elected in 2011. The *Toronto Star*, however, endorsed the social democratic NDP, which at the time was led by the popular former Toronto city councillor Jack Layton.
2. The references to Trump were mere mention of his name in passing. The real story was the extremes to which White House staff used "American intelligence services to manufacture an excuse for Trump's original tweet" about Obama wiretapping his office (Lizzy, 2017).
3. This sentence hints at Godwin's Law, which states that as an online discussion gets bigger, the probability of someone mentioning Hitler increases. The US attorney who coined the phrase, Mike Godwin, said it is sometimes appropriate to do so. See Ohlheiser (2017).
4. It is noteworthy that the teaching of ethics has been a staple of journalism schools in Canada and the United States for decades.

WORKS CITED

Abramson, J. (2017, January 24). "Alternative facts" are just lies, whatever Kellyanne Conway claims. *The Guardian*. Retrieved from www.theguardian.com/commentisfree/2017/jan/23/kellyanne-conway-alternative-facts-lies [January 25, 2017].

Bengtsson, H., & Scruton, P. (2017, February 24). Fox News, Trump and the truth about crime in Sweden—in data. *The Guardian*. Retrieved from www.theguardian.com/world/datablog/2017/feb/24/trump-fox-news-and-the-truth-about-in-sweden-in-data [February 25, 2017].

Bierman, N. (2017, February 14). After Trump calls media an enemy of the people, White House bars many news outlets from briefing. *The Los Angeles Times*. Retrieved from www.latimes.com/politics/washington/la-na-essential-washington-updates-after-trump-calls-fake-news-enemy-of-1487963297-htmlstory.html [February 14, 2017].

Blackwell, T. (2016, November 4). The scourge of the U.S. election: Fake news, exploding on social media, is seeping into the mainstream. *National Post*. Retrieved from news.nationalpost.com/news/world/growing-fake-news-phenomenon-fuels-polarized-u-s-election [February 3, 2017].

Brown, A. (2017, February 22). Buzzfeed media editor Craig Silverman on the impact of fake news, what's next for it, and what, exactly, it even *is*. *The Chicago Reader*. Retrieved from www.chicagoreader.com/Bleader/archives/2017/02/22/buzzfeed-media-editor-craig-silverman-on-the-impact-of-fake-news-whats-next-for-it-and-what-exactly-it-even-is [March 1, 2017].

Bump, P. (2017, February 14). A timeline of Trump's spiraling Michael Flynn–Russia scandal. *Toronto Star*. Retrieved from www.thestar.com/news/world/2017/02/14/a-timeline-of-trumps-spiralling-michael-flynn-russia-scandal.html [February 14, 2017].

Buncombe, A. (2017, February 20). Donald Trump admits "Sweden attack" comments were based on debunked Fox News report. *The Independent*. Retrieved from www.independent.ie/world-news/north-america/president-trump/donald-trump-admits-sweden-attack-comments-were-based-on-debunked-fox-news-report-35465239.html [February 21, 2017].

Cassidy, J. (2017, March 6). Why Trump's latest Obama accusation could backfire. *The New Yorker*. Retrieved from www.newyorker.com/news/john-cassidy/why-trumps-latest-obama-accusation-could-backfire [March 8, 2017].

Dale, D. (2017a, March 26). Donald Trump voters: We like the president's lies. *Toronto Star*. Retrieved from www.thestar.com/news/insight/2017/03/26/donald-trump-voters-we-like-the-presidents-lies.html [March 27, 2017].

Dale, D. (2017b, September 11). All 576 false claims Donald Trump has made as president. *Toronto Star*. Retrieved from www.thestar.com/news/world/2017/09/11/daniel-dales-donald-trump-fact-check-updates.html [September 11, 2017].

DeCosta-Klipa, N. (2017, February 18). Here's how JFK responded to criticism from the media. *The Boston Globe*. Retrieved from www.boston.com/news/politics/2017/02/18/heres-how-jfk-responded-to-criticism-from-the-media [February 20, 2017].

Dickson, J. (2017, January 3). Leitch campaign manager gloats about spreading false info. *iPolitics*. Retrieved from ipolitics.ca/2017/01/03/leitch-campaign-manager-gloats-about-spreading-false-info/ [January 6, 2017].

Donald, B. (2016, November 2016). Stanford researchers find students have trouble judging the credibility of information online. *Stanford Graduate School of Education*. Retrieved from ed.stanford.edu/news/stanford-researchers-find-students-have-trouble-judging-credibility-information-online [February 3, 2017].

English, K. (2017, February 17). The facts about fake news: Public Editor. *Toronto Star*. Retrieved from www.thestar.com/opinion/public_editor/2017/02/17/the-facts-about-fake-news-public-editor.html [February 17, 2017].

Fan, J. (2017, February 2). Donald Trump through a loudspeaker, darkly. *The New Yorker*. Retrieved from www.newyorker.com/news/daily-comment/donald-trump-through-a-loudspeaker-darkly [February 3, 2017].

Gertz, M. (2017, February 28). Donald Trump wants total subservience from interviewers. *Media Matters for America*. Retrieved from mediamatters.org/blog/2017/02/28/donald-trump-wants-total-subservience-interviewers/215494 [March 5, 2017].

Goswami. R. (2017, January 23). India has been a post-truth society for years (and maybe the West has too). *Huffington Post*. Retrieved from www.huffingtonpost.com/the-conversation-global/india-has-been-a-post-tru_b_14349616.html [February 3, 2017].

Grynbaum, M. (2017a, January 26). Trump strategist Stephen Bannon says media should "keep its mouth shut." *The New York Times*. Retrieved from www.nytimes.com/2017/01/26/business/media/stephen-bannon-trump-news-media.html [January 28, 2017].

Grynbaum, M. (2017b, February 17). Trump calls the news media the "Enemy of the American People." *The New York Times*. Retrieved from www.nytimes.com/2017/02/17/business/trump-calls-the-news-media-the-enemy-of-the-people.html?_r=0 [February 17, 2017].

Hunt, E. (2017, January 22). Trump's inauguration crowd: Sean Spicer's claims versus the evidence. *The Guardian*. Retrieved from www.theguardian.com/us-news/2017/jan/22/trump-inauguration-crowd-sean-spicers-claims-versus-the-evidence [January 23, 2017].

Indiana University Bloomington (2016, December 21). Indiana University researchers launch tool to understand spread of fake news. *IU Bloomington Newsroom*. Retrieved from archive.news.indiana.edu/releases/iu/2016/12/iu-hoaxy.shtml [March 1, 2017].

Jackson, D. (2017, February 24). Trump again calls media "enemy of the people." *USA Today*. Retrieved from usatoday.com/story/news/politics/2017/02/24/donald-trump-cpac-media-enemy-of-the-people/98347970/ [February 25, 2017].

Lizzy, R. (2017, April 18). The continuing fallout from Trump and Nunes's fake scandal. *The New Yorker*. Retrieved from www.newyorker.com/news/ryan-lizza/the-continuing-fallout-from-trump-and-nuness-fake-scandal [April 19, 2017].

Miller, G., Demirjian, K., & Barrett, D. (2017, March 22). House Intelligence chair says Trump campaign officials were ensnared in surveillance operations. *The Washington Post*. Retrieved from www.washingtonpost.com/powerpost/house-intelligence-chair-says-its-possible-trumps-communications-were-intercepted/2017/03/22/f45e18ba-0f2d-11e7-9b0d-d27c98455440_story.html?utm_term=.a951375ddc20 [March 25, 2017].

Noack, R. (2016, October 24). The ugly history of "Lügenpresse," a Nazi slur shouted at a Trump rally. *The Washington Post*. Retrieved from www.washingtonpost.com/news/worldviews/wp/2016/10/24/the-ugly-history-of-luegenpresse-a-nazi-slur-shouted-at-a-trump-rally/?utm_term=.08bfffb600e3 [March 4, 2017].

Ohlheiser, A. (2017, August 14). The creator of Godwin's Law explains why some Nazi comparisons don't break his famous Internet rule. The *Washington Post*. Retrieved from https://www.washingtonpost.com/news/the-intersect/wp/2017/08/14/the-creator-of-godwins-law-explains-why-some-nazi-comparisons-dont-break-his-famous-internet-rule/ [May 31, 2018].

Orlowski, P. (2011). News TO the world: The Murdoch phone-hacking scandal & media literacy—Reflections from a media literacy educator. *Our Schools/Our Selves, 21*(1), 115–130.

Orlowski, P. (2014). Critical media literacy & social studies: Paying heed to Orwell and Huxley. In E. W. Ross (Ed.), *The social studies curriculum: Purposes, problems and possibilities* (4th ed.) (pp. 335–352). Albany, NY: State University of New York Press.

Orlowski, P. (2016). Saskatchewan teachers and a study abroad experience in Finland: "I *love* how the Finns respect their teachers!" *Journal of Educational Administration & Foundations, 25*(3), 17–37.

Osborne, S. (2017, January 23). Donald Trump adviser Kellyanne Conway gets shut down by dictionary for calling lies "alternative facts." *The Independent*. Retrieved from www.independent.co.uk/news/world/americas/donald-trump-kellyanne-conway-adviser-lies-alternative-facts-merriam-webster-dictionary-social-media-a7540956.html [January 26, 2017].

Pace, J. (2017, January 24). White House doubles down on Trump's voter fraud claim. *The Globe and Mail*. Retrieved from www.theglobeandmail.com/news/world/us-politics/trump-mixes-bridge-building-with-false-claims-of-voter-fraud/article33714116/ [January 26, 2017].

Rawlinson, K. (2017, February 11). Fake news is "killing people's minds," says Apple boss Tim Cook. *The Guardian*. Retrieved from www.theguardian.com/technology/2017/feb/11/fake-news-is-killing-peoples-minds-says-apple-boss-tim-cook [March 5, 2017].

Revesz, R. (2017, March 19). Donald Trump's approval rating falls to record low, finds Gallup poll. *The Independent*. Retrieved from www.independent.co.uk/news/world/americas/donald-trump-gallup-poll-new-record-low-approval-ratings-russia-healthcare-wiretapping-twitter-a7638601.html [March 21, 2017].

Rucker, P., & Parker, A. (2017, March 20). President Trump faces his hardest truth: He was wrong. *The Washington Post*. Retrieved from www.washingtonpost.com/politics/president-trump-faces-his-hardest-truth-he-was-wrong/2017/03/20/af9cabfc-0d83-11e7-9b0d-d27c98455440_story.html?tid=ss_tw&utm_term=.8687e64bb6f3 [March 21, 2017].

Shepard, A. (2016, December 9). A savvy news consumer's guide: How not to get duped. *Moyers & Company*. Retrieved from billmoyers.com/story/savvy-news-consumers-guide-not-get-duped/ [January 26, 2017].

Short, A. (2017, January 29). Keith Olbermann on how the media should cover Donald Trump and his team's lies. *Alternet*. Retrieved from www.alternet.org/media/keith-olbermann-how-media-should-cover-donald-trump-and-his-teams-lies [January 31, 2017].

Smith, C. (2017, January 23). How universities are tackling the fake news problem. *USA Today*. Retrieved from college.usatoday.com/2017/01/23/how-universities-are-working-to-educate-students-and-the-public-about-fake-news/ [March 5, 2017].

Smith, D. (2017a, January 22). Women's March on Washington overshadows Trump's first full day in office. *The Guardian*. Retrieved from www.theguardian.com/us-news/2017/jan/21/donald-trump-first-24-hours-global-protests-dark-speech-healthcare [January 26, 2017].

Smith, D. (2017b, February 6). Kellyanne Conway's fictitious "Bowling Green massacre" not a one-time slip of the tongue. *The Guardian*. Retrieved from www.theguardian.com/us-news/2017/feb/06/kellyanne-conway-fake-bowling-green-massacre-three-times [February 9, 2017].

Standish, R. (2017, March 1). Why is Finland better at fending off Russian-linked fake news? *Toronto Star*. Retrieved from www.thestar.com/news/world/2017/03/01/why-is-finland-better-at-fending-off-russian-linked-fake-news.html [March 5, 2017].

Taub, A. (2017, January 11). The real story about fake news is partisanship. *The New York Times*. Retrieved from www.nytimes.com/2017/01/11/upshot/the-real-story-about-fake-news-is-partisanship.html?_r=0 [January 28, 2017].

Thrush, G., & Haberman, M. (2017, March 20). Trump's weary defenders face fresh worries. *The New York Times*. Retrieved from www.nytimes.com/2017/03/20/us/trump-obama-wiretap-comey.html [March 21, 2017].

Toronto Star Editorial Board. (2017, February 26). Trump's "dark brilliance" explains why he keeps getting away with lies: Editorial. *Toronto Star*. Retrieved from www.thestar.com/opinion/editorials/2017/02/26/trumps-dark-brilliance-explains-why-he-keeps-getting-away-with-lies-editorial.html [February 26, 2017].

Trilling, D. (2017, June 16). Seen a fake news story lately? You're more likely to believe it next time. *Shorenstein Center on Media, Politics, and Public Policy*. Retrieved from https://journalistsresource.org/studies/society/social-media/fake-news-psychology-facebook-research [September 16, 2017].

Trump, D. (1987). *The art of the deal*. New York, NY: Ballantyne Books.

Wallace, C. (2017, February 4). Journalists are vanishing. Who will fill the void? *Toronto Star*. Retrieved from www.thestar.com/news/atkinsonseries/2017/02/04/journalists-are-vanishing-who-will-fill-the-void.html [February 5, 2017].

Wallace, T., Yourish, K., & Griggs, T. (2017, January 20). Trump's inauguration versus Obama's: Comparing the crowds. *The New York Times*. Retrieved from www.nytimes.com/interactive/2017/01/20/us/politics/trump-inauguration-crowd.html?smid=tw-nytpolitics&smtyp=cur [January 26, 2017].

5. The Public Media Challenge in a Fractured Media Society

If ever there was a government project that defined a country, it was—and continues to be—public media. When communicating with citizens, Canada faced many challenges that could have sent it down a different road, one more like its closest neighbour, the United States. Instead, in the early 20th century, those who made the decisions on how to handle the new medium of broadcasting had a different vision, one that would pave the path to a uniquely Canadian public media system. Yet there are fissures in the system, as the contemporary media environment has exploded with multiple ways for citizens to receive news, information, and entertainment. Where is it going? Tune in …

This chapter will examine the conception and growth of public media in Canada, its history and development, and the challenges it faces in a fast-paced, multi-media society that includes broadcasting, narrowcasting, and new media. The key question to be asked is: if we still need public media, what should it look like and how can it serve today's Canadians?

THE PUBLIC AND THE PUBLIC INTEREST

Public media are based on the premise that there is a public interest in having media that serve and communicate to citizens and are in the best interest of the country. If we were to define the public interest, it is "not only… the long-standing shared aspirations and visions of a nation-state, but also … the interests and objectives that remain to be discovered as new concerns and policy problems arise over time" (McDowell & Buchwald, 1997, p. 709). This tells us that the public interest is embedded in past culture, not one group's interests or the majority's interest, and that the embedding from the past provides the basis for understanding the needs of the public for the future.

In Canada, the concept of public interest is mixed, as our policies seek a balance between public and private interests. Over time, federal governments have carved out what Marc Raboy (1990) calls "particularities" in the Canadian system that give us a specific and unique sense that our institutions form a cornerstone for our culture heritage, that we have a somewhat unique public-private mixed system, and that social groups participate in the policy-making process. This is less so in recent years, with less public participation and more private media influence on the system, but the main thrust of public media remains strong.

But who or what is the public in what we call public service broadcasting? A public is situated within a public sphere, which is the site whereby citizens exercise their citizenship. The site is not necessarily a place so much as it is a public space or a public sphere in which citizens can communicate and debate rationally and democratically with each other and with their government. We often look to Jürgen Habermas to understand that these spaces and the processes that get acted out in them—especially through our ability to participate—are the backbone of democratic communication. The media, which transmit these communications, are a key element in how a public and a public sphere develop and become established. Still, *public* has many interpretations, all of which can be used in the context of public service broadcasting. It can refer to the nation itself, which gives it a political sense. It can be seen as the state or as state-owned, which suggests a hierarchical understanding. It could be the audience itself for public media, giving it a cultural meaning. Finally, the public can be seen as a consumer of broadcasting, which has an economic sense. Each of these can be applied to the Canadian context of being public.

According to the MacBride Commission, a 1980 report of the United Nations Education, Scientific and Cultural Organization (UNESCO, 2000; see Box 5.1), democratic communication has three key elements: *agency*, when an individual is an active partner and not just an object of communication; *multiplicity*, which involves an exchange of messages that have variety and quality; and *quality* itself, when the communication increases not just in its amount, but also in the level of its participation. The MacBride elements raise a question about public service media: Is the communication in such media democratic merely because it is conveyed by the public broadcaster? Further, does having a mandate to serve the public automatically make a broadcaster democratic? Private media

> **BOX 5.1: UNITED NATIONS EDUCATIONAL, SCIENTIFIC, AND CULTURAL ORGANIZATION (UNESCO)**
>
> UNESCO's mission is to contribute to peace and security by promoting collaboration among nations through education, science, and culture. Its main concern is to foster and maintain intellectual solidarity.
>
> Article 1 of the Constitution should not be altered, although there have been contradictory interpretations of the purposes of UNESCO from the origins of the Organization. The Constitution is still valid and of relevance for UNESCO's functions.
>
> According to Article 1 of the Constitution, UNESCO's three main functions are:
>
> - to advance the mutual knowledge and understanding of peoples;
> - to give fresh impulse to education and to the spread of culture; and
> - to help to maintain, increase and disseminate knowledge.
>
> *Source:* www.unesco.org/webworld/taskforce21/documents/holmstrom_en.htm.

networks also make the claim to democratic communication, as do many countries that claim to have democratic media. But if a society isn't democratic, then, as Raymond Williams (1966, p. 34) has asked, how can democratic communication be structured into an undemocratic system? These questions have been debated over the years and will continue for many more, especially as society, and particularly the media, changes.

NATION BUILDING AND PUBLIC MEDIA

Nation building in Canada began long before radio prompted discussions and debates about public media and how it should be used. No history of our public media can be understood without this background, which, in terms of electronic communications, formally began with the development of the telegraph in 1848. After massive shifts in society over the first half of the 19th century, modern society made decisions to develop new forms of transportation, such as railways and steamships, to move people, goods, and raw materials. It also needed new forms of communication, including the telegraph, telephone, and newspapers, which would bring information to citizens, government, labourers, and businesses.

> **BOX 5.2: MACBRIDE COMMISSION 1980**
>
> By 1978, UNESCO, the wing of the United Nations that focuses on culture and social issues, had become aware of and concerned about the changes to media and communication brought about by technology. UNESCO commissioned Sean MacBride to oversee the research and analysis of how media and communication were having an impact on countries around the world, especially those that could not invest in telecommunication and were seen as being left behind, creating a two-tier imbalance in the world's polity.
>
> The report of what has become known informally as the MacBride report was released in 1980, and its focus on *Many Voices*—the title of the report—called for "a new world information and communication order," or NWICO—which was also the report's subtitle. The report became controversial with its key finding that "corporate dominance favoured the objectives of commercial profit over the objectives of social and cultural development" (Hoover, 1993). This prompted the United States, whose media were mostly large and for-profit, to withdraw from UNESCO, destabilizing to an extent UNESCO's global work. Basically, as Calabrese (2005) says, the US "could not control the outcomes," so it withdrew. However, over time, as Hoover (1993) points out, "consumerist trends" have made culture a commodity, and there is less of "global dialogue, of access for marginalized voices, of opportunities for the less powerful and more marginal."
>
> The MacBride report is still seen as a lost opportunity for equality in communication and culture across the world.

Harold Innis (1894–1952) was a Canadian political economy professor at the University of Toronto who studied what he called the "bias of communication." He postulated that each manner (or medium) of communicating has its own bias. The bias of the media helped shape the character of that society. For instance, literate societies like Canada tend to extend themselves over territory or space. That is, they use more portable communication (like paper) that can be taken to any place and can extend their power. He called that a "space bias." This was particularly relevant to a geographically large country like Canada, because our lines of communication were needed and influenced our development as a nation (Vipond, 2011).

Innis said Canada developed northward and westward along our waterways and later along the cross-country railway. It did so for two reasons: first, trade, because we were transferring and exporting goods, like furs, to Europe; and second, settlement, as people moved along the same geographic lines as trade. As people moved along these routes, so did information and communication technologies. Later on, communication and technologies turned southward to serve the needs of trade—such as trading minerals and pulp and paper with the United States.

Knowing this, we can understand why Innis said that Canada emerged as a nation "not in spite of geography, but because of it" (in Vipond, 2011). Canada was an example of how a country had become a unified nation through the development of communication technology—and our somewhat unique geography was at the root of that development.

Yet those outgoing lines of communication that had been opened up also made the new nation vulnerable. Canada was especially assailable to becoming dependent on the communications incoming from the United States. We need to keep in mind that Canada became a nation relatively late in North America, compared to the United States, and it has always been vulnerable lying so close to the American border while it struggled to develop as a nation. Moreover, the country's situation was pretty much the same historically as it is now. It's a vast northern country, but it has a small population, much of it lined up along the American border. Because it is so large, it has a number of strong regional cultures and large provincial governments. It has two official languages now, but even in the early days, there was a split between the two nations (England, which won the battle on the Plains of Abraham, and France) that claimed the country for themselves. Early open immigration policies made the country **multicultural**. It has a large population of Indigenous peoples with their own languages and cultures. Even until 1867, when Canada became a country, European settlement was confined mostly to the East Coast, with isolated settlement elsewhere.

As a vast country, Canada over-relies on information and communications technologies as a way of keeping the country united. They help us foster both information sharing and also cultural and national identity. As Charland (2009) has noted, this is both symbolic and material, in the sense that the connections amongst Canadians both resonate mentally (the symbolic part) and are real physically (the material part). As an example, we see the railway as the *material* manifestation of our nationhood, and it is a *symbol* for us of Canada itself. Many of our government policies related to culture and communication reflect a belief and trust in technology. We understand that communications technology helped us become a unified nation. But we are also concerned about keeping our culture Canadian—so our government policies also intervene to make sure that happens.

The telegraph was a new technology that influenced Canada's development. It was a technology that was developed specifically to fill the need for moving people and goods across great distances. It was a very suitable technology to fit Canada's space bias. Despite this obvious suitability, the telegraph developed slowly, partly because Canada traditionally has been cautious about new inventions generally. Our usual trade partners, the United States and England, have always been more advanced technologically. In Canada, the telegraph as an organized system of communication was tied to other considerations: the state, business, and the press.

At the beginning, there was not a lot of government intervention in the development of the telegraph, but what there was resulted in what could be called Canada's first telecommunication law, the Electric Telegraph Companies Act of 1852. The law actually cleared the way for companies to get charters and start networks. But it wasn't until 1901, after all the struggle in establishing the telegraph was over, that the government began to intervene in its future.

On the other hand, business from the beginning took a keen interest in the telegraph, but only managed to put together a very rudimentary network and do it very slowly. Telegraph companies sprang up and were very competitive. They quickly began to consolidate. Toward the end of this consolidation phase, only two companies were left: the company that became Bell and the company that became Canadian Pacific. Although their charters allowed them to compete in the same areas, instead, the two companies divided up the field between them. Instead of a monopoly, it was a duopoly—two companies held control.

It was the American Press (AP) company in the United States that saw the potential of the telegraph to help collect news and information, so American newspaper publishers were the first big investors in the telegraph. They established the Associated Press in 1846 for the express purpose of getting this new technology to work for them and their needs. For them, the telegraph was a cheap, quick, and reliable way of collecting and distributing information and news. The Americans were so successful in co-opting the telegraph for their own needs that AP and the telegraph companies were actually interdependent in terms of ownership. It was only in the 1870s that Canadian Pacific obtained the rights to AP's telegraph-based news service, and it was only around that time that the strong American influence and control of the telegraph system in Canada subsided.

The second important technology in the development of Canada was the railway. As Innis noted, the lines of communication in Canada have followed the geography of the country. He also said the lines of communication are also the lines of commerce. Our natural resources were exported along those lines, and finished materials and scarce commodities were imported. Trade moved at first from west to east, reflecting our ties to England, and later, from north to south, reflecting our trade ties with the United States.

However, in 1879, the new country of Canada was still concerned about the east-west line of commerce. That was the year of Canada's first economic policy, called the National Policy. The policy was a set of economic initiatives to guide the whole country's economy. The most interesting initiative was a commitment on the part of the government to build a national and transcontinental railway. The railway's purpose was to ensure a full and reliable line of transportation for both people and goods. The idea was that natural resources in their raw state would be carried by rail to the heartland of the country in Ontario, turned into manufactured products and goods, and then shipped back to the rest of the country. It was intended to stop the ongoing export of raw materials to the United States and instead keep the manufacturing in Canada, where our economy would grow and flourish, rather than import finished goods. Two other initiatives in the National Policy supported this. The first was the implementation of a tariff on foreign goods. The tariff was supposed to prevent cheaper manufactured goods from coming into the country and competing with the locally manufactured goods. Because of its small population, Canada simply wasn't able to produce goods in high enough numbers that the price per item would be low enough to complete with foreign goods. The second initiative was a policy on immigration to increase population in the western provinces. The new immigrants would settle the land and produce grain for the eastern markets. The key to this strategy was that the new immigrants would also prevent Americans from crossing the border and laying claim to Canadian land and resources.

Together, these initiatives in the first economic policy by the Government of Canada set a pattern that has been followed since that time: first, it protected the economy, and second, it had a strong underlying purpose of fostering national identity. The railway was one of the first national institutions asked to serve both goals simultaneously (Lorimer, Gasher, & Skinner, 2007, p. 208)—but not the last. Canada's media and communication policies, as well as its cultural policies, have continued to be characterized by the notion that they serve to both protect the economy and foster nation building.

RADIO AND CANADIAN IDENTITY

The idea of nation building through communication has remained solid and significant throughout Canadian history. In 1895, even as we used the railway and the telegraph to move cargo and people across the country, Prime Minister Wilfrid Laurier was funding inventor Guglielmo Marconi to experiment with the idea of transatlantic radio. In 1906, the dots and dashes that Marconi had used to communicate were put aside as Reginald Fessenden, a Canadian inventor, experimented with voice radio. The key shift was from one-on-one communication to broadcasting that was heard by many people all at one time, produced centrally, and, for the first time, distributed on a mass medium. In 1913, the Radiotelegraph Act gave the state the right and power to license the use of the airwaves. At this point, the state felt it could control the airwaves and how those airwaves were being used, as they were considered to be another natural resource no different from furs or pulp and paper.

The shift at this time from the telegraph to the "new technology" of radio also exhibited a pattern that has characterized communication technology and inventions. As we move ahead to something new, something always gets left behind; there is a lot of economic and social upheaval, followed by a period of adjustment, and finally, acceptance of the social and economic change. One incident in particular gave radio a boost and showed governments the usefulness of the new technology: in 1912, when the *Titanic* sank, Marconi radio operators on the ship sent the distress messages. In 1920, the first actual radio station opened in Montreal. (Other telegraph companies in the United States became today's American television stations NBC and CBS.)

Despite the growth of radio, it was not yet a medium used domestically in households. It also wasn't profitable, as once consumers bought a radio receiver, companies had nothing else to sell. The United States found a solution: selling ads. This was not an option for Canada, as we had a smaller population, less production, less strong transmitters, and telegraph lines that couldn't be used for broadcasting. The Canadian government's solution to this was to use the Canadian National Railway system to build and use radio stations along the line. (Radio was also available in the CNR train itself for the enjoyment of passengers.) One of the goals of the government in investing in the railway was to communicate with citizens directly.

By the time the network was running smoothly in the early 1920s, debate was ongoing about the need for a national radio or broadcasting system that would resolve the conditions that had kept Canadian radio broadcasting from realizing its full potential in the way that the United States had. Some wanted our radio system to be entirely publicly owned, while others wanted it to be more like the American system that was completely privately owned. The government's solution was to intervene and establish the Royal Commission on Radio Broadcasting to advise on broadcasting and where it should be going. This was the beginning of many such commissions in Canada over many years that related to publicly owned and operated communication projects for citizens that were focused on nation building.

The Royal Commission on Radio Broadcasting, known as the Aird Commission after its chair, John Aird, reported back to Parliament with a unanimous report in 1929. The report identified some major issues: radio stations were concentrated in urban centres, radio was becoming commercialized, programming was often mediocre, and the Canadian system was overwhelmed by American stations that were close to the Canadian border. The key recommendation was that a broadcasting system for Canada be *one national, publicly owned system*. In one phrase, Canada's broadcasting destiny had been decided. The ideal of a merged public-private system, available nationally, not commercial but publicly owned, marked the first time that the Canadian state was taking ownership and responsibility for a public resource in the public interest. A further recommendation was that an organization be set up to administer broadcasting as "one national publicly owned system"; this became the Canadian Broadcasting Corporation. Altogether, the Aird Commission was making a clear choice for cultural enlightenment, which it saw as quality, Canadian-made programming. Key to the report's recommendations were these passages:

> There has been unanimity on one fundamental question—Canadian listeners want Canadian broadcasting. (Canada, 2003a)

> In a country of the vast geographical dimensions of Canada, broadcasting will undoubtedly become a great force in fostering national spirit and interpreting national citizenship. (Canada, 1929, p. 6)

> [It can be] most effectively used in the interests of Canadian listeners and in the national interests of Canada. (Canada, 2003b)

In other words, the commission specifically and clearly was saying that broadcasting had a nation-building purpose, that communications technologies could be used for nation building, and since it was so important, broadcasting needed to become a public resource. This is the third time, after the railway and the telegraph, that we see public policy used to foster public media and communication with citizens for the purpose of engaging them as citizens.

The Aird report turned out to be one of the few royal commissions in the 20th century that was heeded and then implemented by government. Interestingly, the prime minister of the time, R. B. Bennett, supported a public media approach to radio only after Graham Spry and Alan Plaunt of the newly formed Canadian Radio League (a pro-radio system lobby group) used the evocative slogan of "The state or the United States" to promote a Canadian radio system. The slogan meant that Canadians would get either a state system or the United States' system, as radio station owners in the United States wanted to expand into Canada to increase their scope and revenue.

The victory of the state over the States was not complete. The existing private radio stations were not turned into public stations, as the Aird report had recommended, and the private broadcasters stayed privately owned and operated. In fact, policy making by the government often balanced the interests of both the private stations and the new public system.

The Canadian Radio Broadcasting Act of 1932 put the recommendations from the Aird Commission into law, and that achievement ushered in a time of national purpose in broadcasting (see Nesbitt-Larking, 2007). The idea of the airwaves as a public resource was a very exciting concept for Canada at that point in its history.

World War II increased the interest in news programming, and the war itself made it indispensable to catch the news from the battlefront (or as near to it as it could come). Canadian citizens could listen to war news about their own troops through their own radio network. Altogether, by the late 1940s, almost every household had a radio and enjoyed a large variety of programming, including drama, soap operas, quiz shows, and variety and music shows. By then, advertisers had moved from newspapers to radio, making the stations profitable.

REGULATING MEDIA IN THE PUBLIC INTEREST

Unlike privately owned media, public media have a more stringent mandate to serve their audiences, who are also citizens, and report to government. The 1932 broadcasting act had set out the administration, management, control, and financing of the new broadcasting system (McCausland, 2009). Likely, that was deemed enough for the system to work. However, by the 1950s, broadcasting via television was in almost every household and so a self-standing regulatory body, the Board of Broadcast Governors, was formed in 1958 to handle and regulate broadcasting and to end the situation where the CBC was both competitor and regulator of other media. Prior to that time, its duties had been housed in the CBC. In 1968, the Broadcasting Act, a comprehensive piece of legislation, broadened the law to "protect Canadian culture and strengthen the nation's social, economic and political structures" (McCausland, 2009).

The 1968 act's strong language covered a lot of ground, but the most important provisions spoke to the needs of the public and its members' needs as citizens through three new provisions:

> 1) radio frequencies are public property; 2) broadcast programming provides a public service essential to national identity and cultural sovereignty; and 3) the Canadian broadcasting system should provide a wide range of programming that reflects Canadian attitudes, opinions, ideas, values and artistic creativity by displaying Canadian talent in entertainment programming. (Media Awareness Network, 2008, in McCausland, 2009)

Here, the need for expressions of Canadian identity and creativity in public media are clearly enunciated, along with the need for original Canadian content with quotas to make sure it happens. This was not a small thing to be tucked away and forgotten. The government was signalling that our cultural heritage needed to be protected, or it would be enveloped by the culture of the United States. In 1968, the Board of Broadcast Governors became the Canadian Radio and Television Commission (CRTC); later, in 1976, with satellite communication, "Radio and Television" was changed to "Radio-television and Telecommunication." In the 1960s and '70s, Pierre Juneau, the CRTC's first chair, introduced detailed Canadian content rules (often referred to as "CanCon" or "Cancon") for radio and television programs that are still in effect.

Over the years since the Aird Commission in 1929, many other reports and royal commissions have followed. It may seem that Canadian media and culture are weighed down by rules and regulations. However, these have managed to create, foster, and maintain a strong national culture in a vast multicultural country that shares a very long border with two dominant world powers, each with its own strong media and culture: the United States to the south, and Russia to the north.

EDUCATIONAL BROADCASTING: A DIFFERENT KIND OF PUBLIC MEDIA

When we speak of public media, we are usually thinking about the Canadian Broadcasting Corporation (CBC). Yet there is another layer of public media that seldom gets heard from, despite the considerable impact it has had on

> **BOX 5.3: ROYAL COMMISSIONS AND BROADCASTING ACTS IN CANADA**
>
> Canada has a long history of discussing policy on communication and culture, and enacting legislation to enable public media to protect our culture so that it survives and continues to be valuable to Canadians. The three broadcasting acts and the nine reports demonstrate the growth of Canadian public media. The key legislation and reports are as follows:
>
> **1929** Report of the Royal Commission on Radio Broadcasting (Aird Commission)
> **1932** Canadian Radio Broadcasting Act
> **1951** Royal Commission on National Development in the Arts, Letters and Sciences (Massey Commission)
> **1955** Royal Commission on Broadcasting (Fowler Commission)
> **1968** Broadcasting Act
> **1968** Canadian Radio-television and Telecommunications Commission (CRTC)
> **1970** Special Senate Committee on the Mass Media (Davey Committee)
> **1980** Royal Commission on Corporate Competition (Kent Report)
> **1986** Task Force on Broadcasting Policy
> **1991** Broadcasting Act
> **2003** Standing Committee on Canadian Heritage (Lincoln Report)
> **2003** Senate Transport and Communications Committee Report

Canadians across the country over many years. These are the "educasters"—the public service educational broadcasters. At one time there were six such provincial broadcasters across Canada, the first starting up in Ontario in 1968. Today, only two—TVOntario and its French-language equivalent, TFO, in Ontario, and Télé-Québec—are continuous, full-time educasters with financial allocations from their provinces, but supplemented in TVO's case by private funding. Télé-Québec is funded fully by its province. Along with broadcasters like CBC and Radio-Canada, the educasters have played an important role in "fostering public debate, the construction of community, and awareness of public issues" (Kozolanka, 2012, p. 47). Those that survive receive allocations from their provinces, but over time these allocations have been reduced, and they also have to find revenue elsewhere, often from private donors. Similar to the Public Broadcasting Service (PBS) in the US, Canadian educasters have rebranded themselves to fit the needs of non-governmental funders. Similarly, in the 1990s,

BOX 5.4: HOW DO WE KNOW THAT THE MUSIC WE HEAR IS TRULY CANADIAN?

One of the ways that Canada has developed its own music and the system to support it is through a government plan called the MAPL system—a clear connection to Canada's famous maple syrup.

Back in the 1970s and as part of a plan to stimulate our music industry, the federal government created a system to determine if music was or was not Canadian. The plan was for this system to encourage and strengthen the Canadian music industry. Our proximity to the United States was allowing for the strong and large American music industry to be broadcasted and to overwhelm the work of Canadian musicians.

The MAPL system still exists today. *MAPL* stands for Music, Artist, Performance, Lyrics: the *music* is entirely Canadian-composed; the *artist* who primarily performs either the music or lyrics is a Canadian; the music is recorded or *performed* and broadcast completely in Canada; or the *lyrics* were entirely written by a Canadian. Usually at least two of these four points must describe the music in order for it to be considered Canadian content (Canada, 2009). In addition, there are regulations on defining if musicians are Canadian citizens (see www.crtc.gc.ca/eng/INFO_SHT/R1.HTM).

PBS "survived a major overhaul" and branding process, yet, as Hoynes (2003) has pointed out, it began to lose "its distinctive public service identity ... becoming just another brand competing for consumer attention in an increasingly cluttered commercial marketplace" (p. 128). Although like any other public service media, TVO has struggled, it has avoided the worst aspects of PBS's decline and has less educational material. However, its provincial allocation has dipped from $80 million in 2006 to $62 million in 2016 (Bradshaw, 2016).

WHITHER THE CBC?

A critical political cleavage marks the future of public service media in Canada. Recent Conservative governments have not seen the importance of public media that are funded by government. Under Stephen Harper's governments (2006–2015), the CBC lost 16 percent of its annual parliamentary allocation. Note that Liberal governments of Jean Chrétien and Paul Martin (1993–2006) before Harper also had curtailed the CBC's allocation. (Keep in mind that normally the CBC would have had annual increments, so the loss is much more than 16 percent.)

By 2012, the future of the CBC was looking grim, and the concern about its future spawned a movement to ensure that it survived. Then Canadian Media Guild, which was the union representing CBC employees, and OpenMedia.org, an online organization that lobbies to keep the Internet open and free, joined together in a campaign to support the CBC and ensure it continued as an important part of our heritage and future. Friends of Canadian Broadcasting, a lobbying organization, also has a strong and long history of supporting CBC and public media. They were joined by Leadnow and Gen Why Media. Leadnow (2016) "runs campaigns on the major issues of our time, engages people in participatory decision-making, and organizes in communities across Canada," and Gen Why Media's (2016) mission is to "localize culture through creative engagement and generate a willingness to collectively shape our city, province, country and planet." Altogether, for the campaign to save our public broadcaster, they became ReimagineCBC. Their motivation for joining the movement to save CBC was based on their belief in the importance of public media as being different from the for-profit corporate media and, in this specific case, in having "uniquely Canadian content that could not be accessed elsewhere" (ReimagineCBC, 2017).

The ReimagineCBC movement was also motivated by a then-upcoming CRTC hearing on the CBC's periodic licence renewal. For almost a year leading up to the CRTC hearing in November 2012, ReimagineCBC collected 36,479 signatures on an online petition; held an online "ideas forum" in which 496 ideas were posted in less than three months; had 10,940 people participate in a survey; and finally, submitted a report called "Make it Yours" with recommendations to the CRTC. The response from CRTC was positive, calling the ReimagineCBC report a "guidepost" and a "case study" for how to make media policy, and stating that it "enriched the process of navigating policy for the future of Canadian media" (Yeo & Trusz, 2011, in Mahoney, 2012, p. 18). Yet this positive reaction still needs to be reflected in actual government policy on the future of the CBC.

In 2016, the Liberal government—which, before losing to the Conservatives in 2006, had slightly lowered the CBC's annual operating allocation—did little to recoup lost ground from the previous nine years, announcing additional funding of only $75 million in the first year and $150 million in each of the four following years. Altogether, it didn't fully make up for what was lost in the Conservative years.

The media themselves have also changed rapidly over time, particularly in recent years, in which social media and other new media have become easy to use anywhere and anytime. In the broadcasting environment, "specialty channels" such as Bravo, YTV, Showcase, HGTV, Discovery Channel, Food Network, and HBO Canada serve niche audiences and fragment television audiences. In addition, for a long time now, even the simple television can be connected to devices that tape programs for viewing at some other, more convenient time. Telephone technology has also evolved to the point that hand-held devices such as smartphones and tablets replace heavy, static, and boxy computers. These mini-computers are agile and replete with the many bells and whistles, so to speak, that modern consumers believe they need.

Niche television channels, specialty audiences, and personal hand-held devices are a far cry from the image of the 1950s family audience clustered around a black-and-white television that only had two national channels: CBC and its French-language counterpart, Radio-Canada. Canada's only other channel of the time was CTV, which started broadcasting in 1962. In the **postmodern** media universe, CBC and other public service broadcasters face a middle-age crisis. The same can be said for citizenship.

When radio was established in Canada, it was a nation-building proposition and a risky gamble for the government of the day. But the need was strong and clear: it was a choice of the state or the States. The media environment today is very different. The claims of multiplicity and "something for everyone" are true, but only if we see ourselves as just media consumers. Yet we are more than just consumers; we are also citizens. The purpose of public media was to unify and educate a country. It also can play a significant role in making us mindful and knowledgeable citizens.

Without restrictions on foreign media and without a strong public media sector, a small country like Canada (in terms of population), and especially one that is situated beside the country that is the communication centre of the world, can fast lose its sense of place and belonging. The need to be able to communicate with each other—directly, and specifically as Canadians—is stronger than in most other countries. Taras (2015) says there is a need "for a country to be able to see and speak to itself amid the cacophony created by individualized mass media" (p. 231). He points to Cormack and Cosgrove's view that CBC's "real mission" is to "create a space for a Canadian community to form" (p. 230). In fact, he says that it's not necessarily about whatever CBC is actually broadcasting at any one time, but instead that it is our "ritual of citizenship" (p. 230). In both concrete and symbolic ways, public media continue to define who we are.

Yet others might ask: Aren't public media useful only for nations in their infancy, like a starter kit or a boost up? Do we need them at all?

Paul Attallah (2008) rejected the idea that *only* public broadcasting can defend the public interest in Canadian media and, further, wondered why it should only happen through public broadcasting (p. 12). While he asked who—at the CBC, presumably—gets to decide the content that is in the public interest, his main issue was that it is not clear that the goals of public broadcasting can even enhance democracy, and he instead saw it as paternalistic and distrusting of choices made by citizens. Thus, he said, public media serve in the interest of only an "unrepresentative elite, which enjoys a public subsidy in pursuit of its particularistic interests" (p. 14). Attallah also pointed out that such media have no monopoly on enhancing democracy and wondered if Canadian civil society is weak, with public media used as a stand-in. If that is the case, he concluded, we cannot fix it through public broadcasting (p. 15).

In 2012, political journalist Andrew Coyne also suggested that the CBC isn't necessary in a time of scarce tax dollars and, moreover, that broadcasting itself has changed dramatically. In an environment of narrowcasting, in which large numbers of specialty channels (with one subject and smaller audiences) now populate the television spectrum, he said the CBC shows sameness in its programming and, further, focuses on the "lowest common denominator" in its programs, which all seem "drearily familiar" (Coyne, 2012). He points out that the digital revolution has broken down the former boundaries within the media and overall that broadcast audiences are dwindling. The upshot, Coyne says, is that there is no need for a separate network like CBC, as its programming can be produced anywhere else. (Ironically, given Coyne's view on CBC, he has appeared on a panel on CBC's *The National* for years.)

However, the CBC has remained strong in the minds of citizens, despite sharing the ups and downs of the economy and even after having lost a large chunk of its government allocation in recent years, and despite intrusions from specialty broadcasters and the range of other sites to which viewers have access. In 2013, Nanos Research, a well-respected Canadian public opinion research company, found that 80 percent of those polled would increase or maintain CBC funding from the government, and 83 percent felt that CBC itself plays "an important role in strengthening our culture and identity" (Friends of Canadian Broadcasting, 2013; Csanady, 2014). In 2014, 87 percent of respondents said the same thing, clinching the continued importance of public broadcasting to Canadians.

In addition, while some long-standing public broadcasters in the First World have had their government allocations come into question, other countries in Europe, Asia, and Africa are engaging with public media. These include Hungary, Latvia, Slovenia, Japan, Namibia, and South Africa.

So where are Canada's public media going? The broader Canadian media environment continues to evolve—mostly through takeovers—and has one of the highest media concentrations in the world. At time of writing, the top 10 privately owned media corporations in Canada had a 70 percent share of the market, much higher than in most industrialized countries (Winseck, 2016). This market share has remained virtually the same for some years. Canada has already lost several of the educational public broadcasters to the private sector, which impedes the overall national strength of that sector. With fewer corporations controlling more of our media, there is an increasingly narrow range of perspectives available, especially when newsrooms are amalgamated after takeovers and downsized. If public media are to survive and maintain their symbolic and potential power to enhance citizenship, they must be taken seriously by both governments and citizens.

Under the Conservative government of Stephen Harper (2006–2015), the CBC rebranded itself in different ways to meet the needs of a more fiscally prudent regime. Its social responsibility section on its website says that "[o]ur public value is about serving citizens and *being a good corporate citizen*" (CBC, 2016, emphasis added). The last phrase seems out of place for a public broadcaster, as does another one that mentions its "social, environmental and *business practices*" (CBC, 2016, emphasis added). But both phrases would perhaps be seen by that government as a message that CBC understood the needs of a conservative government that might not fund a public broadcaster unless it could deliver on accountability and balanced budgets. By the time of the annual report of the Office of the Auditor General on CBC in 2012, it was acknowledged that "no other Canadian broadcaster—commercial or public—has the responsibility to provide the same breadth of services or the same scale of operations as the CBC/Radio-Canada" (Canada, 2012). It seemed that the CBC had proven its worth to the government. In 2016, the following government increased funding to the CBC, but did not recoup all of the lost funding from the previous years (Lum, 2016).

It is key to remember, as Skinner & Gasher (2005) point out, that our "communications media have been perceived though a culturist frame," and that even our Broadcasting Act "defines the Canadian broadcasting system as a public service" (p. 71). Despite the struggles and debate over time, they say that our public media have "at least tempered commercial imperatives and provided a critical lens for evaluating and helping to curb creeping commercialism" (p. 71). In effect, while public media may not have the strength and reach of yesteryear, they continue to play an important role in Canadian media and culture.

In his history of broadcasting policy in Canada, Marc Raboy (1990) once wrote that "broadcasting has been more than a traditional means of communication in the Canadian experience; rather, through broadcasting, the Canadian experience has become an experience *in* communication" (p. xii, emphasis in original). In other words, in this huge, expansive country, we come together and see ourselves as Canadians through the process of communication. Moreover, Raboy suggests that struggles around Canadian broadcasting "have left behind a wealthy store of unrealized potential," what he calls "missed opportunities" (p. xiii). It seems we still have work to do on the national project that is the CBC—a project that has played a key role in the development of the country for more than 85 years. That time frame includes a torrent of new ways to communicate to Canadians through different technologies, but there aren't many that specifically speak to us as citizens, as being part of something larger than ourselves that binds us together and helps us understand who we are as a nation. In addition, public media—from Radio-Canada to TVOntario and beyond—have been instrumental through different waves of immigration, and currently with refugees from war-torn countries, in broadening and renewing our sense of who we are. Given this ongoing renewal and potential, perhaps the project of public media in Canada can never be considered finished.

QUESTIONS FOR DISCUSSION

1. Choose a media story from CBC.ca and compare it with the same story on CTV.ca and GlobalTV.ca. Are there any differences or nuances in the wording? Do they use the same experts? As a public broadcaster, should CBC's story be different than the stories of CTV and Global? If so, in what way?
2. In a multi-media universe with an abundance of ways to get information, what role should the CBC play?
3. Choose a commission or broadcasting act from the list in Box 5.3 and research its purpose and key issues, then as a group, review and identify the similarities and differences across time. What are the most enduring issues encountered over time and why might they still be important today?

ASSIGNMENT

Divide into two sides and debate the importance of the MAPL system today. Do we still need it to defend Canadian culture and, specifically, Canadian music? It might be useful to research the opinions of musical artists themselves, as well as the rationale for MAPL. Remember to have specific examples to defend your side.

WORKS CITED

Attallah, P. (2008). What is the public in public broadcasting? In J. Greenberg & C. D. Elliott (Eds.), *Communication in question: Competing perspectives on controversial issues in communication studies*. Toronto, ON: Thomson-Nelson.

Bradshaw, J. (2016, April 16). Leading a very public life. *The Globe and Mail*, p. B2.

Calabrese, A. (2005). The MacBride report: Its value to a new generation. *Global policy forum (Quaderns del CAC, 21*, 23–26). Retrieved from www.globalpolicy.org/component/content/article/157/27023.html [August 26, 2016].

Canada. (1929). *Report of the Royal Commission on Radio Broadcasting* (Aird Commission). Ottawa, ON: F.A. Acland. Retrieved from www.parl.gc.ca/HousePublications/Publication.aspx?DocId=1032284&Language=E&Mode=1&Parl=37&Ses=2&File=57 [July 28, 2016].

Canada. (2003a). A brief history of Canadian content policy. Appendix 8. Retrieved from www.parl.gc.ca/HousePublications/Publication.aspx?DocId=1032284&File=378 [July 28, 2016].

Canada. (2003b). Regulatory history. Background. Chapter 2. Retrieved from www.parl.gc.ca/HousePublications/Publication.aspx?DocId=1032284&Language=E&Mode=1&Parl=37&Ses=2&File=60 [July 28, 2016].

Canada. CRTC. (2009). The MAPL system—defining a Canadian song. Retrieved from www.crtc.gc.ca/eng/INFO_SHT/R1.HTM.

Canada. Office of the Auditor General. (2012). *Spring report of the Auditor General of Canada*. Retrieved from www.oagbvg.gc.ca/internet/English/parl_oag_201304_11_e_38196.html#hd4f [August 1, 2016].

CBC. (2016, May 31). Social responsibility and public value at CBC/Radio-Canada—Citizenship: Inside and out. Retrieved from www.public-value.cbc.radio-canada.ca [August 1, 2016].

Charland, M. (2009). Technological nationalism. In D. Robinson (Ed.), *Communication history in Canada* (2nd ed.) (pp. 50–61). Don Mills, ON: Oxford University Press.

Coyne, A. (2012, October 5). The great Canadian debate: Does Canada still need the CBC? Opening statement. Macdonald-Laurier Institute. Retrieved from www.macdonaldlaurier.ca/opening-statements-from-the-latest-great-canadian-debate-on-the-cbc/ [August 1, 2016].

Csanady, A. (2014). Majority of Conservative voters like the CBC: Poll. Retrieved from www.o.canada.com/news/majority-of-conservative-voters-like-the-cbc-poll [August 1, 2016].

Friends of Canadian Broadcasting. (2013, July 22). Canadians on the CBC by Nanos Research: Executive summary. Retrieved from www.friends.ca/poll/11549 [July 25, 2016].

Gen Why Media. (2016). Mission. Retrieved from www.genwhymedia.ca/philosophy.

Hoover, S. M. (1993). All power to the conglomerate. *Media & values, 61*(Winter). Retrieved from www.medialit.org/reading-room/all-power-conglomerate [August 26, 2016].

Hoynes, W. (2003). Branding public service: The "New PBS" and the privatization of public television. *Television and new media, 4*(2), 117–130.

Kozolanka, K. (2012). Public service educational broadcasting in Canada: Between the market and the alternative margins. In K. Kozolanka, P. Mazepa, & D. Skinner (Eds.), *Alternative media in Canada* (pp. 56–64). Vancouver, BC: UBC Press.

Leadnow. (2016). Vision and mission. Retrieved from www.leadnow.ca [August 25, 2016].

Lorimer, R., Gasher, M., & Skinner, D. (2007). *Mass communication in Canada*. Don Mills, ON: Oxford University Press.

Lum, Z. (2016, March 1). CBC funding increase coming, but not more than what was pledged: Joly. *Huffington Post*. Retrieved from www.huffingtonpost.ca/2016/03/01/cbc-funding-2016_n_9359334.html [August 25, 2016].

Mahoney, T. (2012). The potential of public media: A case study of Reimagine CBC. *Stream: Culture/Politics/Technology, 6*(1): 15–22.

McCausland, T. (2009). Canada Radio-television and Telecommunications Commission. *Mapleleafweb.com*. Retrieved from www.mapleleafweb.com/features/canada-radio-television-and-telecommunications-commission#history [July 28, 2016].

McDowell, S., & Buchwald, C. (1997). Public interest groups and the Canadian Information Highway. *Telecommunications Policy, 21*(8), 709–719.

Nesbitt-Larking, P. (2007). *Politics, society, and the media*. Peterborough, ON: Broadview.

Raboy, M. (1990). *Missed opportunities: The story of Canada's broadcasting policy*. Montreal, QC, and Kingston, ON: McGill-Queen's University Press.

ReimagineCBC. (2017). Reimagine CBC: A New Vision for CBC. Retrieved from www.reimaginecbc.ca [July 28, 2016].

Skinner, D., & Gasher, M. (2005). So much by so few: Media policy and ownership in Canada. In D. Skinner, J. R. Compton, & M. Gasher (Eds.), *Converging media, diverging politics: A political economy of news media in the United States and Canada*. Lanham, MD: Lexington Books.

Taras, D. (2015). *Digital mosaic: Media, power, and identity in Canada*. Trent, ON: University of Toronto Press.

UNESCO. (2000). Task force on UNESCO in the 21st century: Paper prepared for the meeting of the task force, 21–24 February 2000. Retrieved from www.unesco.org/webworld/taskforce21/documents/holmstrom_en.htm [August 25, 2017].

Vipond, M. (2011). *The mass media in Canada* (4th ed.). Toronto, ON: Lorimer.

Williams, R. (1966). *Communications*. London, UK: Chatto & Windus.

Winseck, D. (2016). Introduction and methodology primer. Retrieved from www.cmcrp.org/projectoverview/ [July 31, 2016].

6 The "Science" of Climate Change and the (Mis)Informed Citizen

If you do not change direction, you will get to where you are heading.

—Ancient Chinese saying

Growing numbers of people across the planet are becoming aware of a looming existential crisis for the human species, namely, the warming of the Earth's climate. It is difficult not to be aware of this fact. In North America, we are experiencing massive forest fires, including the raging wildfire that burned an area "larger than Prince Edward Island" in and around Fort McMurray in the summer of 2016 (Giovannetti, 2016). More frequent and more powerful hurricanes and typhoons are also becoming the norm. The polar ice caps are melting at alarming rates (Gillis, 2017).

Numerous climate science research studies have confirmed that these disasters are the result of **climate change** caused by increased levels of greenhouse gases (Klein, 2014). In fact, "based on well-established evidence, 97% of climate scientists have concluded that human-caused climate change is happening" (Molina et al., 2014, p. 1). The increased temperature of the Earth's climate is putting at risk the well-being of humans, myriad other species, and the planet itself. One might think that a problem of this magnitude might garner serious debate around what to do in these circumstances.

Despite the gravity of the situation, however, much of the public discussion around climate change has been far from serious. This appears to particularly describe the situation in the United States. In 2013, 33 percent of Americans claimed that "there is a lot of disagreement among scientists about whether or not global warming is happening" (Molina et al., 2014, p. 2). A year later, scientists conducted a study for the National Climate Assessment that determined "the effects of human-induced climate change are being felt in every corner of the United States" (Gillis, 2014). This study is one of thousands of scientific studies concluding that the effects of climate change are already affecting the planet. Indeed, according to NASA's data, August 2016 was the warmest month ever recorded, continuing "a streak of 11 consecutive months dating back to October 2015 that have set new monthly high-temperature records" (NASA, 2016).

If virtually the entire community of reputable scientists agrees that climate change is human-made and poses a serious risk to all life on Earth simultaneously with new and severe weather patterns, why are so many people skeptical of the scientific research? Where is the misinformation coming from? Is it intentional or misplaced optimism or naivety? Could the "debate" around climate change be a smokescreen for an ideological struggle around the economy? This chapter addresses the issue of climate change, the grave consequences of what is likely to happen if we continue on the path we are currently on, and the role of the corporate media in all of this. To begin, however, a brief discussion on the science of climate change will be helpful.

GREENHOUSE GASES AND GLOBAL WARMING: AN EVER-SO-BRIEF PRIMER

Scientists have been aware of the warming of the Earth's atmosphere since at least the 1980s (Klein, 2014). By the end of that decade, the term *global warming* was used by concerned scientists and activists to describe this phenomenon. Yet, because there seem to be increasingly chaotic weather patterns, especially with a higher frequency of severe winter storms in many parts of the northern hemisphere, "global warming" is today considered to be a misnomer. Hence, the problem has been renamed *climate change*. Whatever it is called, one thing is certain: the amount of carbon dioxide in our atmosphere is increasing, and so is the temperature.

The science around global warming itself seems straightforward enough. There are several types of gases in our atmosphere responsible for its warming. Carbon dioxide (CO_2) is the most notorious, but others include methane, nitrous oxide, and ozone. CO_2 molecules naturally occur in our atmosphere, but only in relatively small amounts. Indeed, nitrogen and oxygen gases comprise 99 percent of the air we breathe. When we burn any of the fossil fuels (e.g., oil, natural gas, coal, wood), we emit carbon into the atmosphere, which bonds with oxygen gas to form more carbon dioxide.

The CO_2 molecules are unable to trap ultraviolet rays from the sun, but are able to capture the infrared rays emanating from the Earth once the surface is saturated from the sun's heat, usually in the afternoon. It explains to some degree why heat is trapped in our atmosphere directly from the Earth's infrared radiation but not from the sun's ultraviolet radiation. This is similar to how a glass greenhouse works, and why the process is often referred to as the *greenhouse effect*. Earth's radiation is trapped within the CO_2 molecules in the troposphere, the lowest of the four layers of our atmosphere, resulting in warmer air temperatures.

Deforestation is another factor in the increase of CO_2 molecules. Trees act like vacuum cleaners of a sort in that they take in carbon dioxide molecules to grow bigger, and release oxygen gas back into the atmosphere. The extensive deforestation that has taken place across the planet in recent decades is one more reason why carbon dioxide levels have increased throughout the past century from 0.00280 percent to 0.00403 percent (Dlugokencky & Tans, 2016). Although this may seem like a miniscule amount, it is an increase of almost 44 percent and is already producing significant and chaotic changes in weather patterns. CO_2 molecules are effective, tiny heat sinks. Carbon dioxide is not the only greenhouse gas, of course, but it is the most prevalent and contributes to the greenhouse effect more than all of the other greenhouse gases combined.

Methane is the second-worst greenhouse gas in the atmosphere, and because of the melting polar ice caps, it is also increasing in our atmosphere. The phenomenon of rising ocean levels from melting polar ice caps, one of several major problems associated with a warmer atmosphere, is now increasing at an alarming rate. Studies by the US National Oceanic and Atmospheric Administration (NOAA) indicate that ocean levels have been rising at an average of over 3 cm per decade since 1992 (NOAA, 2016). The melting of Arctic sea ice is leading to a thawing of offshore permafrost, which in turn is causing the release of large amounts of methane gas (Wadhams, 2016). Other major problems related to climate change include more frequent and larger forest fires, increased desertification, uncertainty over crop yields, shortages of drinkable water, and warmer ocean temperatures that result in decreased sea life and the breakdown of ocean food chains (Gillis, 2017). The political will to take on this impending catastrophe has become a necessity.

CLIMATE SCIENCE AND POLITICAL CONSENSUS

At the Paris Agreement on climate change in November 2015, there was somewhat of a political consensus stating that a 2-degree Celsius increase is the maximum that our atmosphere can accept before we reach a point of no return and experience regular meteorological catastrophes. Many scientists, however, believe that the 2-degree limit is arbitrary and will result in both rising ocean levels that will completely cover many low-lying lands (Shaw, 2013) and more severe droughts in Australia and elsewhere (Hare, Roming, Schaeffer, & Schleussner, 2016). There is a growing acceptance among climate scientists that in order to lessen suffering among living species, the temperature increase must not reach 1.5 degrees Celsius (King, 2016). Scientists believe that more greenhouse gases have already resulted in a 0.8-degree Celsius increase in average global atmospheric temperature since humans began burning coal during the Industrial Revolution (Klein, 2014). Indeed, a new scientific statement released in September 2016 by seven highly respected climate scientists asserts that keeping the warming trend below 1.5 degrees Celsius "has almost certainly been missed" (Mooney, 2016). These scientists, most of whom have held prominent positions with the UN's Intergovernmental Panel on Climate Change, are calling for all national governments in the world to cut CO_2 emissions much more substantially than agreed to in the Paris Agreement. To not do so, they contend, will lead to chaos for life on Earth.

At the time of this writing, 132 countries of 194 signatories have ratified the Paris Agreement (Climate Analytics, 2017). This represents nations that produce over 55 percent of the world's greenhouse gas emissions, enough to begin implementation of the agreement on November 4, 2016, which was four days prior to the American presidential election. The election victory of Donald Trump, however, has put the Paris Agreement in jeopardy. President Trump and many in the Republican Party are climate change deniers (Krauss, 2016), and this will likely result in diminished American support to meet the goals of the Paris Agreement. In other words, the Paris Agreement is on thin ice, pun intended.

If climate science has set firm limits on atmospheric temperature increases for humans to solve the climate change crisis, why are so many people willing to support political leaders that promise to ignore the evidence? Why are they willing to risk the health of the planet that their children and grandchildren will grow up in? Why do they *not* connect disasters like huge hurricanes and frighteningly massive forest fires to the warming of the Earth's atmosphere? Clearly, there is some confusion among the public, likely emanating from a misinformation campaign. It appears that the findings of peer-reviewed climate science research are not being accurately disseminated to the public. It is prudent to explore the role of the media in this convoluted situation.

UNDERSTANDING CLIMATE CHANGE AND THE MEDIA

Why do significant numbers of people believe there is serious disagreement among scientists regarding climate change, when in fact there is not? A metaphor will prove useful to begin this discussion. Let's imagine a scenario where out of the blue a scientist announced his research proves that the Earth is flat. Let's further imagine that the mainstream media jumped on this story and spread the word that there was clear disagreement among scientists about whether the Earth was flat or spherical. Of course, in this hypothetical situation the pseudo-science would not go very far. But with climate change, scientific fakery appears to have legs. The question is this: with the stakes so high, why is this the case?

Part of the answer may reside in the journalist's quest to seek out balance. If an article includes both the perspective of a reputable climate scientist and that of a climate change denier, the reader may get the false impression that both sides have plausible arguments for their respective views. Kovach and Rosenstiel (2014) explain: "Balance, for instance, can lead to distortion. If an overwhelming percentage of scientists, as an example, believe that global warming is a scientific fact … it is a disservice to citizens and truthfulness to create the impression that the scientific debate is equally split" (p. 109). Even if the journalist has good intentions and merely wants to provide two sides to an issue, the result is a skeptical public. The following sections will demonstrate, however, that there are more nefarious forces at work in the so-called climate change debate.

Corporate Media's Coverage of Climate Change

It may appear ironic that, in a chapter that critiques the corporate media's coverage of climate change, there are so many references to articles in the mainstream press. There *are* dedicated journalists, some who are tasked with covering scientific research, doing commendable work in trying to reach the public and warn citizens of the looming crisis around climate change. Many journalists, such as Naomi Klein (2014) and George Monbiot (2007), have written popular books that offer deep analyses around climate change and economic concerns. Yet, in mainstream newspapers, these articles of concerned journalists are not front-page news. Indeed, on television they appear even less frequently over time.

In 2007, three major American news networks—ABC, CBS, and NBC—produced 147 climate-related stories, but in 2011 this number shrank to a paltry *14*. One may speculate that this decrease is partially responsible for the fact that over the same time period, the percentage of Americans who believe that burning fossil fuels affects the climate *also* decreased: from 71 percent in 2007, to 44 percent in 2011 (Klein, 2014). Although the numbers have rebounded somewhat since 2011, the overwhelming majority of conservatives in the United States still reject the evidence produced by the climate scientists. Indeed, a recent study by a team of American sociologists found that over time "partisan polarization widens in the U.S." on climate change (Dunlap, McCright, & Yarosh, 2016, p. 4).

In the summer of 2015, the US Department of Defense released a report calling climate change a security risk "because it degrades living conditions, human security, and the ability of governments to meet the basic needs of their populations." One might think that a report like this in tandem with the climate science would bring the climate change issue to the forefront of American discourse. Yet, in the three presidential debates between Hillary Clinton and Donald Trump during the fall of 2016, there was not one question from the moderators about climate change. They asked the two candidates questions about email usage, abortion, taxes, and Muslims, but completely ignored the biggest political issue of our times. Even more alarming, there were five minutes or so devoted to discussing energy sources, but climate change itself was not addressed.

The political situation in Canada is similar, although perhaps not as stark: in 2013, 41 percent of supporters of the federal Conservative Party, in government at the time, believed that climate change was a problem caused by humans, while 69 percent of Liberal supporters and 76 percent of New Democrats believed it is human-caused (Environics Institute, 2013). Clearly, political ideology matters. (See Chapter 1 for a discussion on the importance of political ideology.)

Rupert Murdoch, executive director and CEO of News Corporation, has long championed neoliberal and socially conservative causes through his media empire (Orlowski, 2011b). Under his leadership, News Corporation has been relentless in dismissing climate science. One of the most influential news outlets in the United States is the Murdoch-owned Fox News. Over the past several years, its coverage has referred to climate change as a "superstition, a scam, and a hoax" (Gerken, 2015). The most frightening aspect of this is that more Americans believed Fox News than believed President Obama on matters pertaining to climate change (Gerken, 2015).

Sociologist Riley Dunlap discussed his recent research on climate change and American political ideology in an interview:

> There are top-down cues from Republican political elites and their supporters from conservative think tanks to conservative media—especially the Murdoch media—that influence voters.... The result is that global warming has joined God, guns, gays, and abortion as core elements of Republican identity. (cited in Readfearn, 2016)

Clearly, in order to garner more political support to constructively take on climate change, new strategies are required. And yes, the media will be instrumental in these new strategies. Civil society needs a strong mainstream media to support it.

Major news outlets in Canada play the same game. Consider the following, written by the former Canadian media mogul Lord Conrad Black (2009) as he sat in a prison cell over convictions of fraud and obstruction of justice:

> Till now, I have avoided more than very limited comment on the whole global-warming carbon emissions controversy. But now that colossal spending and regulating programs impend on these issues, I must say that the Al Gore–David Suzuki conventional-wisdom hysteria is an insane scam.

Very few convicted criminals would be able to have their views on what constitutes sound science appear in a national newspaper. Black was the founder of the socially conservative and neoliberal *National Post*, where his thoughts on climate change appeared, and this undoubtedly was a factor in his views being published at all. Yet, for all the things Black is known for, an understanding of science is not one of them.

Lord Black's column appeared in the newspaper on November 28, 2009, barely a week before the United Nations Climate Change Conference took place in Copenhagen, Denmark. Yet he need not have devoted any time to denigrating climate change scientists and activists. Stolen email messages from one of the world's foremost climate research institutes were circulated to various delegates and media outlets a few days before the Copenhagen Summit (Revkin & Broder, 2009). Within hours, media sources across the world painted a picture of tainted and biased climate science that undoubtedly affected public perceptions (Klein, 2014). Clearly, there are many people who simply do not want government to take action on climate change. The question is, who are these people?

The Climate Change Denial Movement and Access to the Media

The climate change denial movement emanated from a 5,000-word memo written by corporate lawyer (and future US supreme court justice) Lewis Powell and sent to wealthy American conservatives in 1971 (Mayer, 2016). Powell urged these industrialists to wage a propaganda campaign in the media and on college campuses. According to Powell, conservatives needed to control the political debate by demanding "balance" in textbooks, curriculum, and media coverage (Mayer, 2016). Immediately, conservative billionaires such as the Koch brothers, heirs to their Nazi-supporting father's oil empire, gave new think tanks like the American Enterprise Institute (AEI) hundreds of millions of dollars to influence the media. The AEI was one of dozens of American pseudo-scholarly organizations that was created to legitimate the right of oil, gas, and coal corporations to pollute the air and water, as well as pay fewer taxes (Mayer, 2016). This strategy has grown immensely since the 1970s. According to *New York Times* investigative journalist Jane Mayer (2016), the Koch brothers alone have donated nearly $25 million to organizations tasked with propagating the notion that climate change is a hoax perpetrated by left-wing groups to destroy capitalism and, by extension, the American Dream.

Renowned British journalist George Monbiot did an investigation to find out who is *producing* the incorrect data on climate change. In his best-selling book *Heat: How to Stop the Planet from Burning* (2007), Monbiot describes the path his investigation took to uncover the sources of these contrarian views. He began his investigation after reading several accounts in the British media claiming that climate change was a hoax. He found that many of these journalists cited the works of a few scientists who, in turn, cited in their own work a non-existent paper from 1989 in *Science* magazine. Monbiot also used his regular column in the respected British newspaper the *Guardian* to challenge the credentials of those who claim that the research is wrong and that global warming has nothing to do with human activity. For several years, this journalist has been relentless in unmasking the climate change denial movement and its access to the media.

Monbiot discovered that various groups with important-sounding names like The Advancement of Sound Science Coalition use *fake* data from Internet sites such as www.iceagenow.com and www.sepp.org. For example, www.iceagenow.com included false claims that dispute the widespread scientific belief that the world's mountain glaciers are retreating. Here is one such claim: "Since 1980, there has been an *advance* of more than 55% of the 625 mountain glaciers under observation by the World Glacier Monitoring group in Zurich" (Monbiot, 2007,

p. 25, emphasis added). After finding that the claims of these climate change deniers were bogus, Monbiot made a very disturbing discovery: *all* of these groups "have been funded by Exxon" and other Big Oil conglomerates (p. 27). A Drexel University study by environmental sociologist Robert Brulle (2013) discovered that massive donations from the fossil fuel industry itself went to ideologically friendly recipients: "140 conservative philanthropic foundations funneled $558 million to almost 100 climate change denial organizations between 2003 [and] 2010" (see Box 6.1).

Conservative think tanks appear to be increasing their attempts to influence the public relations fight. For example, in August 2016 a new campaign called Fueling U.S. Forward was launched at the RedState Gathering in Denver, Colorado, an annual event where prominent Republicans such as Paul Ryan and media personality Glenn Beck speak to their base. The campaign's stated goal is to "rebrand fossil fuels, focusing on the 'positive' sides of oil, gas, and coal" through media outreach (Kelly, 2016). The Fueling U.S. Forward campaign received its funding from the second-largest privately owned company in the US, oil giant Koch Industries (Negin, 2013).

It is not only the corporate media that are conduits for the climate change deniers. Publishing houses are also involved. In fact, a 2013 study found that 87 percent of climate change denial books (excluding those that are self-published) were "linked to right-wing think tanks" (Klein, 2014, p. 39). Moreover, letters to the editor and online forums at the end of climate change articles created by

BOX 6.1: EXXON SECRETS AND THE FUNDING OF CLIMATE CHANGE DENIAL GROUPS

The list of groups and scientists who claim that climate change has nothing to do with fossil fuels and human activity can be found at www.exxonsecrets.org. This website, sponsored by Greenpeace, relies on data from Exxon's official documents to illuminate the groups and think tanks committed to confusing the public about climate science. The headline that jumps out of the website's homepage explains that from 1998 to 2014 ExxonMobil provided over US$30 million to groups tasked with spewing climate change denial materials, newspaper columns, television shows, and more. The page lists how much funding the oil giant has given to 69 think tanks. Almost all of them are American, but of note to Canadians is the fact that the ultra-right-wing Fraser Institute, based in Vancouver, is also one of the recipients.

some media outlets for the public to engage in conversation and debate are often hijacked by writers connected to these same think tanks (Klein, 2014). Climate change is one of several political issues in which online forums are inundated with pro-corporate and anti-government commentary by people with vested interests.

Perhaps surprisingly, the initial "climate change is a hoax" discourse emanated from the world's largest tobacco company, Philip Morris (Monbiot, 2007, p. 31). In 1993, the tobacco giant hired a public relations firm, APCO, to help it thwart state and city plans to implement passive smoking bans. APCO directed Philip Morris "to create the impression of a 'grassroots movement'—one that had been formed spontaneously by concerned citizens to fight 'over-regulation'" (Monbiot, 2007, p. 32). The PR firm suggested that the company set up a national coalition to help "educate" the media, politicians, and the public. The response of the tobacco company was to provide the funds for a "fake citizens' group" called The Advancement for Sound Science Coalition (TASSC). One of the first tasks of TASSC was to strongly suggest to the media that there was an abundance of "junk science" around the issues of tobacco use, nuclear waste disposal, and global warming.

According to Monbiot, TASSC has "done more damage to the campaign to halt [climate change] than any other body" (p. 34). This has not gone unnoticed by the threatened corporations. Exxon officials have come to understand that their best strategy to keep profits up is to challenge the scientific consensus about global warming and climate change. Corporate media outlets in the United States and Australia have been using Exxon employees and other non-scientists to pose "as serious scientists" (Monbiot, 2007, p. 37). As an example, Fox News hired the TASSC executive director, Steve Milloy, whom they describe as "an advocate of free enterprise and an adjunct scholar at the Competitive Enterprise Institute," to challenge scientific findings that may hurt corporate profits (Monbiot, 2007, p. 35). Milloy writes a column for Fox News called "Junk Science" in which he denigrates any scientific study that, among other things, documents the ill effects of second-hand tobacco smoke or offers proof that climate change is occurring.

This anti-science strategy goes back several years. In 2004, *Harper's Magazine* published a leaked memo from the Competitive Enterprise Institute to a man named Phil Cooney, the chief of staff of the White House Council on Environmental Quality (cited in Monbiot, 2007, p. 38). The memo showed that this group and Cooney were working in tandem to dispute the findings in a report on climate change from the Environmental Protection Agency (EPA). The following year, the environmental columnist for the *New York Times*, Andrew Revkin, revealed that the American Petroleum Institute had pushed for Cooney to work at the White House in that capacity (Revkin, 2005). Moreover, and equally disturbing, Exxon had paid the Competitive Enterprise Institute over $2 million to do this work (Monbiot, 2007, p. 38). Such is the situation with the long-running climate change denial movement in the United States.

Canada is not immune from similar tactics used by the oil industry. Prior to the 2008 federal election in Canada, an Alberta-based group made up of academics and former oil industry insiders named the Friends of Science formed (De Souza, 2008). This group ran a series of ads in the media that called for Canada to renege on its commitments to the Kyoto Protocol—the predecessor to the Paris Agreement—which Canada and other countries had signed in 1997. Some of these ads were presented during the election campaign in Ontario ridings where incumbent Liberal MPs were in danger of losing seats to the Conservatives. During the campaign, the Friends of Science media contact person, Morten Paulsen, became an unpaid spokesperson for Stephen Harper and the Conservative Party. Paulsen also works for Fleishman-Hillard, one of the largest public relations companies in the world, with a specialty in crisis management for many industries, including Big Oil (Orlowski, 2011a). One has to wonder what influence this group had on the Harper government's "mysterious cancellation [of] an 18-month investigation into oilsands pollution" (De Souza, 2010).

In terms of media access, it is difficult for scientists and environmental groups to compete with these extremely well-funded groups bent on distorting or even blocking the scientific research around climate change. One major reason for this is some federal governments refuse to let government scientists discuss their research with the media. (This will be discussed in a subsequent section.) The main point here is that corporate media often appear to be allies of the climate change deniers. In 2014, the *Huffington Post* published a six-part series written by Elliott Negin, the senior writer and scientist for the Union of Concerned Scientists, entitled "Unreliable Sources: How the News Media Help the Kochs and ExxonMobil Spread Climate Disinformation." Negin analyzed eight major news outlets for the ways in which they inform the public about funding for eight different climate contrarian groups who have easy access to the media. The eight groups responsible for disseminating climate disinformation are: Americans for Prosperity, Institute for Energy Research/American Energy Alliance, Heartland Institute, Heritage Foundation, Competitive Enterprise Institute, American Enterprise Institute, Manhattan Institute, and the Cato Institute. It is noteworthy that these eight groups, whom Negin calls the Oil Eight, are funded by the oil industry.

Negin (2013) found that in the 357 media articles pertaining to climate and energy that cited data from these eight groups during 2011–2012, only 32 percent "provided information about the Oil Eight's fossil fuel industry funding." This is significant information in order for citizens to become informed about this extremely important issue. It is even more disconcerting to learn that the *New York Times* and the *Washington Post* are included in the media outlets the Union of Concerned Scientists (2013) studied. The most reliable media source in the study was the *Los Angeles Times*, which reported oil industry funding in 44 percent of its relevant articles. This most likely is a factor as to why the Koch brothers want to purchase this very newspaper (Negin, 2013).

The study done by the Union of Concerned Scientists only examined articles on climate and energy in which it was possible to trace who actually funded the reports cited or the groups who produced the data. This is easier said than done: in the first scholarly inquiry into the organizational underpinnings and funding behind the climate change denial movement, sociologist Robert Brulle (2013) found that much of the funding is "funneled through third-party pass-through organizations that conceal the original funder" (Fischer, 2013). These strategies are designed to keep vital information from the public, and are therefore anti-democratic.

Another tactic Big Oil has utilized is intimidation, especially against journalists who dare to question the ethics of the oil industry. As an example, in late 2015 student journalists at the Columbia School of Journalism collaborated with the *Los Angeles Times* to expose how Exxon "lied to the public and investors about the risks of climate change" (Goodman, 2015). The journalists found that Exxon had covered up scientific data about the fossil fuel connection to global warming as far back as the 1970s. The State of New York proceeded to embark on a criminal investigation against ExxonMobil (as the company is now called). The company complained that the students' work was filled with inaccuracies, and made explicit reference to the $220,000 donation it had made to Columbia.

It gets even more frightening. Responding to the same charge that it had withheld scientific data on climate change dating back to the 1970s, ExxonMobil recently enlisted the help of the US Congress to defend its financial interests. Texas Representative Lamar Smith and the House Committee on Science, Space and Technology issued subpoenas against eight environmental groups involved with the case. The committee even subpoenaed the attorneys general of New York and Massachusetts for launching investigations into the company's decades of deceit around fossil fuels and global warming (Volcovici, 2016). In an archetypal example of the old adage "The best defence is a strong offence," Smith's committee accused the environmental groups and attorneys general of having a "political agenda" and mentioned their "intent to intimidate" (Volcovici, 2016). (It is interesting to note that the *only* coverage of the ExxonMobil intimidation tactics in mainstream on-line news service outlets was found to be in Reuters U.K.)

It is clear that the fossil fuel industry is taking very seriously the threat to corporate profits posed by climate science. The disinformation campaign it funds that claims any scientific study linking human-made greenhouse gases to climate change is merely "junk science" has been very effective. When one considers the role played by corporate media in all of this, the confusion and skepticism among citizens may be understandable. Yet the attacks on the brave journalists who are fighting the power, who want the truth about climate science to be provided to the public, have also had a chilling effect. Further, it is alarming to learn that many elected officials appear to be complicit in this deception, as the ExxonMobil case has demonstrated. The political connections to Big Oil, however, run much deeper than that.

THE BLURRED SEPARATION BETWEEN OIL AND STATE

In Chapter 1, the discussion highlighted that one of the main tenets of neoliberal economic policy is the deregulation of industry. The following quote by former Republican congressman Tom Corcoran clearly explains why it is so difficult to regulate the oil industry in the United States: "There is a desire to reduce the amount of fossil fuels here in the United States. We exist to persuade the government not to do that, and so far with the Congress I think we've been successful" (Dembicki, 2010). When he made this statement, Corcoran was the executive director of the Center for North American Energy Security, a powerful lobby group for the oil industry. That Big Oil has hired former politicians to lobby on its behalf should not come as a surprise, as unseemly as this may appear. What may be disconcerting, however, is how many American and Canadian politicians were former employees of oil companies *prior* to entering politics.

In recent decades, the cabinet of both George W. Bush administrations was probably the most egregious example of the amalgamation of Big Oil and state until Donald Trump became the American president in January 2017. It is instructive to look at the George W. Bush administrations first. Condoleeza Rice was a board member of Chevron Oil, the second-largest American oil company, prior to accepting posts as the national security advisor and secretary of state for President Bush (Gatti & Mouawad, 2007). As well, before becoming the US vice president, Dick Cheney was the CEO of the giant oilfield services and exploration corporation, Halliburton. Probably less known is the fact that as Halliburton's CEO, Cheney was able to almost double the money this company received from the US Treasury (Klein, 2007, p. 351). Halliburton gave Cheney a severance package of $36 million when he left the company to become vice president. Almost immediately, Halliburton benefited tremendously from this golden handshake: by early 2004, the company had already received more than $9 *billion* in contracts associated with the US-led invasion and occupation of Iraq (Teather, 2004). There were other connections between Big Oil and the Bush administrations, but none of them received front-page coverage in American newspapers at the time. Fortunately, members of the Obama administrations were not associated with the fossil fuel industry prior to their cabinet appointments.

The same cannot be said for the Trump cabinet appointees. Indeed, the Trump administration's connections to the fossil fuel industry are roughly on par with the Bush administrations. *The Atlantic* magazine has an online "Donald Trump Cabinet Tracker" that is repeatedly updated as new names are approved (or not) by the Senate to serve in Cabinet (Berman, 2017). There are some noteworthy fossil fuel industry people who have been confirmed to join Trump's cabinet. At time of writing, the secretary of state is Rex Tillerson, who was the CEO of ExxonMobil for the 10 years leading up to the Cabinet position. Tillerson has worked for Exxon since 1975, the only company he has ever worked for. Ryan Zinke of Montana is the secretary of the interior. As a Republican member of Congress, he is a climate change denier and supports mining and drilling for fossil fuels on federal lands. Trump's choice to be the head administrator of the Environmental Protection Agency (EPA) is Scott Pruitt, a leader in the legal battles against the Obama administration's agenda to fight climate change. Pruitt is an outspoken climate change denier. After the election, media critic Noam Chomsky (2016) wrote that President Trump "calls for rapid increase in use of fossil fuels, including coal; dismantling of regulations; rejection of help to developing countries that are seeking to move to sustainable energy; and in general racing to the cliff as fast as possible." Clearly, the citizenry must become informed.

Stephen Harper was the prime minister of Canada from 2006 until 2015. His father was an accountant for Imperial Oil (Nikiforuk, 2010), and Harper himself also worked for Imperial Oil before entering politics (Bunting, 2007). Harper's interim successor as leader of the Conservative Party of Canada was Rona Ambrose, who was also the first minister of the environment that Harper appointed. Like her predecessor, Ambrose's father also worked for Big Oil internationally (Taber, 2007). The election victory of Justin Trudeau's Liberals in late 2015 ended the connection between Big Oil and the Canadian government that had been in place with the previous Conservative government.

Close relationships between the state and the oil industry appear to be strongest when Conservatives form government in Canada and the Republicans are in power in the United States. In recent years, Democratic American governments and Liberal Canadian governments tend to acknowledge that a separation between Big Oil and the state is healthy for democracy. Another important ideological difference relates to governance and climate science, namely, the freedom for Canadian environment scientists to speak to the media about their research.

THE STATE, THE MEDIA, AND ACCESS TO SCIENTIFIC RESEARCH

> It was not a good time for *journalists*. It was not a good time for *scientists* ... and it was not a good time for *Canadian citizens*.
> —Paul Dufour, science-policy analyst at the University of Ottawa
> (cited in Ogden, 2016, emphasis added)

During the 2006–2015 decade in which the Harper Conservatives governed Canada, it became apparent to Canadians that something was amiss around access to information. Articles began to appear in the mainstream press that obstacles were being put in place to keep vital information from the public. This became a particularly burning issue when activists and academics attempted to obtain information pertaining to the environment, specifically around climate change (Klein, 2014). Government scientists, whose salaries are paid for by Canadian citizens, were being muzzled—they were not allowed to speak to the media about their research unless the Conservatives approved of what they could divulge. The muzzling of scientists began almost as soon as the Conservatives came to power. (See Box 6.2 to read about the extent of this censorship.)

In the 18 months leading up to the October 2015 federal election, Canadians learned that the Conservative government demanded that all speaking engagements between its scientists and the media must be vetted by various levels of management (Mortillaro, 2015). Most requests by scientists were denied, and it appeared that this was especially the case if the scientific research yielded results that went against the government's agenda or were perceived to be a threat to corporate profits. As the 2015 federal election moved closer, more and more

> **BOX 6.2: SCIENTIFIC RESEARCH, LITERARY FREEDOM, AND CENSORSHIP**
>
> Under Prime Minister Stephen Harper, Canada's Conservative government forbade its scientists to speak to the media about their research unless they obtained government approval first. Environment minister Rona Ambrose took this muzzling approach much further than merely blocking scientific research from reaching the public. A climatologist at Environment Canada, Mark Tushingham, had written a science fiction novel called *Hotter Than Hell* (2006). Shortly before showcasing the book at an event organized by the publisher, Minister Ambrose phoned the scientist/author. She ordered him not to even attend his book launch, nor to discuss the book with the news media (Austen, 2006). This is an example of extreme censorship.

scientists decided to challenge this policy, most anonymously, while others came out and paid the price for it with their jobs (Watters, 2015). The scientists were beginning to challenge the government-imposed muzzling and its "culture of fear" among its scientific community (Mortillaro, 2015).

The mainstream media were directly affected by the Conservative policy of stopping scientists from explaining their research to Canadians, and with the 2015 federal election looming on the horizon, journalists eventually began to write more about it. More journalists appear to be gaining courage to fight the power that is Big Oil and its friends in government think tanks and government. This in itself provides hope. In order to mount an effective resistance to the climate change denial movement, however, the mainstream media will have to do more.

American environmental scientists also must contend with the same type of censorship that their Canadian peers experienced under the federal Conservatives. A few days after his inauguration ceremony, officials for President Trump informed scientists working at the Environmental Protection Agency and the Department of Agriculture that "they may no longer discuss agency research or departmental restrictions with anyone outside of the agency—including the news media" (Maron, 2017). It is noteworthy that this decree came prior to the president's subsequent "war with the press." Did this Republican president borrow this strategy from Prime Minister Harper? This is unknown. But what is clear is that these acts of censorship are obstacles to an informed citizenry and work toward weakening democracy.

IMPLICATIONS FOR CITIZENS: CLIMATE CHANGE IN AN ERA OF CLIMATE CHANGE DENIAL

Taken at face value, this chapter paints a bleak picture of impending doom. After all, climate science is clear that if countries do not implement stringent policy to limit greenhouse gas emissions, the conditions for life on Earth will undergo significant and uncertain transformations in the not so distant future. The chapter echoes what many climate scientists and environmental activists have been saying for several years, namely, that continuing on the "business as usual" path will lead to certain catastrophe for humanity. Chaos will occur in the Earth's weather patterns, which we are beginning to witness, but it will also appear across the natural world and its ecosystems. This will affect our food production, our economies, indeed, our way of life. As mentioned at the beginning of the chapter, climate change represents an existential crisis such as humanity has never had to contend with before. The ancient Chinese saying that opened the chapter—"If you do not change direction, you will get to where you are heading"—highlights in clear terms the need to change our current approach.

Corporate power is behind the effective climate change denial movement, and its minions in elected office are there to further obfuscate the intersection of concerns around the environment and the economy. The same can be said for media outlets—after all, one axiom that all citizens need to continue to remember is *corporate media have corporate interests*. It is these same corporate interests that are proving to be a major obstacle in combatting climate change on many fronts. Capitalism today is exceptionally rapacious in its treatment of both the environment and civilian populations around the world (McChesney, 2014). As explained in Chapter 1, neoliberalism, the economic paradigm that dominates most of the world's economies today, demands an unfettered version of capitalism that commodifies almost everything and demands government involvement only insofar as it serves corporate interests. And this is the binary that has been presented to citizens in most countries: to fight climate change means to wreak havoc on the global economies. From this perspective, the conundrum is about the environment versus our standard of living. In such stark terms, it is no wonder that many citizens are reluctant to believe that climate change is happening. After all, vast segments of almost every country's citizenry now live in tenuous and fragile economic conditions as more and more of the wealth is concentrated within corporate spreadsheets and the top 1 percent (Klein, 2014; McChesney, 2014).

Existential crises, however, provide great challenges that can bring out the best in humanity. This is perhaps where hope resides. Similar to what occurred among allies in World War II, humanity is going to require a collective effort to take on this challenge. Let's be clear—the World War analogy is not hyperbolic. Environmental activist Bill McKibben (2016) contends our current scenario *is* World War III: "It's not that global warming is *like* a world war. It *is* a world war. And we are losing." McKibben links climate change to the devastating forest fire of 2016 that forced the 90,000 inhabitants of Fort McMurray to evacuate their homes, which may seem obvious. He also connects, however, the terrifying Zika virus in growing numbers of mosquitoes to climate change as well. Because of this virus, seven countries have now urged women to *not* get pregnant, the consequences can be so horrifying. Moreover, much of the world must contend with growing numbers of desperate refugees, the result of wars and desertification caused by climate change.

Only a collective effort across borders provides hope on all of these fronts. Politicians must accept climate science, and if they do not, then they must be replaced by people who understand and accept the scientific research. Our elected representatives must understand the gravity of the situation, and by corollary, the opportunity to help lead us to a better place. The impetus for the climate change denial movement is perceived loss of profits for those corporations who benefit from the status quo around fossil fuel use. Many shareholders in fossil fuel industries likely see green as the new red, meaning the push for alternative energy is a smokescreen for something resembling a socialist economy. Perhaps many citizens share similar concerns, but they should also embrace a more sustainable economy that has a more equitable material distribution embedded in it.

Mark Jacobson, an environmental professor at Stanford University, and his team of scientists concluded that the United States "could generate 80 to 85 percent of its power from sun, wind, and water by 2030, and 100 percent by 2050" (McKibben, 2016). Jacobson's Stanford team has done similar research for 139 countries. A switch of this magnitude to alternative and renewable energy sources is an opportunity to create a new and sustainable economy with decent-paying jobs (Klein, 2014). Joseph Stiglitz (2017), a former recipient of the Nobel Prize in Economics and co-chair of the global High-Level Commission on Carbon Prices, argues in the commission's report that an even stronger economy is possible with a reduction in carbon dioxide emissions. This is exciting, and this is where the corporate media comes back into the picture.

A NEW ROLE FOR MEDIA IN AN ERA OF CLIMATE CHANGE AND NEOLIBERALISM

> If you act like social change for the better is impossible, you guarantee it will be impossible.... Pessimism is self-fulfilling; it is no way to live.
> —Robert McChesney, paraphrasing Noam Chomsky, 2014, p. 5

Citizens in Canada and across the world must have access to the real climate science findings *and* the potential for healthy and sustainable economies such as the Jacobson team's research concludes are entirely possible. In the situation humanity now finds itself in, there can be no more noble a task for journalists today than to inform the public about climate science and sustainable economics. After all, any functioning and stable democracy requires its citizens to be informed and, to a certain extent, activist. As discussed throughout this chapter, most citizens today are bombarded by falsehoods propagated by neoliberal think tanks that receive their funding from the oil industry. Journalists may be forced by their employers to report the pseudo-science from these organizations, but they *must* also make clear to citizens the funding connections to fossil fuel industries. Giving the public fair and accurate information to let them decide the route for society to take is only a first and obvious step.

In order for the mainstream media to help fulfill its role in a functioning democracy, we need a new perspective in how we view the world we live in. Canadian journalist Naomi Klein (2014) explains the situation bluntly:

> Right now, the triumph of market logic, with its ethos of domination, and fierce competition, is paralyzing almost all serious efforts to respond to climate change.... [A] worldview will need to rise to the fore that sees nature, other nations, and our own neighbours not as adversaries, but rather as partners in a grand project of mutual reinvention. (p. 23)

Pointing the finger at neoliberalism, Klein is adamant that this collective process of transformation must occur as soon as possible. Clearly, the mainstream media must play a major role in this project. One clear way for them to do this is through reframing.

The dominant frame used in many mainstream media outlets today is the environment versus the economy. This is a false binary that needs to be critiqued and deconstructed for the public. There are other, related binaries that are commonly used and similarly embedded with negative connotations on both sides of the coin. For example, *poisoning versus poverty* is a frequently considered binary in conversations across many tables in kitchens and pubs in North America (Klein, 2014). This extremely bleak binary refers to a choice of a functioning economy combined with an environment polluted with fossil industry by-products and oil spills, or a cleaner environment with an alternative energy–based economy that fails to provide for its citizens. In places such as Alberta, a common binary is *austerity versus extraction*, implying that if the oil industry is not allowed to grow, the government will be forced to implement austerity measures in which common Albertans will have to suffer even more. As Stiglitz and others point out, these binaries are false.

Mainstream media can and should present binaries that are more reflective of reality, and more hopeful. An example of a progressive binary around decision-making and resource extraction would be *local community versus corporate power*. Regarding support for energy sources, a binary might be presented along the lines of *oil subsidies versus green job support*. In Canada, the oil industry receives well over $3 billion a year in public monies (McDiarmid, 2015). The public should be presented with this information and then decide if this money would be better spent developing alternative energy sources that are renewable. Citizens may come to understand that to rise up to the challenge of climate change, the economy need not be decimated. Indeed, a more sustainable economy that is socially progressive may well be possible.

Not all of this situation can or should be put onto the shoulders of journalists. Governments have a role to play in supporting both mainstream and alternative media outlets. They must protect journalists who write about climate change and the so-called dark money behind the climate change denial movement. Indeed, legislation that protects whistle-blowing should be extended to scientists. Politicians and civil servants should likewise be removed from possible lawsuits brought forth by vindictive fossil fuel industries. Scientists who have important research findings to share must not be censored. If a government attempts to censor its scientists, as we have seen with recent Conservative and Republican governments, mainstream media must alert citizens with a public awareness campaign. Democracy itself will be strengthened by all of these measures.

With any major crisis, opportunity for positive growth and wisdom also exists. This is true of the current scenario humanity finds itself in surrounding climate change and the economy. The time has arrived for human ingenuity to focus on solutions to this existential threat to life on Earth. Citizens need to be informed in order to effectively employ agency for change. Journalists in the mainstream media have a vital role to play in the transformation toward this new worldview.

QUESTIONS FOR DISCUSSION

1. What is the official mandate of the Environmental Protection Agency (EPA) in the US? When was it created and under which president? What regulations has it imposed on industry? How has the status of the EPA changed since then?
2. What does the 2015 Paris Agreement on climate change request of all countries that signed? What is the position of the current Canadian government toward this agreement? What is the position of the current American government toward this agreement?
3. The chapter includes a brief discussion around reframing issues related to climate change as binaries. Can you think of any others not mentioned in the chapter? What are they? Explain their usefulness.

ASSIGNMENTS

1. The list of 69 groups and think tanks that claim climate change has nothing to do with fossil fuels and human activity can be found at www.exxonsecrets.org. It is telling that each of the recipient groups must produce reports insisting that climate change is not occurring or that, if it is, it is not caused by human activity. Choose one of the larger recipient groups. Go to its website, locate any climate change denial pieces, and summarize the main points.
2. David and Charles Koch are American billionaires who have spent exorbitant amounts of their own money to influence public opinion on major political issues, including climate change. Research their family background, what industries they are involved in, and the positions they take and hope the public takes on various issues. For a resource, see Jane Mayer's (2016) book *Dark Money: The Hidden History of the Billionaires behind the Rise of the Radical Right*.
3. Compare articles on the environmental website 350.org to environmental articles in a mainstream newspaper over the past two months. How do the topics differ? What are the discernible ideological influences? Who benefits from the perspective of the articles? (See Chapter 1 for background information on political ideology.)

WORKS CITED

Austen, I. (2006, May 1). Debate on global warming helps produce a brisk seller. *The New York Times*. Retrieved from www.nytimes.com/2006/05/01/business/worldbusiness/01environment.html [October 9, 2016].

Berman, R. (2017, March 2). The Donald Trump cabinet tracker. *The Atlantic*. Retrieved from www.theatlantic.com/politics/archive/2017/03/trump-cabinet-tracker/510527/ [March 5, 2017].

Black, C. (2009, November 28). Conrad Black: A teeming rainforest of irrelevant climate claims. *National Post*. Retrieved from network.nationalpost.com/np/blogs/fullcomment/archive/2009/11/28/conrad-black-a-teeming-rain-forest-of-irrelevant-climate-claims.aspx [August 8, 2010].

Brulle, R. (2013). Institutionalizing delay: Foundation funding and the creation of the U.S. climate change counter-movement organizations. *Springer Science, Business, Media*. DOI: 10.1007/s10584-013-1018-7

Bunting, L. F. (2007, March 4). Black and Harper ... the old Canada and the new Canada ... or just the same old Canada? Retrieved from www.counterweights.ca/2007/03/new_canada/ [August 9, 2010].

Chomsky, N. (2016, November 14). Trump in the White House. *Information Clearing House*. Retrieved from www.informationclearinghouse.info/article45844.htm [November 28, 2016].

Climate Analytics. (2017, February 16). Paris Agreement Ratification Tracker. *Climate Analytics*. Retrieved from climateanalytics.org/hot-topics/ratification-tracker.html [February 20, 2017].

Dembicki, G. (2010, June 28). "We got that deleted": Canada's oilsands lobby twisting Washington's arm. *The Tyee*. Retrieved from thetyee.ca/News/2010/06/28/OilSandsTwistsWashington/ [August 8, 2010].

De Souza, M. (2008, February 17). Elections Canada to investigate anti-Kyoto group. *The Edmonton Journal*. Retrieved from www.canada.com/edmontonjournal/news/story.html?id=b2307acc-cc2a-42dc-b562-3ed737847a4d&k=81087 [August 10, 2010].

De Souza, M. (2010, July 6). Politicians cancel oilsands pollution probe, tear up draft reports. *CanWest News Service*. Retrieved from www.canada.com/business/Politicians+cancel+oilsands+pollution+probe+tear+draft+reports/3242727/story.html [August 8, 2010].

Dlugokencky, E., & Tans, P. (2016). Trends in atmospheric carbon dioxide. *National Oceanic & Atmospheric Administration 2016 Report* (U.S. Department of Commerce). Retrieved from www.esrl.noaa.gov/gmd/ccgg/trends/global.html [February 20, 2017].

Dunlap, R., McCright, A., & Yarosh, J. (2016). The political divide on climate change: Partisan polarization widens in the U.S. *Environment: Science and Policy for Sustainable Development, 58*(5), 4–23. Retrieved from www.tandfonline.com/doi/full/10.1080/00139157.2016.1208995 [March 5, 2017].

Environics Institute Poll on Climate Change. (2013, November). Focus Canada 2013: Canadian public opinion about climate change. *Environics Institute*. Retrieved from www.environicsinstitute.org [January 7, 2017].

Fischer, D. (2013, December 23). "Dark money" funds climate change denial effort. *Scientific American*. Retrieved from www.scientificamerican.com/article/dark-money-funds-climate-change-denial-effort/ [January 15, 2017].

Gatti, C., & Mouawad, J. (2007, May 8). Chevron seen settling case on Iraq Oil. *The New York Times*. Retrieved from www.nytimes.com/2007/05/08/business/08chevron.html [August 9, 2010].

Gerken, J. (2015, April 2). More Americans trust Fox News than Obama on climate change, poll finds. *Huffington Post*. Retrieved from www.huffingtonpost.com/2015/04/02/americans-fox-news-climate-change_n_6993360.html [April 2, 2015].

Gillis, J. (2014, May 6). U.S. climate has already changed, study finds, citing heat and floods. *The New York Times*. Retrieved from www.nytimes.com/2014/05/07/science/earth/climate-change-report.html [January 18, 2017].

Gillis, J. (2017, January 18). Earth sets a temperature record for the third straight year. *The New York Times*. Retrieved from www.nytimes.com/2017/01/18/science/earth-highest-temperature-record.html [January 19, 2017].

Giovannetti, J. (2016, June 4). Fort McMurray wildfire "most likely human caused," Alberta senior wildfire manager says. *The Globe and Mail*. Retrieved from www.theglobeandmail.com/news/national/fort-mcmurray-wildfire-most-likely-human-caused-alberta-senior-wildfire-manager-says/article30279836/ [June 30, 2016].

Goodman, A. (2015, December 2). As NY State probes Exxon, oil giant targets the journalists who exposed climate change cover-up. *Democracy Now*. Retrieved from www.democracynow.org/2015/12/2/as_ny_state_probes_exxon_oil [November 20, 2016].

Hare, B., Roming, N., Schaeffer, M., & Schleussner, C. (2016, August). Implications of the 1.5 degree limit in the Paris Agreement for climate policy and decarbonisation. *Climate Analytics*. Retrieved from climateinstitute.org.au/verve/_resources/ClimateAnalytics_Report_FINAL_23082016.pdf [September 29, 2016].

Kelly, S. (2016, August 14). New Koch-funded group "Fueling U.S. Forward" aims to promote the "positives" of fossil fuels. *DeSmog*. Retrieved from www.desmogblog.com/2016/08/14/new-koch-back-campaign-rolled-out-red-state-gathering-aims-promote-positives-fossil-fuels [August 16, 2017].

King, E. (2016). Adaptation takes centre stage as IPCC prepares 1.5 degree study. *Climate Home*. Retrieved from www.climatechangenews.com/2016/08/24/adaptation-takes-centre-stage-as-ipcc-prepares-1-5c-study/ [January 29, 2017].

Klein, N. (2007). *The shock doctrine: The rise of disaster capitalism*. Toronto, ON: Alfred A. Knopf Canada.

Klein, N. (2014). *This changes everything: Capitalism versus the climate*. Toronto, ON: Alfred A. Knopf Canada.

Kovach, B., & Rosenstiel, T. (2014). *The elements of journalism*. New York, NY: Penguin Random House.

Krauss, L. (2016, August 21). Trump's anti-science campaign. *The New Yorker*. Retrieved from www.newyorker.com/news/news-desk/trumps-anti-science-campaign [August 29, 2017].

Maron, D. (2017, January 24). Trump Administration restricts news from federal scientists at USDA, EPA. *Scientific American*. Retrieved from www.scientificamerican.com/article/trump-administration-restricts-news-from-federal-scientists-at-usda-epa/ [February 4, 2017].

Mayer, J. (2016). *Dark money: The hidden history of the billionaires behind the rise of the radical right*. New York, NY: Penguin Random House.

McChesney, R. (2014). *Blowing the roof off the twenty-first century: Media, politics and the struggle for post-capitalist democracy*. New York, NY: Monthly Review Press.

McDiarmid, M. (2015, November 12). G20 countries spend $450B a year on fossil fuel subsidies, study says. *CBC News*. Retrieved from www.cbc.ca/news/politics/g20-fossil-fuel-subsidies-450b-1.3314291 [December 21, 2016].

McKibben, B. (2016, August 15). A world at war. *New Republic*. Retrieved from newrepublic.com/article/135684/declare-war-climate-change-mobilize-wwii [December 21, 2016].

Molina, M., McCarthy, J., Wall, D., Alley, R., Cobb, K., Cole, J., ... Shepherd, M. (2014). What we know: The reality, risks, and responses to climate change. *AAAS Climate Science Panel Report*. American Association for the Advancement of Science.

Monbiot, G. (2007). *Heat: How to stop the planet from burning* (Canadian ed.). Toronto, ON: Random House of Canada.

Mooney, C. (2016, September 29). Scientists fear we're about to blow past the red line for climate change. *Toronto Star*. Retrieved from www.thestar.com/news/world/2016/09/29/scientists-fear-were-about-to-blow-past-the-red-line-for-climate-change.html [December 21, 2016].

Mortillaro, N. (2015, May 20). Breaking the silence: Government scientist speaks about culture of fear. *Global News*. Retrieved from globalnews.ca/news/2007611/breaking-the-silence-government-scientist-speaks-about-culture-of-fear/ [May 24, 2015].

NASA. (2016, September 12). NASA analysis finds August 2016 another record month. *Goddard Institute for Space Studies*. Retrieved from data.giss.nasa.gov/gistemp/news/20160912/ [October 28, 2016].

Negin, E. (2013, November 5). Unreliable sources: How the media help the Kochs & ExxonMobil spread climate disinformation. *Huffington Post*. Retrieved from www.huffingtonpost.com/elliott-negin/unreliable-sources-how-th_b_3255192.html [March 3, 2017].

Nikiforuk, A. (2010). *Tar sands: Dirty oil and the future of a continent*. Vancouver, BC: Greystone Books.

NOAA (National Oceanic and Atmospheric Administration, U.S. Department of Commerce). (2016, September 12). Is sea level rising? Retrieved from oceanservice.noaa.gov/facts/sealevel.html [November 3, 2016].

Ogden, L. (2016, May 3). Nine years of censorship. *Nature: International Journal of Science*. Retrieved from www.nature.com/news/nine-years-of-censorship-1.19842 [July 13, 2016].

Orlowski, P. (2011a). Separate oil & state: Using the media for a critical eco-pedagogy in the classroom. *Our Schools/Our Selves, 20*(3), 91–119.

Orlowski, P. (2011b). News TO the world: The Murdoch phone-hacking scandal & media literacy–Reflections from a media literacy educator. *Our Schools/Our Selves, 21*(1), 115–130.

Readfearn, G. (2016, August 31). Americans now more politically polarized on climate change than ever before, analysis finds. *DeSmog*. Retrieved from www.desmogblog.com/2016/08/31/americans-now-more-politically-polarized-climate-change-ever-analysis-finds [November 3, 2016].

Revkin, A. (2005, June 8). Bush aide softened greenhouse gas links to global warming. *The New York Times*. Retrieved from www.nytimes.com/2005/06/08/politics/08climate.html

Revkin, A., & Broder, J. (2009, December 6). Before climate meeting, a revival of skepticism. *The New York Times*. Retrieved from www.nytimes.com/2009/12/07/science/earth/07climate.html [August 10, 2010].

Shaw, C. (2013). Choosing a dangerous limit for climate change: Public representations of the decision making process. *Global Environmental Change, 23*, 563–571.

Stiglitz, J. (2017, July 16). Trump & climate change. *ZNet*. Retrieved from https://zcomm.org/znetarticle/trump-climate-change/? [July 20, 2017].

Taber, J. (2007, June 2). Silence of the lamb. *The Globe and Mail*. Retrieved from www.theglobeandmail.com/focus/silence-of-the-lamb/article102833/ [May 5, 2010].

Teather, D. (2004, February 18). Halliburton suspends bill for army meals. *The Guardian*. Retrieved from www.guardian.co.uk/world/2004/feb/18/iraq.usa [August 1, 2010].

Tushingham, M. (2006). *Hotter than hell*. St. John, NB: Dream Catcher Publishing.

Union of Concerned Scientists. (2013, May 13). U.S. news media help Koch Brothers and ExxonMobil spread climate disinformation, UCS investigation finds. Retrieved from www.ucsusa.org/news/press_release/us-news-media-help-koch-0382.html [November 3, 2016].

U.S. Department of Defense. (2015, July 29). DoD releases report on security implications of climate change. Retrieved from www.defense.gov/News/Article/Article/612710 [October 28, 2016].

Volcovici, V. (2016, July 13). U.S. House panel subpoenas New York, Massachusetts attorney general. *Reuters U.K.* Retrieved from uk.reuters.com/article/exxon-mobil-climatechange-idUKL1N19Z1EI [November 3, 2016].

Wadhams, P. (2016, September 26). As Arctic Ocean ice disappears, the global climate impacts intensify. *Yale Environment 360*. Retrieved from e360.yale.edu/feature/as_arctic_ocean_ice_disappears_global_climate_impacts_intensify_wadhams/3037/ [October 28, 2016].

Watters, H. (2015, August 28). Federal scientist put on leave over Harperman protest song. *CBC News*. Retrieved from www.cbc.ca/news/politics/harperman-tony-turner-scientist-investigation-1.3207390 [October 28, 2016].

7 The Other: The Canadian Mosaic Hits a Roadblock?

It started like any other news story we'd heard many times before: A lone gunman mows down six people at worship on a Sunday evening. But this time it wasn't in the United States. This time it was in Quebec City, it was 2017, and those who died were Muslim Canadians at evening prayers.

A "lone gunman"—that's what they say in the United States when someone fatally shoots other people—a lone gunman shot them and then waited for police to arrest him. The shock swept across the country. In the days that followed, vigils were kept and slowly the details emerged along with the dirty linen and secrets that always follow such tragedies. Here, however, the media latched on to one part of the puzzle of such madness: the many talk radio programs in Quebec City that fostered anger against new Canadians who had emigrated from countries with high populations of Muslims and who brought their faith with them to their new country.

Only after the murders did it come out that three years earlier in 2014, a professor at Laval University had already published a report on talk radio in the city that concluded that such radio in Quebec City had "a toxic culture driven by competition for ratings, advertising and the desire to cause a stir on social media" (Woods, 2017). It was such a bad radio environment that the CRTC did not renew the licence for one of the radio stations. Also, the radio hosts had been "encouraged to take provocative positions on issues of the day," picking issues ranging from "feminist groups to government bureaucrats to labour unions to practicing Muslims" (Woods, 2017).

No single trajectory led to these murders. Instead, there is a combination and a confusion of laws, policies, history, values, and racism.

This chapter discusses the delicate but necessary history of immigration and the changing values and mores in the current environment that has seen suspicion, fear, and terror within Canada since the 9/11 attacks in 2001. It also addresses and assesses the uncertainty and upheaval of challenges that come from continuing acts of violence such as the Quebec mosque murders in Canada and in many countries around the world. The chapter does so by applying the concept of "the Other" (Said, 1979), which provides a useful analytical tool to understand how we have reacted as a nation to these unprecedented, difficult, and changing times. The chapter also probes how contemporary citizens—such as LGBTQ+ individuals (those who identify as lesbian, gay, bisexual, transgender, queer, and other minority genders), Indigenous peoples, and other marginalized groups—continue to be challenged by a frame of "Otherness," and how they are lobbying and engaging in activism that will make for a truly open and inclusive Canadian society.

BUILDING CANADA

For many years, Canada has signified a new life and opportunity for many hundreds of thousands of immigrants. Early settlement in the 18th century came from England and France, and later on from the United States, although racialized Americans were not allowed at that point; later, the Underground Railroad brought them to settle in Nova Scotia. In the 19th century, immigrants from Scotland and Ireland followed. By the mid-20th century, Canada was opened to most Europeans, many of them populating the prairies and farther west. After World War II, southern Europeans arrived. In 1967, changes to the Immigration Act made it even easier for immigrants to come to Canada, and emigrants from South Asia, China, Hong Kong, Africa, and the Caribbean also began to settle here.

Unlike the United States, which had a "melting pot" approach to immigration where new Americans would adapt and assimilate to the new country, Canada was generally open to immigration in which newcomers would bring their different cultures with them, but would still "become" Canadians. Over time, it was thought, immigrants would themselves naturally begin to act, dress, play, and eat like homegrown Canadians. Basically, 20th-century immigration accepted the unspoken rule of "becoming Canadian."

However, immigration to Canada in the 21st century has been very different and often contentious. This is partly because of an often unsteady economy that makes Canadians cautious about bringing in immigrants and refugees while jobs are scarce. The Canadian Encyclopedia (n.d.[a]) notes a further issue that made immigration more careful and concerning. The events of September 11, 2001, have made countries cautious and their immigration policies restrictive. Since that time, Canada has still brought in more than one million immigrants from Asia and the Middle East (57 percent of all immigrants), non-European immigrants (African at 12.5 percent; and Caribbean, and Central and South American, altogether at a further 12.3 percent) (Canadian Encyclopedia, n.d.[a]). While it is clear that immigration has been an important aspect of the Canadian fabric, culture, and economy for many decades, now it is also clear that immigration has changed, while Canada itself has changed as well.

Previous immigrants in the 19th and early 20th centuries from Europe and the United States were agreeable to "becoming Canadian" (or perhaps found it necessary to do so) in any way they could to fit in and as fast as possible. More recent immigration, which spans the world, has arrived in a Canada that, just like many other Western countries, is not as open as it was previously. Some Canadians, even though they themselves are descendants of earlier immigrants, might nonetheless find it difficult to welcome new immigrants, perhaps thinking that those new arrivals might take their jobs. In this troubling environment, the atmosphere at times can become rife with frustration and anger—and fear.

We tend to point with pride to our bilingualism and our multiculturalism as the key attributes of being Canadian. In the 1960s, the Royal Commission on Bilingualism and Biculturalism examined the concept of an "equal partnership" between English- and French-speaking citizens that would include protecting the French language and culture (Canadian Encyclopedia, n.d.[b]). A further part of the mandate of the commission was to report on the state of ethnic groups, specifically on how to preserve their cultural contribution to Canada. The commission found that French-speaking Canadians were "not well represented" in the economy or in government and were not getting an adequate education in their language outside of Quebec. Unlike the criticism that follows most Royal Commissions for not amounting to anything, this commission "lay the groundwork for functional bilingualism throughout the country and for increased acceptance of cultural diversity" (Canadian Encyclopedia, n.d.[b]). This is when we began to speak of Canada as being both bilingual and multicultural, particularly after Canada specifically adopted a policy of multiculturalism in 1971.

Yet, although we can acknowledge that Canada was built on and has valued both our common Canadianness and our separate identities, no matter if we were born in this country or came to it later on, this took place in a better economy and in a different time. There are cracks in what we have called our ethnic "mosaic," a mosaic that we have treasured, and those cracks have widened since the events of 9/11. The events of that day signified a disturbing change in Western societies. Moreover, it seemed that the media in Canada were no better equipped than other citizens to handle such terror. Without complete information because of the need for censorship, the media had to rely on whatever politicians and security officers told them.

Into this environment of anger and fear came resentment and, unfortunately, racism. It is fair to say that our pride in a multicultural, multi-ethnic society hit a roadblock that is still with us through the continuing upheaval in a world that formulates acts of terror. Moreover, with the 2017 murders of Muslims in their mosque in Quebec City, Canada itself became another victim, as we struggle to understand what happened and to know what path to take to move ahead together as a nation.

9/11 CHANGES EVERYTHING?

The unthinkable tragedy of 9/11—in which the two World Trade Center towers in New York City were deliberately struck by two airplanes, resulting in the towers crumbling to the ground, and in which two other airplanes also crashed, altogether killing 3,000 people and wounding 6,000 others—can be seen as an event that both horrified Canadians and changed their understanding of the world around them. It also focused us on issues that were confusing as well as upsetting about how we see ourselves and those around us: Why would anyone do such a thing? When and where would the next attack come? While a normal response to such a huge tragedy, these seeds from the events of 9/11 have grown and become a part of our society over time. Canada and many other Western countries have been slow to recognize how their societies have changed. Where once immigrants to Canada were eager—and expected—to "become Canadian," now that had a specific meaning (or perhaps a warning?) as immigration shifted away from European and Commonwealth countries and included Asian and Middle Eastern countries. The time of the "melting pot" immigration (a term mostly used in US immigration) that saw new Canadians shedding old customs, cuisine, language, and clothing, had passed. The terror of 9/11 fostered suspicion at every turn, and now-cautious citizens, who over and over again had seen media images of bombers elsewhere, worried about new arrivals to our country. Much of the fear focused on an easy and visible target: new female immigrants who continued to wear hijabs (head scarves) and, rarely, other clothing normal in their birth countries that covered completely their arms and legs, although that also is extremely rare. Sadly, in the heightened environment of security and terror, this became a lightning rod for some Canadians to think there was something suspicious and unlawful under this clothing that, for instance, could lead to a suicide bombing here.

As improbable as it is that such an enormous terrorist tragedy would take place again, given the stepped-up vigilance and security, Canadians were genuinely concerned and needed to be reassured. It didn't help that the authorities themselves were finding it difficult to pinpoint who or what a potential adversary looked and acted like. For example, early on after the events of 9/11, many Western countries swiftly passed broad legislation to give police and security sweeping powers. Canada was no exception. Our Anti-terrorism Act (2001, 2003) included changes to the Official Secrets Act that did not go through the usual procedures of full parliamentary and public debate. It also did not establish a joint oversight committee to review the act and audit security intelligence matters. The new act also had a controversial provision to exclude security-related data from the public record for indefinite periods, without a review or way to revoke them, or way for the public to access that information (Rubin & Kozolanka, 2014, p. 203). This was a departure from the way other security issues had been handled; here, there was no disclosure of information and no way for citizens to review their files. The new act was seen as a way to widen considerably what records could be classified as security-related (p. 204). In short, and unlike other previous legislation, the new law was not accountable to the public, and it was challenged by many lawyers and by civil liberty associations (Daniels, Macklem, & Roach, 2001).

Very soon after the swift enacting of the Anti-terrorism Act, the case of Maher Arar demonstrated the new realities and problems with security and Canadians who had emigrated from other countries, some from those at war or with non-democratic governments. In September 2002, Arar, a Syrian-born Canadian citizen, was returning from a vacation in Tunisia when he was detained by American officials during a stopover in New York. Acting on unknown information from the RCMP, Arar, who had a Canadian passport, was deported not back to Canada, where he lived, but instead to Syria. The secrecy of the Anti-terrorism Act made it almost impossible for Arar to defend himself, while the RCMP had access to all his records. In 2004, when Ken Rubin, who has a distinguished and knowledgeable reputation in access-to-information cases over many years, requested the Arar files from the federal Foreign Affairs and International Trade department, one-quarter of the 240 pages on Arar were blanked out completely (although, oddly, some of the information was later found to be in open-source material). Later, in 2006, an inquiry concluded there was no evidence to link Arar to terrorist activity (Rubin & Kozolanka, 2014, p. 205). In 2007, Arar received an apology from the Canadian government and the RCMP and $1.5 million in compensation. Arar's case demonstrated how information (even information that was already public) could be concealed and used as a reason to hastily enact legislation that was a knee-jerk response to a tragedy such as 9/11. It also demonstrates the precarious situation of Canadian citizens who were not born in Canada, but who emigrate from countries that are now seen to be troubled or divided internally and that are considered to engage in terrorist acts. Arar was not the only Canadian to have been targeted by the RCMP and then released after many months in jail. Four other Canadians born in Syria and Egypt were detained. Perigoe and Eid (2014) have concluded that these detentions "demonstrate a long-standing double standard in Canada in which minority groups are treated, at best, with suspicion and hostility and, at worst, with systemic racism" (p. 7).

NEW CENTURY, OLD HABITS

Canada is seen by many as a democratic country that welcomes immigration and refugees, but there is also an underside for those who reach our shores and cross our borders. This has been exacerbated by the events of 9/11, with security remaining high in countries around the world.

On the 10th anniversary of the attacks of September 11, 2001, Eid and Karim (2011) evaluated "what we have learned—and not learned—about communication and conflict" within the "new pattern of global conflict" left by that day (p. 1). It is a sobering analysis for those who cherish the much-promoted idea of Canada as a cohesive mosaic of many races, ethnicities, genders, and religions. Their review of the literature on global conflict hits many valuable but worrisome tones about the challenges faced before and after 9/11. Eid and Karim remind us that Said saw the East (he called it by its traditional name, "The Orient") as the opposite of Western societies, noting the West's "sense of superiority" over The Orient (p. 3), a concept that remained salient throughout the following East-West wars and conflicts (pp. 3–4). Eid and Karim (2011) note that conservative American Samuel P. Huntington, along with other Western authors, framed these conflicts as a "clash of civilizations," a phrase that seemed to stick with other analysts who followed, and who perpetuated the sense of "them" versus "us" (p. 4). Over the following decade, the events of 9/11 also firmly associated Islam with terrorism, "so much so that the terms 'Muslim' and 'terrorist' have become almost synonymous" (p. 4). Finally, Eid and Karim note that since 9/11, "the themes of violence and militancy are commonly associated with Muslims," and there is a further tendency to "label Muslims as terrorists," with the latter label having "grown steadily over the last three decades" (p. 5).

Unfortunately, Eid and Karim's research also found what they called "lessons (not) learned" that underline the further impacts of 9/11. Specifically, these lessons not learned include a fear of Muslims and a "negative influence on public perceptions of immigration" (p. 5). Muslim Canadian citizens also have themselves been targeted through what is now known as **Islamophobia** (p. 5).

In addition, and over time, many studies and much public opinion research on race and immigration have opened our eyes to the problems facing Canada. While we can say that our media environment is "relatively progressive," research shows us that can be true only in comparison with those of other countries (Hier, in Fleras, 2011, p. 56). Our sense of being a multicultural nation tends to obscure the many "barriers and contradictions" that Augie Fleras says still exist (p. 56). Since 2001, Fleras has conducted research on representations of diversity. His research indicates that the media tend to see minorities, and to process them in stories about diversity, "along racialized lines," and thus frame them in their stories as "troublesome constituents, who are problems, who have problems, and who create problems" (p. 56). In effect, Fleras finds that minorities are reduced to being only either good or bad, and we mostly hear about the bad. This brings into focus the research of Eid and Karim (2011), which notes the fear of immigration, something that can only be seen as a **systemic bias** (p. 57). Systemic bias occurs when conclusions are made about people based solely on the group they belong to, which can be their gender, race, country of origin, or many other ways of making sweeping comments that confer attributes on a group. It is usually used to keep groups of people as outliers who can then be isolated or dismissed from society as inferior or unwelcome.

Are we aware of systemic bias? For the most part, no. But that doesn't mean it doesn't exist, and in fact, that's the point: it is something that is often so engrained in society that it is not even visible or debated. Systemic bias is usually only recognized at the rare times when it becomes so blatant that it is named and brought to our attention. Such bias challenges us to crack open our long-held understandings of who we are and who we can be, and take a long and hard examination of our society. Often systemic bias is so entrenched that it is difficult to dislodge and can take many attempts to change. Some groups, such as Jews and the Roma (formerly known as gypsies), can trace such unwarranted bias back hundreds of years.

An example of systemic racism from Canada's past is the fate of Sikh immigrants on the *Komagata Maru* freighter ship in 1914. After arriving in Vancouver's harbour, the ship's passengers waited for two months until being told that only 22 of them were allowed to disembark, while the other 354 had to return to Hong Kong and Japan. Through no fault of their own, the boatload of would-be Canadians were expelled because of past events that took place in Canada. A year earlier in 1913, during a mine workers' strike involving Chinese- and Japanese-born labourers, White Canadian-born citizens had been afraid that the workers would "take over the country." By the time the *Komagata Maru* innocently sailed into the Vancouver harbour, restrictions had been placed on Asian immigration that were impossible to overcome. Local Sikhs rallied in sympathy and endorsed a message of concern to Prime Minister Borden and then quietly dispersed. Yet the next day's newspaper headline "caused waves of panic to sweep through the white community" with its headline that "Hindus hold Mass Meeting and Preach Sedition and Treason" (Kozolanka, 1980, p. 27). The local member of Parliament clinched the fate of the *Komagata Maru* when he said that if Canada allowed such immigrants, "there would be left practically not a vestige of the civilization of which we are so proud" (p. 27). Only in 1967 was the quota for Indians such as Sikhs abolished in favour of a points system and only in 2017 did the Canadian Parliament apologize for the incident.

Another example is the internment of Canadians who had immigrated to Canada for a new and better life, and then were interned as "enemy aliens" in camps for the duration of World War I or World War II. Because civil liberties were restricted in wartime, authorities had the right "to arrest, to detain, to censor, to exclude, to deport, to control or to capture all persons and property considered as a potential threat to Canada" (Canada, 2012). In World War I and after the war, 24 camps held 8,579 men, women, and children, most of them Ukrainian, who were relocated mostly in remote northern areas (Barnes, 2014). Only 3,138 of the internees were legitimate prisoners of war, and all were forced into labour, although that was against the various wartime agreements. Many also died from tuberculosis and pneumonia. Some were still locked up two years after the war ended. Another part of this sad history was that Canada had enticed Ukrainians to immigrate to the Canadian prairies beginning in the late 1890s, as Ukraine has a similar climate (Barnes, 2014). When the war started a generation later, many of these same immigrants (and sometimes their families) were imprisoned.

Ethnic groups were also detained in World War II; that time, it was German and Japanese Canadians (Canada, 2012). Only one day after the beginning of the war, the government started the procedures to construct internment camps for so-called "enemy" prisoners. After 1941 and the Japanese attack on Pearl Harbor in Hawaii, the passing of the War Measures Act allowed for the interning of Canadians of Japanese descent and seizing of their assets. The detentions in camps included many other groups as well: Italians (after Italy joined the war in 1940), Jews, and Mennonites (Canada, 2012).

Systemic racial bias also tends to have its own hierarchy. The Pew Center in the United States confirmed this in its 2010 media study. The study involved 67,000 national news stories in the US for a full year. The three groups with ethnic or cultural origins (often called "visible minority" groups) in the survey were very poorly represented in the media stories: 1.9 percent for African Americans, 1.3 percent for Latinos, and 0.2 percent for Asians. Although all three groups were represented very poorly, the difference between African Americans with the highest representation and Asians with the lowest suggests a hierarchy even within these minorities. The coverage percentages were also nowhere near as high as the percentages of the country's population that these groups represent (Fleras, 2011, p. 59).

Given that, as of 2011, one in five (20.6 percent) Canadians is a member of a racialized group, we should be able to see much more diversity on our screens (Canada, 2011), yet these groups are grossly under-represented as journalists and in newsrooms across the country. It also needs to be said that disabled and Indigenous peoples are also still under-represented in Canadian media (Pedwell, 2017). Without diversity within journalism and newsrooms, news stories cannot claim to have achieved "all the news that's fit to print," the motto of the *New York Times*. However, in 2017, after the retirement of CBC's main news anchor, Peter Mansbridge, the CBC took a leap forward when it chose to replace him with four revolving journalists: two women, and two men who are members of racialized groups.

In addition, we can point to very few television programs that feature Canadian actors who are members of racialized groups in starring roles. Some of the exceptions include CBC's *North of 60* (1992–1998), *Little Mosque on the Prairie* (2007–2012), *Arctic Air* (2012–2014), and *Kim's Convenience* and *Second Jen*, both of which debuted in 2016. Even then, as Hirji (2011) points out, "it is clear that television after 9/11 has not evolved in its depiction of the Muslim woman," who are still "underrepresented and stereotyped when they do appear" (p. 44).

Interestingly, a national survey conducted by Environics for the Canadian Race Relations Foundation in 2015 showed that Canadian Muslims, for their part, "are embracing Canada's diversity, democracy and freedoms, and feeling more positive about the country than ever before" (CRRF, 2015). This goodwill provides an opportunity to reach out to Canadian Muslims, as well as the "other Others" in our society.

Although 9/11 wasn't the beginning of racism or other such problems in Canada, as the examples here demonstrate, it gave us an "enemy" to blame and to focus on that more or less gave us permission to band together against immigration. Unfortunately, the fear that was engendered at that time has made it more difficult to dislodge racism, as smaller acts of terror continue throughout the Western world. There are choices to be made by countries—Western countries in particular, but also around the world, as no one country is exempt—to protect their citizens at home and abroad. How far should they go to reduce or annihilate terror—or is that starting at the wrong end of the problem? And what is the impact on democracy? Will the way we in Canada treat new citizens make a difference? How can the media contribute to diversity and a truly inclusive Canadian mosaic? Right now, the ideal of a multicultural country, for all its genuine full-heartedness, may be slipping away.

OTHER OTHERING

In the post-9/11 world, the "Othering" of Canadians that were born elsewhere and emigrated here continues. It is not likely to soften if governments take a hard line against their citizens who were born in countries that are deemed, as in Maher Arar's situation, to be suspicious with little or no cause.

There are other ways of Othering—"other Othering"?—that, unfortunately, also live and breathe in democratic societies. Although it is true that being born in the Near East is the very epitome of the Othering set out by Said in 1979, over time, his concept has been applied to various subaltern groups in modern society. The best-known groups include genders, races, and religions. Over time, many different people have become aware that they belong in a different kind of society than the simple male-female dichotomy, with women as subordinate. The acknowledged first break from this dichotomy was the separation of women from men, that is, it was based on gender.

In 1949, French author and essayist Simone de Beauvoir published *The Second Sex*. It was a groundbreaking analysis on what became feminist theory. De Beauvoir pinpointed the relationship between men and women as being one of opposites, with men seen as the true, first human being, and women as "the

Other," or what is different from men. Until then, being different as a woman had also been seen as being inferior to men. De Beauvoir looked at this from a very different perspective: women were not born to be inferior, in the same way that men were not born to dominate or be superior to women. Rejecting the narrow sense of the dominant-inferior dichotomy, instead, de Beauvoir believed that both men and women are defined by **socialization**. In other words, all human beings, male or female, become who they are when they are socialized, and that of course only takes place after they are born (Routledge, 2016). In Canada, sociologist Dorothy Smith critiqued the overarching male perspective that focused on the exclusion of women from sociology. Instead, her work started with and focused on the standpoint of women, an **ethnological** approach that foregrounded everyday life experiences and led to what she saw as a "sociology for people" (Routledge, 2016). It was the beginning of a different point of view on gender.

By the 1960s and '70s, most Western countries were coming to grips with women and women's organizations lobbying for equal rights with men. There were many achievements that were built on over the following decades. In 1970, the Royal Commission on the Status of Women recommended that the government take steps to ensure equal opportunities with men. The National Action Committee on the Status of Women (NAC) was formed in 1972 to lobby the government to honour the recommendations of the Royal Commission's report and was very vocal in the 1970s and '80s. In 1977, the newly enacted Canadian Human Rights Act gave basic rights to all Canadians, and in 1982, Canada repatriated its constitution from England and enacted a new Charter of Rights and Freedoms. Even with that, Canadian women had to wait until 1985 to be guaranteed equality of rights under the law.

Canadian women have lobbied and continue to lobby for equal rights with men. For instance, even with the strength of legislation and lobbying over many decades, in Canada, women are still not paid the same as men. In 2014, based on the 34 countries in the Organization for Economic Cooperation and Development, Canada had the seventh-highest wage gap between women and men (Canadian Women's Foundation [CWF], 2014). That may sound good, but the breakdown of wages for women of different groups shows a different story. Much higher rates of poverty for women in Canada include: Indigenous women living away from their community, at 37 percent; women with disabilities, at 33 percent; visible minority women, at 28 percent; Métis and Inuit women, at 23 percent; and single mothers, at 21 percent (CWF, 2014). One reason could be that there is a wide wage gap between women and men in Canada—and it is getting wider. In 2009, women made 74.4 percent of what men made, while in 2011 they made only 72 percent (Evans, 2016). Altogether, it is a serious, ongoing, and unequal environment in which women, who usually bear the brunt of keeping a family together, cannot afford child care, nutritious food, clothing, and decent housing.

> ### BOX 7.1: "YOU'VE COME A LONG WAY, BABY"?
>
> In 1968, an America company that made cigarettes launched a new product for women in a time when North American women were beginning to assert their equality with men. The slogan for the advertisement for the new cigarette was "You've come a long way, baby." While it was true that gender inequality was changing, the ad campaign was seen as inappropriate (if not insulting with the use of the word *baby*) by many women who saw how slowly society was moving toward that goal of equality. Here are some various situations that show that, even decades later, there is still much room for improvement:
>
> - According to the video *Joystick Warriors*, "atrocious levels of misogyny and online harassment ... pervade video game culture" (Media Education Foundation, 2014). The video points out how game culture normalizes "violent masculinity."
> - The princesses in Disney films are getting more sexy over time, from lip-plumpers to bikini poses to low-cut tops, "teeny" waists, and "wavy locks," with girls as young as six "beginning to think of themselves in sexual terms" (Cooper, 2014). (At the same time, some Disney heroines are more independent—a strange juxtaposition.)
> - As an experiment, a 24-year-old woman wearing jeans and a black T-shirt walked the sidewalks of New York City with a hidden camera and was harassed by 108 men in 10 hours (Sullivan, 2014).
>
> Over time, we have also learned not to make rash conclusions that see all women and their views on equality in the same way. For example, modern discourses on wearing hijabs focus on the oppression of women—but that's not how the women wearing hijabs see it. Many of these women "find empowerment in rejecting the idea that women can be reduced to their sexual allure" (Yusuf, 2015).

During the many years of lobbying for equal rights with men, other "feminisms" in Canada were also growing. Indigenous women shared some of the same issues as their non-Indigenous counterparts across the country; however, their key issues revolved around colonialism and cultural discrimination that most other women in Canada did not share. Another key divide was the issue of the "strongly anti-natal and anti-family stance" of mainstream feminists, who were distancing themselves from having large families at a time when Indigenous peoples were "rebuilding their own nations" in ways that included a baby boom (Dhruvarajan & Vickers, 2002). (For more on Indigenous women in Canada, see the next chapter.)

As with Indigenous peoples, racialized women and men in Canada also have a different and more difficult history than other Canadians. Unfortunately, Canada's approach to diversity of all kinds had no better understanding than its neighbour, the United States. For example, we often forget that we also engaged in slavery. In 18th-century Lower Canada (Quebec), it showed one's prestige or status to own slaves. It is estimated that one-third of slaves were racialized, while the other two-thirds were Indigenous people (Everett-Green, 2014). The last slave sale took place in 1797, and slavery was abolished here in 1833.

Moreover, although we tend to think of ourselves as having a more open society, the US has a strong and longer history of civil liberties and human rights. For example, the American Civil Liberties Union (ACLU) has been defending rights and liberties for almost 100 years, with a strong federal constitution behind it. In Canada, the Canadian Civil Liberties Association was founded in 1964, and the Canadian Federation of Civil Liberties and Human Rights Associations (1972–1991), a more grassroots-based organization, had many small member organizations across the country that focused on both local and national issues.

Despite these issues, our history and recent events indicate that we, too, have a long way to go. In addition, racialized women face the double hurdle of race and gender. Since 2013, the Black Lives Matter (BLM) movement in both Canada and the United States has shown how racialized persons and their supporters can coalesce into a strong social movement that is also led by racialized women (#BlackLivesMatter). In 2016, it was BLM, which was invited to march in the annual Gay Pride Parade in Toronto, that called for the Toronto Police Force (which had been taking part in the parade for many years) not to take part in future parades, because of the police force's detaining of racialized people in proportions far higher than that of the racialized population. In 2017, Pride Toronto voted to remove the police floats in future parades. The response from the police demonstrates the cleavages emanating from the issue, with its spokesperson suggesting "some people are choosing division over inclusion" (CBC News, 2017). BLM has also called for a commitment to increase diversity in Pride Toronto.

The case of BLM at the Pride Toronto parade is also an example of **identity politics**, which is politics based on social movements of marginalized citizens seeking meaningful inclusion in society. To some, it is a controversial way of handling issues, as it involves groups identifying themselves solely by their gender or race or (dis)ability, etc., and lobbying as a group to take part in mainstream society and politics. Political parties often pay disproportionately more attention to the multiplicity of minority groups who can, as a group, vote for them. Identity politics can be very successful when groups lobby or when politicians reach out to them for votes; however, it also can be very divisive within those groups (many of whom may feel differently politically).

Women, minorities, and many other "Others" noted here have gained increasing acceptance in Canadian society, and, over time, other groups of citizens are "coming out of the closet" (an old term that was used to indicate the moment of revealing one's true sexuality). For example, where once we spoke of gays and lesbians, today we have a better awareness of the many ways that people have come to understand who they are, and instead we acknowledge LGBTQ+ as an abbreviation for many other ways to be: Lesbian, Gay, Bisexual, Trans[gender], Queer, and Questioning—along with the inclusive understanding that more options might also exist.

LET'S NOT CELEBRATE JUST YET

In early 2017, the Canadian government released a brand new $10-dollar bill with great pride. For the first time, a racialized woman, Viola Desmond, graced a currency bill, for her refusal to sit in a segregated theatre back in 1946 in New Glasgow, Nova Scotia. This is one of the many ways that countries like Canada are coming to grips with a past that subjugated their citizens based on race and gender, and, of course, we look forward to many more such additions to remind us of our full heritage. However, governments will be seen as only appeasing their citizens through token gestures such as the Desmond bill if they do not also focus on the roots of discrimination and exclusion of all kinds. As Mark Twain and many others who fight for equality have said, "Denial ain't just a river in Egypt."

This chapter has probed into the different ways that Canadians have changed over time. Our mainstream history often focuses on the highlights of immigration as an open door and the building of a broad and cohesive Canadian mosaic. However, over time, immigrants and even their Canadian-born descendants have seen the "other" side that can also arise and that needs to be addressed: intolerance and racism. And yet, we live in a country where one in five Canadians is a member of a visible minority (Elghawaby, 2014). This chapter has pointed out the differences between early immigration and contemporary immigration. It has also touched on the complicated and ongoing sense of varied gender orientations, which include approximately 4 to 7 declared percent of the population that identify as LGBTQ+ (Allen, 2017).

Today's global environment, with all its modern ways, is also rife with issues we never had to consider previously. This has an impact on how we see ourselves, how we see those around us, and how we see those who come to join us in Canada. It also should have a strong impact on our media. Will it be a Canada of inclusion and tolerance, or will we let fear divide us and build a roadblock in our minds?

QUESTIONS FOR DISCUSSION

1. What can we do to ensure that all Canadians feel safe and included in society?
2. Do Canada's bilingualism and multiculturalism need to be updated for the 21st century? If so, why, and how can this be achieved?
3. What other ways can Said's (1979) concept of Othering be applied?
4. How might a broader or different education on our history contribute to a better and more holistic society? What would it need?
5. How could the media develop a stronger understanding of issues related to Othering?
6. What are the pros and cons about identity politics?

ASSIGNMENTS

1. Given racial divides and changes in immigration over time, research how new Canadians are making a positive difference to our society.
2. Fleras (2011, pp. 57–67) identifies four generalized representational frames found in all media stories that racialize minorities: *invisibility, stereotyping, problem people,* and *whitewashing* (see Fleras for details). Dividing into four groups, with each group researching the details of one of Fleras' four frames, and using your local media (online or offline), identify these frames as they relate to the Other.

- Which of the four frames are the most prevalent (by numbers of stories, by the length of the stories)?
- How are Others, as noted in the chapter, mentioned in the story? Is what you read fair comment? Compare what you have read in the media you have selected to a tabloid newspaper. If you see differences, use your research and what you have learned to suggest how these minorities *could* have been portrayed instead of how they were actually portrayed.
- Watch for binaries, that is, portraying one group in a particular way and then portraying a different group as its opposite. For example: us or them; weak or strong; superior or inferior; modern or backward; different or normal; and so on.
- If photos are part of the news story, when the photos show different races or genders, can the photos seem to be revealing those differences deliberately to make a point?
- What information does the story put first and what is buried later in the story? Does that make a difference as to how different people in the story are seen?
- Check out the rest of the news in the media chosen: does one story only use sources who are White, and if so, what would that mean?

3. Either in a group or singularly, choose a contemporary Canadian organization to profile that focuses on race, religion, or gender. Research the organization's purpose, history, and any other information that is useful for a complete profile.

    Together, discuss each other's organizations with a focus on comparing how they reach out to Canadian society (for making connections, informing about their organization, lobbying or funding, and so on) and how our society reaches out to them. What issues does your organization face in society? What communication and tactics does it use to publicize its work? How do your group's organization and its members get portrayed in the media, and is it different from or the same as other social groups in Canada? For example, do they have a clear purpose for what they are doing? How and when do they communicate with their own members and also to the general public? Share and compare your organization's profile with the other groups in your class.

4. Debate the following: "Be it resolved that anyone can march in the annual Pride Parade." Research the different views that were taken on the standoff in the 2016 Pride Parade in Toronto and review the parades after 2016. Be sure to research other such parades elsewhere and how they would or did handle the issue.

WORKS CITED

Allen, S. (2017). Just how many LGBT Americans are there? *The Daily Beast*. Retrieved from www.thedailybeast.com/articles/2017/01/14/just-how-many-lgbt-americans-are-there.html [April 22, 2017].

Barnes, D. (2014). Some internees were locked up until 1920, nearly two years after the First World War ended. *Edmonton Journal*. Retrieved from ww1.canada.com/homefront/dark-memories-endure-of-canadas-internment-of-enemy-aliens [February 23, 2017].

Canada. Canadian Heritage. (2016). Rights of women. Retrieved from www.canada.pch.gc.ca/eng/1448633334004 [February 24, 2017].

Canada. Collections Canada. (2012). Internment camps in Canada during the First and Second World Wars. Retrieved from www.collectionscanada.gc.ca/lepublic/005-1142.27-e.html [February 23, 2017].

Canada. Statistics Canada. (2011). 2011 Census—Immigration and ethnocultural diversity in Canada. Retrieved from www12.statcan.gc.ca/nhs-enm/2011/as-sa/99-010-x/99-010-x2011001-eng.cfm [June 5, 2018].

Canadian Encyclopedia. (n.d.[a]). Immigration. Retrieved from www.thecanadianencyclopedia.ca/en/article/immigration/ [February 14, 2017].

Canadian Encyclopedia. (n.d.[b]). Royal Commission on Bilingualism and Biculturalism. Retrieved from www.thecanadianencyclopedia.ca/en/article/royal-commission-on-bilingualism-and-biculturalism/ [February 21, 2017].

Canadian Women's Foundation (CWF). (2014). The facts about women and poverty. Retrieved from www.canadianwomen.org [February 14, 2017].

CBC News. (2017, January 18). Pride Toronto AGM vote reaffirms Black Lives Matter request for no police floats at parade. Retrieved from www.cbc.ca/news/canada/toronto/black-lives-matter-pride-1.3940642 [April 22, 2017].

Cooper, G. (2014, September 6). Curse of the sexy Disney princesses. *The Ottawa Citizen*, p. F6.

CRRF. (2015.) Canadian Race Relations Fund. Retrieved from www.canadahelps.org/en/charities/canadian-race-relations-foundation/

Daniels, R., Macklem, P., & Roach, K. (2001). *The security of freedom: Essays on Canada's anti-terrorism bill*. Toronto, ON: University of Toronto Press.

De Beauvoir, S. (2011). *The second sex*. New York: Vintage.

Dhruvarajan, V., & Vickers, J. (2002). *Race, gender, and nation: A global perspective*. Toronto: University of Toronto Press.

Eid, M., & Karim, K. H. (2011). Ten years after 9/11—What we have learned. Editorial. *Global Media Journal—Canadian Edition, 4*(2), 1–12.

Elghawaby, A. (2014, March 3). Why are visible minorities invisible in Canadian media? *Rabble.ca*. Retrieved from http://rabble.ca/news/2014/03/why-are-visible-minorities-invisible-canadian-media [April 17, 2017].

Environics Institute. (2015). Canadian public opinion about immigrants and multiculturalism. *Focus Canada*, Spring, 1–10. Retrieved from www.environicsinstitute.org/uploads/instituteprojects/environics%20institute%20%20focus%20canada%20spring%202015%20survey%20on%20immigration-multiculturalism%20-%20final%20report%20-%20june%2030-2015.pdf [February 22, 2017].

Evans, P. (2016, March 7). Women's wage gap getting wider in Canada, new report indicates. *CBC News*. Retrieved from www.cbc.ca/news/business/wage-gap-oxfam-1.3478938 [April 8, 2017].

Everett-Green, R. (2014, March 3). 200 years a slave: The dark history of captivity in Canada. *The Globe and Mail*. Retrieved from www.theglobeandmail.com/opinion/200-years-a-slave-the-dark-history-of-captivity-in-canada/article17178374/ [April 8, 2017].

Fleras, A. (2011). *The media gaze: Representations of diversities in Canada*. Vancouver, BC: UBC Press.

Hirji, F. (2011). Through the looking glass: Muslim women in television—an analysis of *24*, *Lost*, and *Little House on the Prairie*. *Global Media Journal, Canadian Edition*, 4(2). Retrieved from www.gmj.uottawa.ca/1102/v4i2_hirji_e.html [April 17, 2017].

Jedwab, J. (2016, October 12). How Angus Reid, CBC got it wrong about multiculturalism. Commentary. *Toronto Star*. Retrieved from www.thestar.com/opinion/commentary/2016/10/12/how-angus-reid-cbc-got-it-wrong-about-multiculturalism.html [February 23, 2017].

Kozolanka, K. (1980). The Canadians that never were: Sikh immigrants rejected on doorstep. *Droits et Libertés/Rights and Freedoms*, *34*, 26–27.

Kozolanka, K. (2007). Reading between the lines and crossing borders: Critical media literacy, good citizenship and democratic media. Editorial. *Our Schools/Our Selves*, *17*(1), 17–25.

Media Education Foundation. (2014). *No Girls Allowed*. Video. Retrieved from www.mediaed.org/its-all-fun-games-until-the-haters-are-exposed/ [April 5, 2017].

Pedwell, T. (2017, September 23). Look in the mirror and what do you see? Not enough diversity, says report. *The Globe and Mail*. Retrieved from www.theglobeandmail.com/feeds/canadian-press/entertainment/look-in-the-mirror-and-what-do-you-see-not-enough-diversity-says-report/article35702189/ [September 23, 2017].

Perigoe, R., & Eid, M. (2014). *Mission invisible: Race, religion and news at the dawn of the 9/11 era*. Vancouver, BC: UBC Press.

Routledge. (2016). Woman as Other. *Social Theory Re-wired: New connections to classical and contemporary perspectives*. Retrieved from www.routledgesoc.com/category/profile-tags/woman-other [February 25, 2017].

Rubin, K., & Kozolanka, K. (2014). Managing information: Too much publicity, not enough public exposure. In K. Kozolanka (Ed.), *Publicity and the Canadian state: Critical communications perspectives* (pp. 195–214). Toronto, ON: University of Toronto Press.

Said, E. W. (1979). *Orientalism*. New York, NY: Pantheon Books.

Sullivan, G. (2014, October 30). Video sparks debate on street harassment. *The Ottawa Citizen*, p. C3.

Woods, A. (2017, February 3). "Trash radio" creates culture of intolerance in Quebec. *Toronto Star*. Retrieved from www.thestar.com/news/canada/2017/02/03/trash-radio-creates-culture-of-intolerance-in-quebec.html [February 3, 2017].

Yusuf, H. (2015, June 24). My hijab has nothing to do with oppression. It's a feminist statement. *The Guardian*, Opinion Videos. Retrieved from www.theguardian.com/commentisfree/video/2015/jun/24/hijab-not-oppression-feminist-statement-video [June 5, 2018].

8 Indigenous Representation in the Media

> Media coverage of Aboriginal peoples often contains misinformation, sweeping generalizations and galling stereotypes.... [The] Commission would prefer that journalists are well versed and informed on the history of Aboriginal peoples and issues that would affect their lives.
> —Truth and Reconciliation Commission Report Executive Summary, 2015

In the mid- to late 1990s, the provincial government of British Columbia attempted to right a historical wrong by negotiating the first treaty with a First Nations people since the province entered Confederation in 1871. It was a historical wrong because the legislation that led to the creation of Canada, the **British North America Act of 1867**, mandated negotiations of land treaties between three parties: the federal government, the provincial government, and the First Nations.[1] When British Columbia joined Canada it refused to negotiate treaties or acknowledge Aboriginal title. The 1973 Calder Decision by the Supreme Court of Canada led the federal Liberal government to attempt to begin the treaty process with First Nations in British Columbia. However, the BC Social Credit government refused. During the 1990s, however, the BC NDP was committed to using the treaty process to successfully negotiate with the First Nations (Harcourt, 1996).

As the negotiations between the federal Liberal government, the provincial NDP government, and the Nisga'a people of northwestern BC moved toward a signed treaty, a major problem became evident—it seemed that no one had explained to the journalists in BC that treaties were required by law. Newspaper headlines seemingly designed to rile the public became more frequent. In early February of 1998, the front-page headline of the *Vancouver Sun* screamed, "BC

Indian Chiefs Lay Claim to Entire Province, Resources" (Ouston, 1998). Three weeks later a column entitled "How to Make Indian Land Claims Go Away" appeared (Lautens, 1998), followed by another front-page article, with the headline "Native Leaders Reject Public Referendum on Nisga'a Deal" (Rinehart, 1998). Two more of the countless articles created to foster opposition to these first treaty negotiations in BC had the following headlines: "Cost of the Nisga'a Deal: $490 Million and Counting" (Palmer, 1998), and "What You Get from Behind Closed Doors" (Yaffe, 1998). It appeared that the mainstream media were opposed to land treaties with the First Nations in British Columbia.

Three things became evident from the media coverage. First, the mainstream media were being provocative either to oppose the Nisga'a Treaty on some sort of principle or simply to sell more newspapers. Whatever the reason, opposition to the treaty, especially in northern BC, rose as the media coverage became more negative and at times hysterical. Second, the journalists writing these articles had very little understanding of treaties and the important foundational role they have played in the development and body politic of Canada. Third, these journalists were using common stereotypes of Indigenous peoples from the colonial and nation-building periods, such as "trouble makers."

The rigorous **Truth and Reconciliation Commission** (TRC) report (2015) recommends that journalists in Canada become better informed about the history of treaties, title, and all major issues past and present that affect the lives of Indigenous peoples. This chapter is a beginning in this education of journalism students. In this way the chapter has a different focus from all of the other chapters in the book. The next section briefly describes racial discourses and forms of racism. The following section explains treaties, title, and the Canadian laws that support these important concepts. Lastly, the chapter discusses the ways in which mainstream media coverage of contemporary Indigenous issues utilizes common negative stereotypes.

A BRIEF LOOK AT RACE THEORY FOR JOURNALISTS

The notion of race is fraught with complications and challenges, including blurred racial boundaries and persuasive arguments that race is only a social construction. Yet, no one can deny the existence of racism. There is a tendency for many people to personalize racism—they fail to see it as systemic, institutional, or interwoven into the social relations of society (Orlowski, 2001). This interpretation of a few bad racist apples has the effect of leaving structural forms of racism that are embedded throughout society unchallenged, thus maintaining current hegemony around race relations.

Forms of Racism

A significant number of White people articulate overt racism such as racist name-calling as the only form they are aware of (Orlowski, 2001; Elliott & Fleras, 1993). This is especially the case with people of European ancestry. It is clear to most people living in the United States and Canada that overt racism is no longer acceptable.[2] Consequently, this form of racism that was so common in the past occurs less frequently today, replaced by a much more covert form that attempts to hide one's racist attitudes. For example, a parent who is unhappy that their child's new teacher is of First Nations ancestry may request that their child be moved into another class without being upfront about the reason. Another term for this is polite racism.

One form of racism that has been almost completely expunged from Canadian society is called *institutional*—this refers to racist laws passed by the state. First Nations children forced to attend residential boarding schools throughout much of the 20th century is an obvious example of institutional racism. In fact, the colonization of First Nations people in general is an example of institutional racism of gargantuan proportions. First Nations people were the last group to be enfranchised in Canada, finally receiving the right to vote in 1960—this was institutional racism.

Another more insidious form of racism, *systemic* racism, influences social relations long after racist legislation has been abolished. Systemic racism refers to *attitudes* that work to discriminate against a person because of their race. It is one thing for a society to abolish racist laws; it is another altogether to rid a society of racist attitudes. Most people today can understand how racist laws in Canada's history were unfair. The problem is that they cannot see how the *legacies* of longstanding racist laws still influence race relations today, nor can they comprehend the power of systemic racism. A critical perspective on Canadian history demonstrates that the degree to which a person experiences privilege or oppression has everything to do with what side of the colonial divide they were born into.

Paradoxically, systemic racism can be part of a seemingly benign situation. For example, the colour-blind discourse promotes **meritocracy**, or the idea that anyone can succeed provided they work hard enough. Therefore, many non-Indigenous Canadians rationalize the poverty that the majority of First Nations people experience as being the result of laziness. Most White Canadians are unaware of the privilege that their race grants them. Indeed, many get upset when they hear about White privilege from Indigenous scholars. One of the reasons for this lack of awareness is that most Canadians cannot comprehend the suffering that First Nations people have experienced from colonization that included a century of abuse in residential schools (TRC, 2015). Further, most journalists in Canada are White, as are most teachers, doctors, politicians, lawyers, judges, and police officers.

As members of the dominant society, people in these important roles are also recipients of the practices, meanings, and values of the dominant culture. White privilege structures sociocultural relations in Canada, including the way minorities are portrayed in the media. If more journalists were aware of how White privilege is embedded in our dominant culture, the discourses and perspectives they use in their work might also increase the awareness of White citizens. For example, the angry White backlash evident in the support for President Trump's immigration policies, and the anger toward social protestors at Standing Rock in North Dakota and in Black Lives Matter, might dissipate if more mainstream media outlets took the lead in explaining the reasons why these protest movements have arisen. Of course, many people do not receive their news from those media sources like the *Toronto Star* and CBC that do tend to balance their portrayal of these social movements. Some conservatives prefer to get their news from far-right outlets such as Rebel Media in Canada, and Breitbart News and Fox News in the US. Another factor in mainstream media's lack of critique of White privilege is the dearth of diversity among journalists in a newsroom. The majority of journalists working in Canadian newsrooms today are middle-class White people. This is a difficult situation to remedy in the current context of staff reductions amid falling revenues (see Chapter 3).

Racial Discourses

Frankenberg (1993) describes the three competing racial discourses from the 1700s to the present. Each of these discourses works to either further entrench or challenge the dominant view toward people of other races or ethnicities. Frankenberg calls these three discourses essentialist, colour-blind, and race-cognizance.

The Essentialist Discourse on Race
The first discourse in Frankenberg's taxonomy, which she refers to as *essentialist*, ascribes an overall superiority to a race because of a supposed biological

birthright. Ever since the European imperialist agenda developed, essentialist racial hierarchies were socially constructed that positioned Europeans on top of all other racial groups. This was the dominant hegemonic discourse in North America as it underwent a process that transformed it from the land of the Indigenous peoples into British colonies and then into the newly formed nations of the United States and Canada. As well, White ethnic groups were also positioned in relation to each other—in Canada, the British were almost always atop the others (see Figure 8.1).

This discourse influenced European attitudes toward each other and the racially marginalized Other (see the previous chapter for further discussion of Othering), eventually forming a system of race and ethnic relations that privileged White people of northwestern European extraction at the expense of everyone else, with the exception of the Irish, who were positioned with the other lower-status Europeans. The essentialist discourse dominated public debates throughout the colonial and nation-building periods of the United States and Canada.

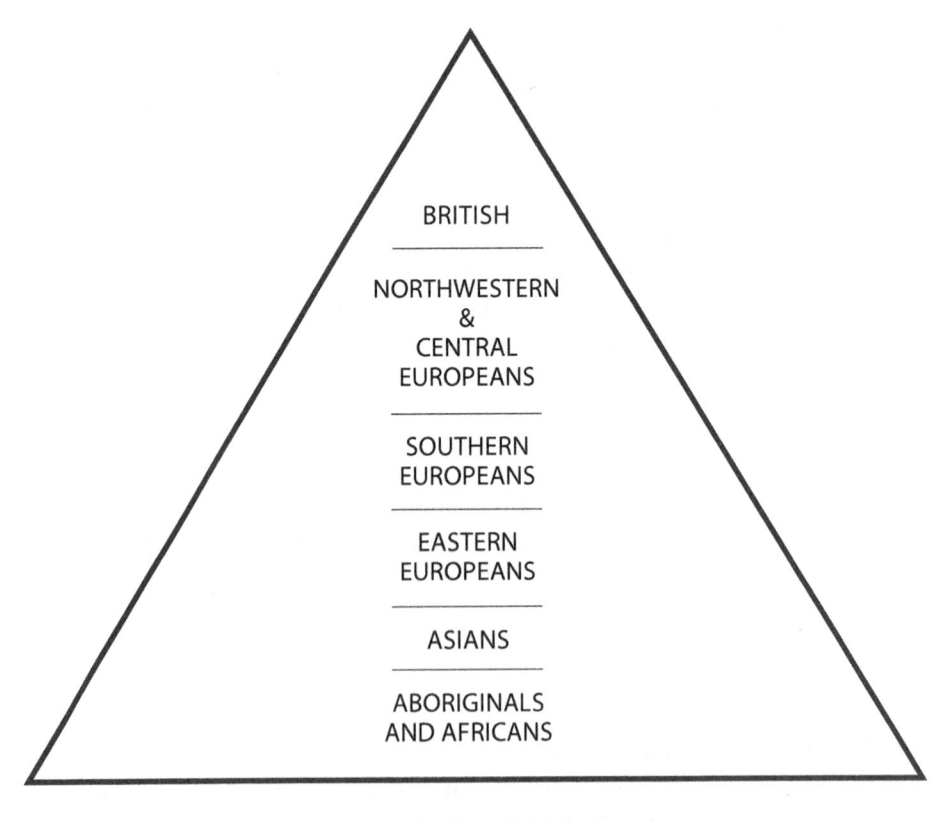

Figure 8.1: Racial Hierarchy during British Empire

According to Frankenberg, there was no reason for a White person to hide racist attitudes during this period because it was in keeping with the norm. In other words, the essentialist discourse had a normalizing and regulating effect that enabled White supremacy to go, for the most part, unchallenged. The effects of this discourse were present everywhere Europeans set out to conquer other peoples during the empire-building period of European expansionism (Young, 1995). It justified the theft of Indigenous peoples' lands and the enslavement of African peoples, destroying many of these Indigenous cultures in the process. Clearly, present-day Canada and the United States were founded on the essentialist discourse.

The essentialist discourse was related to the racist cultural ranking system developed by British philosopher Herbert Spencer in the 19th century. According to Spencer (cited in Francis, 2007), every society can be categorized as *civilized* (e.g., western Europe), *barbaric* (e.g., India, China, and Japan), or *savage* (e.g., Indigenous and African peoples). The legacy of this system is still in effect today with the preponderance of the *cultural-deficit* discourse. This discourse posits that rather than genetic deficiency, it is the cultural practices and values of certain social groups that inhibit many of them from experiencing success. As an example, a conservative perspective on the low graduation rates of First Nations high school students will point to an assumed cultural trait that does not place enough value on formal education. This discourse assumes that the problem resides in the culture itself rather than in a school system that uses a Eurocentric curriculum that does not acknowledge the histories, art forms, or perspectives of Indigenous peoples.

The Colour-Blind Discourse on Race

The second racial discourse in Frankenberg's taxonomy is referred to as *colour-blind*. Its major tenet is that beneath the skin, everyone is equal. This core assumption was born out of the Enlightenment, yet it rose to prominence much later, during the second half of the 20th century. The United Nations produced the *Universal Declaration of Human Rights* in 1948, an important political document intended to promote racial and religious tolerance. This was the result of acknowledging the horrors of the Holocaust during World War II.

A clear example of the colour-blind discourse can be found in this statement taken from a 1995 *Globe and Mail* editorial: "Ours is a modern nationalism: liberal, decent, tolerant and colour blind" (cited in Mackey, 2002). The statement attempts to conceal the more sordid parts of Canadian history. It overlooks the effects of historical factors like the colonization of Indigenous peoples and the horrors of the residential school policy. It is worth noting that when this editorial was published in 1995, the last residential schools were still in existence in BC (TRC, 2015).

The colour-blind discourse works in concert with the notion of meritocracy to justify the stratification of contemporary society in terms of socioeconomic status. In other words, an individual's low standard of living as an adult can be explained by a lack of skill or work ethic, or both. In North America, the colour-blind discourse is still the most dominant one in the mainstream media, although it is currently being challenged by an angry White backlash discourse on the right as well as more race-sensitive discourses coming from the left. In contemporary North America, the former position is represented by supporters of President Trump, while the latter is represented by protest movements such as Idle No More, Standing Rock, and Black Lives Matter.

The Race-Cognizance Discourse

The third discourse, according to Frankenberg, emerged out of debates among White feminists, socialist feminists, and scholars of colour during the 1980s. Called *race-cognizance*, it is a reaction to both of the other more influential discourses, acknowledging that the amounts of privilege or oppression people receive are dependent on their skin colour as well as other factors such as their social class, gender, sexuality, culture, religion, and geographical location. People who adhere to this perspective consider the colour-blind discourse based within the liberal individualist paradigm to be *power-blind* because it overlooks the effects of historical factors and societal structures and institutions. With its support for meritocracy, the argument goes, colour-blindness insidiously supports White privilege.

The race-cognizance discourse has been unable to displace the dominance of the colour-blind discourse in public debates today, however. The main reason for this is that this discourse attempts to illuminate society's unearned privileges as being major root causes of racism, sexism, and poverty. In other words, it demonstrates that the idea of meritocracy is a myth. Further, the race-cognizance discourse demands an analysis of society based on **intersectionality**. For example, intersectionality explains that a First Nations woman is discriminated against because of her race and because of her gender. Many White people, especially White males, feel threatened by the ideas within the race-cognizance discourse, including intersectionality.

Race-cognizance calls for institutional and social change and is most closely related to the critical left ideology (see Chapter 1). As mentioned above, Idle No More and Black Lives Matter are examples of protest movements based on race-cognizance. Further, the inquiry into Murdered and Missing Indigenous Women and the federal-government-sponsored Truth and Reconciliation Commission are examples of state recognition of the role that race has had in oppressing Indigenous peoples in the past and in present-day Canada. Think about these forms of racism, discourses, protest movements, and government responses as you read the next sections on colonization, land treaties, and Aboriginal title.

A BRIEF HISTORY OF LAND TREATIES AND ABORIGINAL TITLE IN CANADA

Colonialism, typically, is legitimated by myths of superiority, inevitability, and racism, and is enforced by colonizers' socio-political institutions. Canadian colonialism was justified by the *essentialist* racial discourse that framed Indigenous peoples as alien "Others" to emerging provincial and national identities based on Christianity, Anglo-Saxon cultural norms, and capitalist ideals of progress and wealth acquisition. It was assumed that this biological superiority conferred an attendant right to dictate the fate of all other races. Thus, a model of **colonization** was developed and implemented to gain control over Indigenous peoples, a model that began on the continent of North America before Canada or the United States came into existence.

The **Royal Proclamation of 1763** is the foundational legal document that structures Indigenous/non-Indigenous relations in North America. This document was produced by the British government and contained three very important points for contemporary Canadian society. First, it stated that the British government and only the British government can and must engage in land treaty negotiations with First Nations (see definition of **treaty** in the glossary). This was to provide a legal obstacle to White whiskey traders and their ilk from dealing with First Nations peoples for land, especially in the 13 colonies that a few years later became the United States. Second, Aboriginal **title** exists, meaning that First Nations peoples are legally allowed to hunt and fish on "Crown" land to feed their communities. Aboriginal title is why all-Native fisheries occur at various times and in different locations across Canada. Considering that First Nations peoples had year-round access to all the land and waterways prior to European settlements, receiving title is minute compensation. Third, "Indian" peoples belong to *nations*, and as such, negotiations must adhere to nation-to-nation international law. The British government negotiated treaties with the First Nations in British North America prior to the formation of Canada. These pre-Confederation treaties cover much of the land in what is now eastern Canada.

Most Canadians know that Canada became a nation in its own right through the passing of the British North America Act of 1867. Far fewer are aware that the statements pertaining to the First Nations in the Royal Proclamation of 1763 were also included in the British North America Act. There was one important difference in the two documents: the legal requirement to engage in land treaty negotiations with the First Nations passed from the British government to the federal government of Canada. Aboriginal title was enshrined in Canada's original Constitution, as it continues to be in the Charter of Rights and Freedoms created by the Trudeau Liberal government in 1982. Many non-Indigenous Canadians today are unaware of the concept of title, and often express anger when Indigenous peoples have hunting and fishing rights that they do not have. A former Conservative MP claimed the federal Liberal government was "acting illegally and in a racist manner by granting aboriginal fishermen exclusive rights to fish for sockeye salmon" over a weekend (Kennedy, 2002). This politician was invoking the colour-blind discourse, and in doing so, highlighted the discourse's shortcomings in that it ignores history. First Nations people lack the support of other people for title because non-Aboriginals do not even know it exists as a legal concept. In the *Globe and Mail* article that described this protest against the all-Native fishery, not once was title mentioned or the misinformed views of the White fishermen challenged (Kennedy, 2002). Whether intentional or not, this is an example of omission as a hegemonic strategy.

Schools and mainstream media have clearly failed to foster an informed citizenry around the legal rights inherent in Aboriginal title. For example, if the media explained that Aboriginal title is what was left for First Nations peoples after their land was taken from them and they were moved onto tiny reserves, many more Canadians would come to understand that it is the least the government and mainstream society could agree to offer them. Further, if the media described the unfulfilled promises made to Indigenous peoples in the signed treaties, more Canadians would support treaties and their role in the development of Canada.

To understand the *contemporary* situation in Canada around land treaties, it is important to examine what transpired shortly after the British North American Act was signed in 1867. Treaties negotiated between the British government and First Nations in much of eastern Canada occurred prior to 1867. The discussion, therefore, will focus on western Canada chronologically—first, treaties in British Columbia; and second, treaties on the prairies. Although the British North America Act stated that land treaties had to be negotiated, this was in the context of the racist essentialist discourse that dominated race relations in

Canada from Confederation up until the 1950s. Moreover, many White politicians have refused to acknowledge what pertained to First Nations peoples in the Royal Proclamation of 1763 and the British North America Act. The media has only exacerbated the situation.

British Columbia's Contrarian Views on Treaties and Title

> Shall we allow a few red vagrants to prevent forever industrious settlers from settling on the unoccupied lands? Not at all.... Locate reservations for them on which to earn their own living, and if they trespass on white settlers punish them severely. A few lessons would soon enable them to form a correct estimation of their own inferiority, and settle the Indian title too.
> —Editorial in the *British Colonist* newspaper, 1863, cited in Friessen & Ralston, 1980, p. 267

This excerpt from a Vancouver Island newspaper editorial in 1863 is a clear example of the media's use of the racist essentialist discourse that posited British people as superior to First Nations people. The newspaper was championing a racist perspective that was extremely popular among White settlers in the British colony. White settlers were outraged at James Douglas, the governor of the British colony on Vancouver Island, for negotiating 14 small land treaties with the First Nations peoples living there. They were concerned that the First Nations were *taking* some of the best land, when they felt they should be the recipients (Campbell, Menzies, & Peacock, 2003).

Once Governor Douglas retired and moved back to England, a more virulent version of institutional racism became the norm in the British colony. Many of the First Nations people were removed from the reserve lands negotiated in the Douglas Treaties. Others had their reserve lands significantly decreased to allotments smaller than elsewhere in what eventually became Canada (Friessen & Ralston, 1980). Moreover, all of this took place as the Indigenous peoples living on the west coast were struck by a major smallpox epidemic that killed approximately 70 percent of the population (Campbell, Menzies, & Peacock, 2003, p. 87). White leaders simply forced the remaining weakened survivors to take their dead relatives by boat away from White settlements (Barman, 1991).

The media were complicit in these callous and inhumane actions. In 1865, at the height of the smallpox epidemic ravaging west coast First Nations communities, the *British Columbian* newspaper reflected upon and also influenced the prevailing attitudes among White settlers:

> Colonization necessarily involves the contact, and practically the collision, of two races of men—one superior, and one inferior, the latter being in possession of the soil, the former gradually supplanting it. The history of every civilized country illustrates the truth of this supposition. Everywhere, in obedience to what appears to be a natural law, the uncivilized native has receded before the civilizer. (Cited in Perry, 2001, p. 125)

This newspaper editorial is an example of how the essentialist discourse could rationalize the most savage of behaviours toward First Nations peoples. The racist attitudes prevalent in the colony of British Columbia were soon brought to the discussions with the federal government about it joining Canada as a province.

Shortly after Confederation, Prime Minister John A. MacDonald negotiated with the White settlers of British Columbia to join Canada. MacDonald was committed to blocking the United States from claiming British Columbia, and offered the White representatives from the colony the promise of a railway line from BC to Ontario. Apparently, this was the deciding factor—British Columbia was going to join Canada on the promise of rail travel to the east. Prior to the official signing, the prime minister stated that land treaties with First Nations would have to be negotiated and that Aboriginal title to the land existed in law. BC land commissioner Joseph Trutch responded with his now infamously racist statement that Native people "had no more right to the land than a panther or a bear" (Dickason, 1992, p. 261). Despite the illegality of this essentialist position toward treaties and title, British Columbia became part of Canada in 1871.

The provincial government of British Columbia refused to negotiate land treaties with First Nations people until the 1990s when NDP premiers Mike Harcourt and Glen Clark agreed to negotiate with the First Nations and the federal Liberal government. Despite the massive opposition led by the mainstream media described near the beginning of this chapter, the first treaty in the history of the province was successfully negotiated by the Nisga'a people of northwestern BC, the federal Liberal government, and the provincial NDP government. The Nisga'a Treaty received royal assent in 2000 (Campbell, Menzies, & Peacock, 2003).

After British Columbia had agreed to join Canada, Prime Minister MacDonald focused his attention on the Canadian prairies. The next section focuses on the numbered treaties on the Canadian prairies that were negotiated during the 1870s. The details differ from what took place in British Columbia, but there are many sordid components to this history as well. Deception is a crucial part of the story.

The Prairie Treaties of the 1870s

Despite the prevailing myths of "social harmony and a tradition of cooperation" on the prairies (Green, 2006, p. 19), this region also very much comprises a jurisdiction with a race problem rooted in a problematic colonial history. From the time the Canadian federal government followed British precedent in utilizing treaties as instruments of nation building, formal agreements that guaranteed reserve lands and other rights, including education, were negotiated with Indigenous groups in the 1870s (Dickason & McNab, 2008). These numbered treaties constituted the benign face of Canadian colonialism and arguably also represented attempts on the part of prairie First Nations to achieve an accommodation with Euro-Canadian society by accessing formal schooling and other technologies of modernity. Much more malign were subsequent federal policies of dispossession, removal, and transformation through which Indigenous autonomy was coercively appropriated.

In order to make a strong case for the prairies to become part of Canada in the 1870s, the federal government desired European immigrants to farm the land. Yet, the land belonged to the prairie First Nations, many of whom were nomadic hunters of the buffalo. The majority of the buffalo were being slaughtered by White buffalo hunters in the 1800s (Dickason, 1992), but the land had not yet been ceded to the federal government. This was a necessary condition to persuade European farmers to immigrate to the plains. To that end, the prime minister sent Alexander Morris, the main treaty commissioner of the federal government, to negotiate on behalf of Canada with the First Nations leaders. After long negotiations, treaties were agreed upon and signed.

The European settlers would receive parcels of land as the First Nations people were to be moved to (quite tiny) reserves. The newcomers would be able to live in peace because the First Nations agreed to this. They would also be able to practice their various European-based religions. In exchange for this, the First Nations people would receive education in day schools located on or next to the new reserves—the Cree leaders wanted the next generation to know how to read and write in order to better understand the ways of the Euro-Canadians. They were to receive medical help, and agricultural tools to change from buffalo hunters to farmers. Clearly, *all* of the people living on the prairies in those days were treaty people.

The First Nations people honoured the promises they made in the treaties (Dickason, 1992). They were soon to find out, however, that honouring one's word did not go both ways. For example, whenever the First Nations people became successful at farming and out-competed the settlers, as occurred in the Qu'Appelle Valley, they were quickly relocated to less arable land (Dickason, 1992). There were far more duplicitous actions by the federal government that the First Nations would experience, however, with extremely disastrous consequences. At the same time that Morris and the leaders of the prairie First Nations were engaged in treaty negotiations, the federal government was developing another legal document in Ottawa, one that had *absolutely no input from First Nations people*. Once it became law it changed the lives of every single Indigenous person in Canada from the 1870s until today. It was called the Indian Act.

Prairie Treaty Promises about Education Become Meaningless

The Indian Act of 1876 brought legal and political dimensions to the colonization of Indigenous peoples in Canada. This legislation, a clear example of how the racist essentialist discourse led to government policy, defined Indigenous peoples as wards of the state and empowered the federal government to enforce aggressive assimilation policies as a means of rendering them into acculturated Canadian citizens (St. Denis, 2007). A mass system of segregated education was seen as critical to the achievement of this goal and was formalized through the Indian Act and the infamous Davin Report of 1879 (Milloy, 1999). Education as a tool in the cultural transformation of Indigenous peoples found particularly graphic expression in residential schools, which operated between the 1880s and the 1990s as partnerships between the Canadian state and various Christian churches (Cappon, 2008). Indigenous children were forcibly removed from their homes at the age of 6 to residential schools where they would remain until 16. Parents were not allowed to visit their children in these schools, which were located extremely far from the reserves. Children could see their parents only during the summer months. *Thousands* of them died either in the schools or trying to escape from them to find their way home. In some cases, parents never found out what happened to their children (TRC, 2015).

The residential school system for First Nations children was created under the auspices of assimilating them into mainstream Canadian society. This system was flawed right from its outset, however, as the policy was "not for assimilation but for inequality" (Barman, 1995, p. 57). A lack of understanding of First Nations cultures, inadequate funding leading to poor food, and inferior instruction doomed this educational project to failure. The state's policy on Indigenous education "made possible no other goal than Aboriginal peoples' absolute marginalization from Canadian life—a goal schools achieved with remarkable success" (Barman, 1995, p. 75). The underpinnings for this project were based on the essentialist discourse of White supremacy. The Canadian government wanted Native people to assimilate, at least as farm workers and domestic servants, because they were fearful of violent conflict and "Indian wars," such as were occurring in the United States (Milloy, 1999). The schools embarked on a philosophy of "kill the Indian to save the man," resulting in **cultural genocide**. First Nations people's worst fears about what these schools were doing to their children were being realized—they were being beaten even for speaking their native language. The mandate to eradicate First Nations languages and traditions led to a culture of violence within the schools in which the children had no one to protect them—parents were forbidden to visit their own children. At best, government intentions were to train First Nations people to assimilate into mainstream society as members of the lowest part of the working classes.

First Nations leaders demanded that the federal government adhere to what was promised in the signed treaties. In particular, they wanted day schools to be on or near the reserves as was agreed upon in the treaties. The cruel response was that the Indian Act negated anything the government had promised in the signed treaties. In other words, the treaty promises made by the federal government through its representative Alexander Morris were virtually meaningless. The anguish experienced by Indigenous parents and children as a result of this egregious and duplicitous policy of institutional racism is incomprehensible to most White people (TRC, 2015). As an example of this ignorance, a Saskatchewan newspaper editorial published in August 2017 lamented how often First Nations leaders speak of the racism they experience (cited by Hunter, 2017). Called "When Will It End?" the editorial claimed that "racism is a daily reality … for everyone," yet First Nations people are the only ones "claiming racism." The coverage by the CBC and other larger media outlets to call out the *Melfort Journal* managing editor's "ignorant views of Indigenous people" demonstrates a positive step toward reconciliation.

Canadian authorities have recently acknowledged that residential schools were responsible for brutalizing children emotionally, psychologically, physically, spiritually, culturally, and sexually. The narratives of survivors of the residential school system included in the Truth and Reconciliation Commission report (2015) make explicit the pain and suffering of Indigenous peoples at the hands of a racist federal government steeped in the belief that colonization of the "savages" was for the best. The findings of the Truth and Reconciliation Commission report are illuminating—it was not a "civilized" people educating "savages" as the government claimed and the media of the day portrayed; rather, the opposite appears to be closer to the truth.

BOX 8.1: "WHY DON'T RESIDENTIAL SCHOOL SURVIVORS JUST GET OVER IT?"

Senator Murray Sinclair is Ojibway and a former judge in Manitoba. He was the chair of the Truth and Reconciliation Commission. His response to the commonly heard question was part of the CBC radio program *The Current* at a public forum on March 29, 2017. His response was also in part to address the comments made by fellow senator Lynn Beyak, who had staunchly defended the "well-intentioned" residential school system. Here is Senator Sinclair's response:

> Many people have said over the years that I've been involved in the work of the Truth and Reconciliation Commission: Why can't we just get over it and move on? And my answer has always been, Why can't you always remember this? Because this is about memorializing those people who have been victims of a great wrong. Why don't you tell the United States to get over 9/11? Why don't you tell this country to get over all of the veterans who died in the Second World War, instead of honouring them once a year? Why don't you tell your families to stop thinking about all of your ancestors who died? Why don't you turn and burn down all of those headstones that you put up for all of your friends and relatives over the years? It's because it's important for us to remember. We learn from it. And until people show that they have learned from this, we will never forget, and we should never forget even once they have learned from it, because this is a part of who we are. It's not just a part of who we are as survivors and children of survivors and relatives of survivors, but part of who we are as a nation, and this nation must never forget what it once did to its most vulnerable people.

The government's insistence on separating children from their families over multiple generations resulted in a significant incapacitation of the cohesiveness and social sustainability of First Nations families and communities. This created a "complex situation where a high level of *dependency* toward the state is combined with a *profound distrust* of that same state" among most Indigenous peoples (Papillon & Cosentino, 2004, p. 1). In other words, the legacy of the racist residential school policy very much exists today. The social problems and low economic status of large segments of Indigenous peoples today are evidence of that. Most Canadians, however, are unaware that the federal government has not lived up to the promises negotiated in the numbered treaties of the prairies. Nor are they conscious of the fact that the First Nations *have* lived up to all of the promises they made in the treaties. For example, many non-Indigenous people own property on the prairies, demonstrating a promise kept. The mainstream media could do a much better job of educating citizens about treaties. The discussion turns to the ways in which the media represent Indigenous peoples in contemporary Canada.

STEREOTYPES OF INDIGENOUS PEOPLES IN MAINSTREAM MEDIA

> Whether we're aware of it or not, reporters use stereotypes. A lot. News happens fast, and we need quick ways to simplify our storylines to make sure our audience "gets it".... Unfortunately, there's ample evidence of journalists basing stereotypes about Aboriginal peoples on false assumptions. By repeating stereotypes, we have the power to transform assumptions about Aboriginal peoples into "realities," which reinforces discrimination and prejudice.
>
> —Duncan McCue, CBC journalist, 2014

Stereotypes are a common feature of stories in general, not only in the media, and not only of Indigenous peoples. Indigenous peoples, however, are particularly vulnerable to issues arising from ubiquitous negative stereotyping because of the problems associated with over two centuries of colonization. According to acclaimed Canadian Indigenous author Thomas King, up until recently any depiction of "Indians" in the Hollywood film industry was based on one or a combination of three stereotypes. "There was the bloodthirsty savage, the noble savage, and the dying savage" (King, 2012, p. 34). Television, especially in the United States, was no better. It was not until Indigenous filmmakers and television producers came on the scene that more nuanced and complex Indigenous characters appeared.[3] Although the stereotypes used to represent Indigenous peoples in mainstream news reports are somewhat more varied, the depictions are still unidimensional.

In 1990, international headlines were focused a land dispute involving the Mohawk First Nation and the (mostly White) town of Oka, Quebec. At issue was a piece of land that the Oka town council had approved for a golf expansion from a 9-hole course to an 18-hole course. The problem was that the expansion was going to be on "disputed territory—including on a Mohawk burial ground"

(Valiante & Rakobowchuk, 2015).[4] The confrontation highlighted one of a set of common stereotypes journalists often use when covering Indigenous peoples and issues affecting their lives—the warrior. For several weeks, media coverage of the tensions surrounding the town of Oka and the nearby Mohawk village of Kanehsatake included dramatic photos of Canadian soldiers facing off against Mohawk warriors clad in military fatigues and masks. Canadians were led to believe that a major battle was soon to break out between the military and the Mohawk warriors.[5] Fortunately, this did not come to pass.

Duncan McCue is Anishinaabe and a veteran CBC journalist who writes a blog called *Reporting in Indigenous Communities*. The blog is "an online educational guide to assist journalists who report in Indigenous communities" (2014). McCue highlights five stereotypes that journalists often use in stories about Indigenous peoples. These stereotypes comprise a set that McCue humorously calls the WD4 Rule. For an Indigenous person to make it on the news they must fit into at least one of these stereotypes: be a *Warrior*, beat your *Drum*, start *Dancing*, get *Drunk*, or be *Dead*. McCue admits that this is a provocative stance, but he wants to emphasize to journalists that news reports about Indigenous communities "tend to follow extremely narrow guidelines based on pre-existing stereotypes" (McCue, 2014, p. 5).

A major problem arises when stereotypes are the main source of information that the dominant society receives about an oppressed group such as Indigenous peoples. When the public sees repeated images of any group of people whom they are mostly unfamiliar with, they begin to see members of that group in the ways they are depicted. The stereotypes "become etched in the public consciousness" (McCue, 2014, p. 4). In other words, the stereotypes become the realities for mainstream society, another example of how knowledge is a social construction.

As a result of the Oka crisis, the federal government created the Royal Commission on Aboriginal Peoples (RCAP) in 1991 to study one important question: What are the foundations of a fair and honourable relationship between the Aboriginal and non-Aboriginal people of Canada? In 1996 they released their report, which included an analysis of the ways Indigenous peoples are represented in the media. According to RCAP, there are three stereotypes that are consistently repeated in the Canadian media: *pathetic victims*, *angry warriors*, and *noble environmentalists*. The repetition of these unidimensional representations effectively reinforces "old and deeply embedded notions of 'Indians' as alien, unknowable and ultimately a threat to civil order" (RCAP, 1996, p. 5). As discussed earlier in the historical sections of this chapter, however, this civil order has almost always been *exclusionary*. Using stereotypes exaggerates the divide between Indigenous and non-Indigenous Canadians. This is of course unjust.

In arguably the definitive work on Indigenous representation in Canadian newspapers, *Seeing Red: A History of Natives in Canadian Newspapers*, Anderson and Robertson (2012) claim that there has been little improvement since the colonial period. They contend that the demeaning unidimensional representations that journalists continue to use will effectively block non-Indigenous Canadians from truly seeing Indigenous peoples, and thus will pose an insurmountable obstacle to reconciling with them. Their investigation uncovered overwhelming evidence that the racist discourses and stereotypes of the colonial and nation-building periods still dominate Indigenous representation in contemporary newspaper coverage. This imagined inferiority, according to Anderson and Robertson, is a major influence in the marginalization of Indigenous peoples in Canada today. Because of this, they claim Canadians are in denial about this marginalization as they cling to the image of the tolerant, decent nation that supports the cultural mosaic.

The question arises about whether this commitment to negative portrayals of Indigenous peoples is intentional or unconscious. Mackey (2002) analyzed the ways in which the dominant culture in Canada has almost always been able to successfully manage how minorities, especially Indigenous peoples, have been represented. According to Mackey, since Confederation it has always been an implicit expectation that the state needs to control Indigenous peoples. The main reason for this is economic—the land and the resources that the First Nations have a legal claim to. Treaties and title are the foundation that Canada was founded on. Access to land and resources, which is what treaties and title ultimately represent, would also help Indigenous peoples get out of poverty. The legality of this is sound and the rationale sensible.

If a large segment of the public supported treaties and Aboriginal title to "Crown" land, it is likely that a more equitable arrangement around the division of resources could be negotiated. Mainstream media could have a positive influence on public perceptions of treaties and title. Media coverage of two recent Indigenous campaigns is worth exploring to see what stereotypes were being used, if any. The first one is very much an issue of control over an important resource, namely, fresh water.

Idle No More

In 2012, Canada's Conservative government used its majority to pass two massive omnibus bills, C-38 and C-45, that critics correctly claimed were anti-democratic because of the impossibility to properly debate all of the proposed legislation. Even worse, buried deep within these documents were changes to environmental laws that the *Globe and Mail* benignly described as an "effort to streamline and expedite approval of resource projects" (Hoekstra, 2014). In reality, however, the Harper Conservatives were weakening environmental protection laws for almost all of Canada's lakes and rivers using one of the staples of neoliberal policy, namely, the deregulation of industry (see Chapter 1). Almost immediately, four women in Saskatchewan launched an Indigenous protest movement they called Idle No More that burgeoned into a massive social force across Canada as well as in other countries. In fact, Idle No More became "the largest Canada-wide social action movement since the civil rights movement of the 1960s" (Sinclair, 2014). Flash gatherings occurred in public places across the country, often with traditional drumming. Road blockades were also utilized. The mainstream media began to cover it in earnest, focusing on the drumming, the dancing, and the blockades rather than the reasons for the protests.

First Nations peoples have title to Canada's fresh waterways to sustain their communities through fishing. They understand the potential for devastation as lethal industrial pollutants enter the lakes and rivers. One of the most vulnerable groups in the country stood up for *all* Canadians to resist the neoliberal agenda and demand continued protection for the nation's lakes and rivers. After all, many non-Indigenous Canadians eat fresh water fish as well. Yet, from the reaction to mainstream media coverage in online forums and talk radio, one would get the impression that much of the public despised Idle No More or were at least annoyed at being inconvenienced by their tactics. It is not that the media called for industrial pollutants to destroy Canada's lakes and rivers—they simply ignored what it was the protestors were calling for. Most non-Indigenous Canadians also appeared oblivious to what was at stake. Ignoring the reasons for the protests, however, was not the worst part of the media coverage.

Indigenous scholar Leanne Simpson (2013) describes the mainstream media's coverage of Indigenous issues and Idle No More: "With few exceptions ... the mainstream media reports Indigenous issues through the lens of the colonial ideology that permeates every aspect of Canadian culture. Since the beginnings of Idle No More, they have consistently chosen to exaggerate and manufacture controversy and crisis, rather than to create open dialogue." Mainstream media outlets pushed fear over understanding. Conservative Party advisor Tom Flanagan (2013) wrote in the *Globe and Mail* that the "indigenist ideology" at the root of Idle No More "is a direct challenge to the existence of Canada as a state." He failed to mention even once that the movement was resisting the federal government's plans to allow industrial pollutants into the country's freshwater sources.

In support of the Idle No More movement, and in an attempt to influence the federal Conservative government to help alleviate the suffering on the Attawapiskat reserve, Chief Theresa Spence went on a hunger strike. Her first goal was to get a meeting with Prime Minister Harper to help him understand the suffering of the people on the reserve. How did the mainstream media respond? After attempting to destroy Chief Spence's credibility to even speak for her people, columnist Christie Blatchford (2012) added in her popular *National Post* column: "It is tempting to see the action as one of intimidation, if not terrorism." Canadians know—indeed, most people in the world know—that invoking the word *terrorism* is a sure-fire way to spread fear. The *warrior* stereotype was being transformed into the more frightening *terrorist* stereotype. The Blatchford piece was indicative of other sharp attacks on these Indigenous acts of resistance in other conservative media outlets such as the now-defunct Sun News.

Murdered and Missing Indigenous Women

> The legacy of Aboriginal representations in the Canadian context dates back to early French and English colonization.... What is noteworthy is that these representations changed when it became strategically necessary to discredit Aboriginal claims to land and nationhood.
>
> —Jiwani, 2009, p. 3

An RCMP report released in 2014 stated that between 1980 and 2012, "there were 1,181 police-reported cases of homicides and long-term disappearances involving indigenous women and girls" (Baum, 2016). Other sources claim that unreported disappearances put the figure around 4,000. Indigenous women are "four times more likely to go missing or be murdered than other Canadian women" (Paquin, 2015). Indigenous groups had been calling for an inquiry into this tragic phenomenon for several years. With the publication of the RCMP report, the CBC asked Conservative prime minister Stephen Harper about the possibility of a national inquiry. His answer: "It really isn't high on our radar" (Paquin, 2015). Harper's position was that the violence was not a "sociological phenomenon" and the police were best suited to deal with crime (Baum, 2016). To understand this seemingly callous perspective, it is wise to examine the history of Indigenous female representations from the colonial period to today.

Newspapers in colonial British Columbia were complicit in degrading First Nations women: "First Nations women were represented as overtly sexual, physical, and base. White men were simultaneously attracted and alarmed by what they saw as Aboriginal women's sexual availability" (Perry, 2001, p. 51). Indigenous women were misconstrued to be sexually available because they were judged through a White, Christian, patriarchal lens in which the taboos that were normalized in 19th-century European societies had no counterpart in Indigenous societies (Barman, 1997/98). Moreover, the race and gender dynamics in colonial British Columbia made it possible for "men in power to condemn Aboriginal sexuality and at the same time, if they so chose, to use for their own gratification the very women they had turned into sexual objects" (p. 240). According to Barman (1997/98), "By the time British Columbia became a Canadian province in 1871 Aboriginal women had been almost wholly sexualized," while their White counterparts had been constructed to be almost at the other extreme (p. 249).

In the late 20th and early 21st centuries, representations of Indigenous women in newspaper stories and popular culture have used two main stereotypes: the Indian princess who helps White men, and the "lascivious squaw [who] does what white men want for money or lust" (Jiwani, 2009, p. 4). The latter depiction encourages a conservative moral perspective that the missing and murdered Indigenous women had been living on the edge. From this perspective, it was their chosen lifestyle that had brought violence upon them. The connection between the "wholly sexualized" Indigenous woman of the 1870s and the contemporary "squaw" stereotype is visible. This connection may have influenced the Harper government's decision to ignore calls to do something about the massive numbers of missing and murdered Indigenous women.

Shortly after Harper's CBC interview, the body of 15-year-old Tina Fontaine was pulled out of Winnipeg's Red River. Mainstream media began to give the missing and murdered Indigenous women story the attention it deserved. Harper's controversial "sound bite" of indifference inadvertently helped propel coverage of the Fontaine murder into the public consciousness (McCue, 2014). The federal Liberals and NDP announced support for a national inquiry, and after Harper retired from politics, the Conservatives agreed (Baum, 2016). Most coverage in the mainstream media got behind the initiative for a national inquiry (see Box 8.2).

The media began to point to the history of colonization rather than blaming dysfunctional Indigenous communities. The squaw stereotype has been replaced by one of victimhood. The release of the Truth and Reconciliation Commission report in 2015 appears to have also supported this process.

BOX 8.2: AL JAZEERA AND INDIGENOUS ISSUES

Al Jazeera is a media outlet owned by the government of Qatar in the Middle East. Beginning in 1996, it originally covered news in Arab countries. In recent years, it has expanded its coverage to many parts of the world, and provides counter-hegemonic perspectives to stories in mainstream Western media outlets. Al Jazeera often carries stories about Indigenous issues in North America that challenge the dominant narrative. For example, in one story it encouraged readers to view police violence against Indigenous Americans in Arizona "through the lens of 'settler-colonialism'" (Newton, 2017), a position that is not heard in mainstream media outlets in North America.

CBC journalist Duncan McCue (2015) offers his perspective on why Al Jazeera's coverage of Indigenous issues is so powerful, and why in particular their work on Murdered and Missing Indigenous Women (MMIW) was so effective:

> I think it's very, very intriguing to compare Al-Jazeera to North American media coverage, in particular American media coverage. In a very short time period, they've done a better job of covering Native American issues than any mainstream American outlets. I think their mission is to report the underbelly of America in a way that American media don't like to do and Native America is the underbelly of the U.S. It's very interesting to watch what they're doing. So obviously if that's your mission, and they make no qualms about that, then [Missing & Murdered Indigenous Women] fits in beautifully to that mission.

CONCLUSION

The Truth and Reconciliation Commission report (2015) recommended that Canadian journalism programs require education for their students on the history of Indigenous peoples, including residential schools. The report calls for journalists to try to understand Indigenous peoples' perspectives on contemporary issues that are affecting their lives today and are likely to affect them long into the future, as well. This chapter is a partial response to this recommendation.

Journalists should understand aspects of critical race theory such as the various forms of racism and the racial discourses that have been instrumental in shaping race relations in contemporary Canada. All citizens should have a basic grasp of the importance of land treaties in the development of Canada, and should also realize that in many cases the federal government has reneged on its promises made in signed treaties from over a century ago. All Canadians should know what Aboriginal title means and why it exists. These are still important concepts in contemporary Canada.

The Royal Commission on Aboriginal Peoples (1996) stated that there is a dire need for public education to deconstruct the effects of false and debilitating images and stereotypes of Indigenous peoples in the media, in popular culture, and in school textbooks. This chapter discussed some of these stereotypes and the persistence of some of them in the history of Canada to the present day. The media covered the 1991 Oka crisis by instilling fear in the public with the warrior stereotype. Despite its honourable intentions, the Idle No More protest movement that began in 2012 demonstrated that there is much room for improvement in terms of social and ecological justice in the media.

There are signs, however, that some journalists and media outlets in Canada are beginning to understand the power of representation and related effects on

BOX 8.3: AN INDIGENOUS JOURNALIST EXPLAINS HOW TRUST IS CRUCIAL WHEN INTERVIEWING INDIGENOUS PEOPLES

The *Toronto Star* employs a journalist of Ojibway heritage, Tanya Talaga, to cover Indigenous affairs. Talaga contends that the increase in the number of stories depicting Indigenous issues in recent years is because of "the Idle No More movement, the rise of social media, the Truth and Reconciliation Commission, and an awareness of missing and murdered Indigenous women and girls" (Wallace, 2017). She feels that what is crucial to her working with grieving people who have just lost a family member to suicide or other tragedy is to develop trust. Recognizing that each First Nations community is unique in how it deals with trauma is an important first step. She will often call an official from the community to find out if family members even feel like speaking with her.

Being compassionate and sensitive to the people involved while probing into the story is necessary. According to Talaga, the aim is "to look at the broader issues behind each death, such as intergenerational trauma brought on by residential schools. We try very hard to make sure our stories are not gratuitous or disrespectful" (Wallace, 2017). These are important ideas for all journalists to consider when reporting on suffering and marginalized communities.

the lives of Indigenous peoples. It would seem that the release of the Truth and Reconciliation Commission report in 2015 has had a positive effect. Media support for a national inquiry into the missing and murdered Indigenous women and girls grew exponentially after the report was released. This led to two of Canada's three major federal parties immediately calling for the inquiry. Public support increased as citizens became aware of the tragedy that had been taking place in Canada for many decades.

Another positive sign in the mainstream media was the immediate condemnation of comments made by Lynn Beyak (Tasker, 2017). The Conservative senator called the findings of the Truth and Reconciliation Commission report skewed, and that there were many positives from the residential schools that had not been mentioned. The media's position on Beyak's insensitive and misguided stance demonstrates that progress has been made in supporting Indigenous peoples in the media. However, that a Canadian senator can make these remarks and receive support from her Conservative Party colleagues indicates that there is still a long way to go in fostering a citizenry that understands how Indigenous peoples have been mistreated and misunderstood throughout Canada's history. Indeed, there is an acute need for citizens to understand the importance of treaties and to create an inclusive society for Indigenous peoples and everyone in Canada. Media representation and analysis have a major role in this noble endeavour.

QUESTIONS FOR DISCUSSION

1. (a) The Canadian government outlawed the Sun Dance in the 1880s, and then made it legal again in 1951. Why do you think the government outlawed this traditional ceremony? Why do you think it rescinded this ban in 1951? (Hint: Think about the racial discourses you read about in this chapter.) (b) If a powerful culture were to overtake your country and outlaw ceremonies such as Christmas and Easter, what do you think the long-term result would be?
2. (a) What was the stated intention of the Canadian government to forcibly send Indigenous children to residential schools? Do you believe that this was the actual intention? Why or why not? (b) Speculate as to what might have occurred had the mainstream media of the day provided counter-arguments to the residential school policy. Would this presentation of counter-arguments by the media even have been possible? Explain.
3. Why do you think that there is so little mentioned in the mainstream media about broken treaty promises and what Aboriginal title means? (Hint: Think in economic terms.)

4. What do you think journalists can do to help improve the lives of Indigenous peoples? What might be better ways to represent Indigenous peoples and issues than what has been the norm in most Canadian media outlets?

ASSIGNMENT

Research and analyze from an ideological perspective how the mainstream media in Canada covered issues pertaining to Aboriginal title in each of the following:

1. The Delgamuukw Court Case (1997)
2. Lobster fishing at Burnt Church, New Brunswick (1999–2002)
3. Northern Gateway Pipeline (2014–2017)

NOTES

1. Throughout this chapter, several terms are used to represent the original inhabitants of North America. *Indian* is used only when it refers to historical documents such as the Indian Act. *First Nations* is the preferred term in Canada, and this term is used instead of *Indian* in most cases. *Aboriginal* is an inclusive term representing First Nations, Inuit, and Métis people. *Indigenous* has also become an accepted term, and appears to be preferred in many circles today. This term is used whenever applicable here. In some instances, either *Aboriginal* or *Indigenous* could have been used.
2. The election campaign of Donald Trump and his subsequent victory to become the president of the United States appears to have inspired a resurgence of overt racism in that country. This seems to be an anomaly, however, as the trend has been a decrease in this form of racism since the civil rights movement of the mid-1960s.
3. King makes the case that Canadian broadcasters are more progressive than Americans in representing Indigenous peoples. He highlights the Canadian-produced Aboriginal Peoples' Television Network (APTN) as a case in point.
4. After a 78-day standoff, a deal was brokered. The Mohawks would take down their road barricades in return for the cancellation of expanding the golf course. The disputed land issue has yet to be settled.
5. For an in-depth investigation of the Oka crisis from an Indigenous perspective, see *Kanehsatake: 270 Years of Resistance*, a powerful two-hour documentary made by filmmaker Alanis Obomsawin.

WORKS CITED

Anderson, M., & Robertson, C. (2012). *Seeing red: A history of Natives in Canadian newspapers*. Winnipeg, MB: University of Manitoba Press.

Barman, J. (1991). *The west beyond the west*. Toronto, ON: University of Toronto Press.

Barman, J. (1995). Schooled for inequality: The education of British Columbia Aboriginal children. In J. Barman, N. Sutherland, & J. D. Wilson (Eds.), *Children, teachers and schools in the history of British Columbia* (pp. 57–80). Calgary, AB: Detselig.

Barman, J. (1997/98). Taming Aboriginal sexuality: Gender, power, and race in British Columbia, 1850–1900. *BC Studies, 115/116*, 237–266.

Baum, K. (2016, August 31). Nine things to know about the national inquiry into missing and murdered indigenous women. *The Globe and Mail*. Retrieved from www.theglobeandmail.com/news/national/nine-things-to-know-about-the-national-inquiry-into-missing-and-murdered-indigenous-women/article31654434/ [September 1, 2016].

Blatchford, C. (2012, December 27). Inevitable puffery and horse manure surrounds hunger strike while real Aboriginal problems forgotten. *National Post*. Retrieved from http://news.nationalpost.com/full-comment/christie-blatchford-inevitable-puffery-and-horse-manure-surrounds-hunger-strike-while-real-aboriginal-problems-forgotten [April 2, 2017].

Campbell, K., Menzies, C., & Peacock, B. (2003). *B.C. First Nations Studies*. Victoria, BC: British Columbia Ministry of Education.

Cappon, P. (2008). *Measuring success in First Nations, Inuit, and Métis learning*. Ottawa, ON: Canadian Council on Learning. Retrieved from http://ccl-cca/NR/rdonlyres/ODOA5F71191-43D9-A460-13D7C9BECAB/0/Cappon_PolicyOptions.pdf [March 5, 2013].

CBC Radio. *The Current*. (2017, March 29). Senator Murray Sinclair responds to Lynn Beyak's defence of residential schools. *CBC News*. Retrieved from www.cbc.ca/news/politics/murray-sinclair-lynn-beyak-residential-schools-1.4045465 [April 2, 2017].

Dickason, O. (1992). *Canada's First Nations: A history of founding peoples from earliest times*. Norman, OK: University of Oklahoma Press.

Dickason, O., & McNab, D. (2008). *Canada's First Nations: A history of founding peoples from earliest times* (2nd ed.). New York, NY: Oxford University Press.

Elliott, J., & Fleras, A. (1993). *Unequal relations*. Scarborough, ON: Prentice-Hall.

Flanagan, T. (2013, January 25). Native talks with the Crown challenge Canada's very existence. *The Globe and Mail*. Retrieved from www.theglobeandmail.com/opinion/native-talks-with-the-crown-challenge-canadas-very-existence/article7779669/ [March 31, 2017].

Francis, M. (2007). *Herbert Spencer and the invention of modern life*. Ithaca, NY: Cornell University Press.

Frankenberg, R. (1993). *White women, race matters: The social construction of Whiteness*. Minneapolis, MN: University of Minnesota Press.

Friessen, J., & Ralston, H. (1980). *Historical essays on British Columbia*. Montreal, QC: McGill-Queen's University Press.

Green, J. (2006). From Stonechild to social cohesion: Anti-racist challenges for Saskatchewan. *Canadian Journal of Political Science, 39*(3), 507–527.

Harcourt, M. (1996). *Mike Harcourt: A measure of defiance*. Vancouver, BC: Douglas & McIntyre.

Hoekstra, G. (2014, December 22). Ottawa should have consulted First Nation over omnibus bills C-38 and C-45's sweeping legal changes: Federal Court. *Vancouver Sun*. Retrieved from www.vancouversun.com/technology/Ottawa+should+have+consulted+First+Nation+over+omnibus+bills+sweeping+legal+changes/10674431/story.html [April 4, 2017].

Hunter, A. (2017, August 2). Melfort journalist's column criticized for "ignorant" views on Indigenous people. *CBC News*. Retrieved from www.cbc.ca/news/canada/saskatchewan/column-from-melfort-journalist-receives-criticism-for-ignorant-views-on-issues-facing-aboriginal-people-1.4232574 [August 9, 2017].

Jiwani, Y. (2009). Symbolic and discursive violence in media representations of Aboriginal missing and murdered women. In D. Weir & M. Guggisberg (Eds.), *Violence in hostile contexts e-book*. Oxford, UK: Inter-Disciplinary Press.

Kennedy, P. (2002, August 5). MP charged in B.C. fishery protest. *The Globe and Mail*. Retrieved from www.theglobeandmail.com/news/national/mp-charged-in-bc-fishery-protest/article1025334/ [March 31, 2017].

King, T. (2012). *The inconvenient Indian: A curious account of Native peoples in North America*. Toronto: ON: Anchor Canada.

Lautens, T. (1998, February 28). How to make Indian land claims go away. *Vancouver Sun*, p. A23.

Mackey, E. (2002). *The house of difference: Cultural politics and national identity in Canada*. Toronto, ON: University of Toronto Press.

McCue, D. (2014). News stereotypes of Aboriginal peoples. *Reporting in Indigenous communities*. Retrieved from http://riic.ca/the-guide/at-the-desk/news-stereotypes-of-aboriginal-peoples/ [April 2, 2017].

McCue, D. (2015). On Canadian media coverage of #MMIWG—Missing and Murdered Indigenous Women and Girls. *Reporting in Indigenous communities*. Retrieved from http://riic.ca/on-canadian-media-coverage-of-mmiwg-missing-and-murdered-indigenous-women-and-girls/.

Milloy, J. (1999). *"A national crime": The Canadian government and the residential school system, 1879 to 1986*. Winnipeg, MB: University of Manitoba Press.

Newton, C. (2017, April 27). Police violence against Native Americans in Arizona. *Al Jazeera*. Retrieved from www.aljazeera.com/indepth/features/2017/01/police-violence-native-americans-arizona-170111083205542.html [May 1, 2017].

Orlowski, P. (2001). Ties that bind and ties that blind: Race and class intersections in the classroom. In C. E. James & A. Shadd (Eds.), *Talking about identity: Encounters in race, ethnicity, and language* (pp. 250–266). Toronto, ON: Between the Lines Press.

Ouston, R. (1998, February 2). BC Indian chiefs lay claim to entire province, resources. *Vancouver Sun*, p. A1.

Palmer, V. (1998, July 23). Cost of the Nisga'a deal: $490 million and counting. *Vancouver Sun*, p. A14.

Papillon, M., & Cosentino, G. (2004). *Lessons from abroad: Towards a new social model for Canada's Aboriginal peoples* (Report No. 40). Ottawa, ON: Canadian Policy Research Networks.

Paquin, M. (2015, June 25). Unresolved murders of indigenous women reflect Canada's history of silence. *The Guardian*. Retrieved from www.theguardian.com/global-development/2015/jun/25/indigenous-women-murders-violence-canada [April 11, 2017].

Perry, A. (2001). *On the edge of empire: Gender, race, and the making of British Columbia, 1849–1871*. Toronto, ON: University of Toronto Press.

Rinehart, D. (1998, July 23). Native leaders reject public referendum on Nisga'a deal. *Vancouver Sun*, p. A1.

Royal Commission on Aboriginal Peoples (RCAP). (1996) (5 volumes). Indigenous & Northern Affairs Canada. Retrieved from www.aadnc-aandc.gc.ca/eng/1307458586498/1307458751962 [April 2, 2017].

Simpson, L. (2013, February 27). Idle No More: Where the mainstream media went wrong. *The Dominion*. Retrieved from http://dominion.mediacoop.ca/story/idle-no-more-and-mainstream-media/16023 [April 20, 2017].

Sinclair, N. (2014, December 7). Idle No More: Where is the movement 2 years later? *CBC News*. Retrieved from www.cbc.ca/news/indigenous/idle-no-more-where-is-the-movement-2-years-later-1.2862675 [April 21, 2017].

St. Denis, V. (2007). Aboriginal education and anti-racist education: Building alliances across cultural and racial identity. *Canadian Journal of Education, 30*(4), 1068–1092.

Tasker, J. (2017, March 8). Conservative senator defends "well-intentioned" residential school system. *CBC News*. Retrieved from www.cbc.ca/news/politics/residential-school-system-well-intentioned-conservative-senator-1.4015115 [March 10, 2017].

Truth and Reconciliation Commission of Canada (TRC). (2015). *Honouring the truth, reconciling for the future: Summary of the final report of the Truth and Reconciliation Commission of Canada*. Winnipeg, MB: Truth and Reconciliation Commission of Canada.

Valiante, G., & Rakobowchuk, P. (2015, July 7). Oka crisis, 25 years ago, inspired Native movements around the world. *Huffington Post*. Retrieved from www.huffingtonpost.ca/2015/07/07/1990-oka-crisis-events-i_n_7741628.html [August 9, 2015].

Wallace, K. (2017, August 4). How the Star's Tanya Talaga approaches her coverage of Indigenous affairs. *Toronto Star*. Retrieved from www.thestar.com/trust/2017/08/04/how-the-stars-tanya-talaga-approaches-her-coverage-of-indigenous-affairs.html [August 9, 2017].

Yaffe, B. (1998, November 10). What you get from behind closed doors. *Vancouver Sun*, p. A19.

Young, R. J. C. (1995). *Colonial desire: Hybridity in theory, culture and race*. London, UK: Routledge.

9 War and Terror: Militarization and the Fearful Citizen

September 11, 2001. There it is: the date that changed Canadian society. Is that too strong? Did it really change us? Should it have?

Many of us see that date as important for any number of reasons—and perhaps particularly because of the historical and close geographical relationship we have with the US—but the reasons themselves are less important than the end result: a change in how we see the world around us from a somewhat bountiful and generally comfortable country to a society whose citizens have normalized fear in anticipation of terrorist attacks. Who can blame us? We have witnessed terror first-hand in the heart of our country in one man's attack on the Parliament buildings in 2014, and in the shootings in a Quebec City mosque in 2017.

We can't erase images of terror from our collective memory and, of course, we need to be vigilant, but it is not clear how vigilant or what kind of vigilance our country needs. Despite that, governments since 2001 have stepped up their efforts to keep us safe. They are being cautious—after all, it is the role of the government to protect its citizens—but they are also being political: it is in their political interest to show Canadian citizens that they have strongly responded on issues of public safety.

A little history: After World War II, Canada earned a reputation as a peacekeeping nation. We have sent our military forces to many countries in difficulty and where the presence of neutral troops between countries or between factions within countries was able to ramp down conflicts. Our success as peacekeepers was well known internationally as, on behalf of the United Nations, we intervened and have helped keep the peace in more than 26 countries, beginning with the Suez Canal crisis of 1956. Unlike the US, we have kept out of waging war and have focused instead on our role in peace and security, and on cultivating relationships beyond the United States around the world. This strategy of diplomacy and peacekeeping has kept conflict far from our own borders, even as our American neighbours have engaged actively in both skirmishes and wars, notably its war against Vietnam in the 1970s and its war with Iraq in 1991 and 2003.

Yet the road that Canada took in this post–World War II era has changed over time. Since 1999, when Canada sent troops to Bosnia, Canada's troops are less likely to do their global peacekeeping work under the auspices of the UN and instead do so through the North Atlantic Treaty Organization (NATO). NATO has a different mandate than the UN. Its purpose is "to safeguard the freedom and security of its members through political and military means" (NATO, 2016). In contrast, the charter of the United Nations indicates it will take "effective collective measures for the prevention and removal of threats to the peace" (United Nations, n.d.). This approach kept a Canadian military contingent in post–World War II Germany until 1993 and in Kosovo, Bosnia, in 1999. The UN notes that it will do so "through collective measures" and "by peaceful means"—not by declaring war. Our most recent military engagements were with NATO in Libya and Afghanistan, both in 2011.

At the same time, however, security issues are changing. We have a long and porous border with the United States. It has often been called the longest undefended border in the world. However, in times of security threats, it is easy for those who do not have peace and friendship in mind to slip into or out of either country. We also have to consider the issues that might arise from the melting polar mass in our far north, which opens up waterways that used to be iced over for most, if not all, of the year. In this political and natural environment, both our northern and southern borders are now more vulnerable. Generally, however, as Elinor Sloan (2010) points out, unlike the US, Canada has not had a direct military threat since World War II (p. 488).

This chapter will examine Canada's history in wartime and the aftermath of the events of September 11, 2001. Beginning with the quick enactment of the Anti-terrorism Act, the chapter demonstrates how Western countries responded to these terror acts. It also follows the chronology of Canada's endorsement of and participation in the response to that event (which also included some participation in two wars in Iraq), and the stern legislation that was passed in Canada and in other countries in the hope of preventing further such events. In so doing, the government of the time launched a war of persuasion to convince Canadians to support the importance of going to war. In this situation, Canadian journalists had to choose between patriotism and the needs of their profession in reporting on war and terror. In addition, in today's 24-hour news cycle environment, the expectation of media is to get a story of any kind or importance out instantly.

> **BOX 9.1: CANADA AND PEACEKEEPING: DOES CANADA STILL KEEP THE PEACE SINCE 9/11?**
>
> **Under the United Nations (UN): Peacekeeping**
> "The UN takes effective collective measures for the prevention and removal of threats to the peace" (United Nations, n.d.).
>
> | | |
> |---|---|
> | 2004 | Haiti |
> | 2005–2009 | Sudan |
> | 2009 | Darfur (Sudan) |
>
> **Under the North Atlantic Treaty Organization (NATO): Not Peacekeeping**
> "NATO's essential purpose is to safeguard the freedom and security of its members through political and military means" (NATO, 2016).
>
> | | |
> |---|---|
> | 2001–2003 | Afghanistan |
> | 2011 | Libya |

THE ANTI-TERRORISM ACT (2001)

Immediately after September 11, 2001, the Liberal government very quickly implemented the Anti-terrorism Act, which tightened and broadened security measures. Both the United States and the United Kingdom passed such laws as well. The speed with which Canada and other countries enacted those laws is not surprising, since it wasn't clear what security problems lay ahead. At the same time, many legal and security experts warned that the new laws were overly harsh and even inappropriate in democracies. In addition, there wasn't any provision or deadline to review the law, despite the swift process it had undergone. Only two areas—investigative hearings and preventive arrests—would be reviewed after three years (Canada, 2006).

Legal expert Kent Roach (2003) pointed out that parts of the Anti-terrorism Act were "massive and hastily drafted" and included many new legal concepts and powers to the point that lawful protests and even strikes by citizens could be considered terrorist activities (p. 8). Some of the aspects of the legislation seemed to have been included to pacify the Americans, who enacted their own legislation, the Patriot Act, in October 2001, in their own response to 9/11. That porous border between the two countries that had been a sign of friendship over many years took on much stronger security measures. Partly this was enacted due to the erroneous belief that 9/11 terrorists entered the US from Canada. Now the new law included stricter measures for tourist and commerce travel to the US, while border crossings for citizens were tightened.

Perhaps more importantly, Roach (2003) pointed out—or even warned—that the new laws would put "pressures on the courts to readjust the balance between liberty and security" toward security and, indeed, liberty was curtailed by the Supreme Court several months after 9/11 (p. 9). The court unanimously decided that Canadians travelling abroad could not expect privacy on the information on their customs declarations. (Interestingly, a huge amount of trade continued to flow between the two countries mostly effortlessly [Roach, 2003, p. 11].)

One troubling post-9/11 Canada-US border issue raised by many was **racial profiling**. The concern was that Canadian citizens were being detained by American customs based on their Middle Eastern heritage and their Muslim religion. This came to a head in 2002 when Canadian Maher Arar was detained while returning home through the US after a vacation in Tunisia.

As noted in Chapter 7, Arar's flight stopped over in New York, where the US detained him and then deported him—to Syria, his birthplace, not to Canada where he was a citizen. It was later revealed that the RCMP had given false information to the US officials. Originally, our attorney-general, the RCMP, and the Canadian Security Intelligence Service denied having anything to do with Arar's deportation, but information obtained through access to information hinted that all three were exchanging information—or misinformation—on the case. The Arar case demonstrates why passing legislation hurriedly outside of the normal parliamentary process and public debate raises problems. Particularly, such fast legislation does not allow for careful scrutiny by the media and civil liberty organizations. Without proper time to evaluate and understand such legislation, media reports are rushed and may not have a full understanding of the issues.

The new security law did not have the usual parliamentary and public debate that is normal in a democracy, and left considerable secret control in the hands of the government (Rubin & Kozolanka, 2014). In addition, there is no question that Canada "followed the American lead in the war against terrorism" (Roach, 2003, p. 14), which worried many Canadians. Eventually, Arar was released from prison in Syria, where he had been tortured.

Unfortunately, Arar was not the only Canadian to be detained during this post-9/11 time. A 15-year-old Canadian, Omar Khadr, spent 10 years in the American prison at Guantanamo Bay at the eastern tip of Cuba. He was

> **BOX 9.2: RACIAL PROFILING**
>
> Racial profiling is any action undertaken for reasons of safety, security, or public protection that relies on stereotypes about race, colour, ethnicity, ancestry, religion, or place of origin, or a combination of these, rather than on a reasonable suspicion, to single out an individual for greater scrutiny or different treatment...
>
> Stereotyping becomes a particular concern when people act on their stereotypical views in a way that affects others. This is what leads to profiling. Although anyone can experience profiling, racialized persons are primarily affected.
>
> Typically but not always, profiling is carried out by persons in positions of authority, and can occur in many contexts involving safety, security, and public protection issues.
>
> *Source:* Excerpt from Ontario Human Rights Commission. (2016).

wounded in a firefight between American soldiers and suspected al-Qaeda soldiers in Afghanistan and at one point, while wounded, threw a grenade that the Americans said killed one of their soldiers. The US put him on trial for war crimes, the only underage person ever to have been prosecuted for war crimes. Only lobbying by Canadians and his lawyer drew attention to Khadr's plight and he was finally released in 2015 into the care of his lawyer. Interestingly, the Canadian governments during that decade—both Liberal and Conservative—did very little to ensure Khadr's release from the US prison, appeasing the US while joining with its war effort in the Middle East.

Many Canadian groups and individuals were concerned about the Anti-terrorism Act (C-36 and C-42) and its impact on civil liberties. These included the British Columbia Civil Liberties Association, La Ligue des droits et libertés, the National Association of Women and the Law, the Canadian Arab Association, lawyers, and prominent Canadians such as David Suzuki. Groups representing Muslim and Arab Canadians were also concerned about how broad the law was. Because of the huge amount of criticism, the bill included a sunset clause that meant Parliament would review it after five years. However, in the anger, fear, and shock that came after 9/11, there was little toleration for lawful dissent such as demonstrations and free speech. With our proximity to the US, and while the US was building to retaliate for 9/11, Canada seemed to be following along behind. This raised troubling concerns about our sovereignty, as well as our ability to allow other voices to be heard. One prominent Canadian dissenting voice was a university professor, Sunera Thobani, who suffered through extremely negative responses and harsh media stories when she challenged what she called the "bloodthirsty" rhetoric of President George W. Bush (Roach, 2003, p. 119). American professor Lee Artz has pointed out the US use of propaganda on this issue, writing that "the entire premise of the global war on terrorism ... is unsupportable and constituted only by constant government and media repetition" (Artz, 2011, p. 213). Thobani's rhetoric was strong, but it brought attention to the use of ongoing propaganda by the American administration to build support within its country and with allied countries like Canada that might assist with military retaliation for 9/11.

The intensity of the backlash Thobani experienced for her challenge to government rhetoric and speed was disturbing because it suggested that Canadians should not be able to speak openly about contemporary issues that are also divisive, especially when there is a perceived threat to the country. However, in the same way that fear can drive our emotions, someone who has a different point of view can be labelled as being on "the other side," whatever that might be. For instance, in the case of the 2003 war with Iraq, especially since it came as a result of a shocking incident such as 9/11, those with a different point of view, who were against the war, were often seen not just as dissenters, but as "riding with the terrorists" or "riding with Osama [bin Laden]," who was considered the mastermind of the 9/11 attacks. Sometimes they were even seen as being out-and-out terrorists. These were phrases in quotes in media stories, social media, and commentary that were used often at that fearful time.

CHANGING GOVERNMENT, CHANGING CANADA

By early 2003, the US had decided on how to retaliate: it invaded Iraq, claiming that al-Qaeda—the group led by Osama bin Laden, a Saudi citizen—had been given haven there by the government. Canada declined to join the US and British invasion, which was not supported by the United Nations.

This is not to say that Canada continued just as it had prior to 9/11. In different ways, Maher Arar and Omar Khadr experienced a different Canada than the one that existed before 9/11, as did Sunera Thobani, who has always been outspoken on important social and economic issues. In addition, as Roach points out, we have to acknowledge that Canada was already changing and had been for some time. As an example, by the late 1990s, the Liberal government was more conservative, with more conservative ideas and policies. The Liberals made huge cuts to government and society that broke with many of the policies and traditions of Canadian post–World War II society. Until then, Canada was seen as an open and democratic society where—to the extent possible—citizens had rights, freedoms, and assistance from their government in many ways. For example, starting near the end of World War II, families received a monthly family allowance, informally called the "baby bonus," for each child, and later, and over time, seniors over the age of 70 received old-age security, and retirees received pensions from the government. And there were still other supports to ensure equality for all Canadians (Canadian Encyclopedia, n.d.).

However, in the 1990s, Canada encountered an economic recession, experiencing high unemployment and high interest rates on borrowing. Spurred on by organizations such as the National Citizens' Coalition and the Canadian Taxpayers Association that demanded less government, many citizens became worried about their futures and demanded less taxation to fund universal social programs for those who needed it so that they could use their wages in their own way for their own families rather than have the government redistribute "wealth." It was in this precarious environment in 1995 that the Liberal government made huge cuts to government and these supports for citizenship.

Thus, the reaction of the same Liberal government to 9/11 through its hasty anti-terrorism legislation was already foreshadowed to be overcautious and conservative, if not draconian in the way that it could, for instance, be used to stop legitimate dissent and protests—not just against the new law, but also for any instance that someone might see as linked to terror. This, of course, would be of interest and concern to the media. There was an abundance of information from the government to use in stories, but how much did we see and hear from those who had a different, reasonable, and dissenting point of view, such as the Canadian Centre for Policy Alternatives, to add to the conversation?

Overall, it is not an exaggeration to say that the open and broad society of the post–World War II era in Canada, with all its democratic policies and open citizen discussion in building a just society, was breaking down under the challenge of a major shift in world politics.

MILITARIZING CANADA

Although Canada didn't join the US in the invasion of Iraq in 2003, Canadians still participated in it. Media of all kinds made Canadians aware every day of what was happening, even though they didn't have "boots on the ground." The US vice-president at the time used the phrase "shock and awe" to describe the American assault on Baghdad that started the Iraq war, and indeed, the visuals were spectacular, almost unreal and movie-like. The onslaught was intended to lead to quick surrender by spreading fear and demonstrating the miltary might of the United States. But for whom? The followers of al-Qaeda were not part of the Iraqi government. It seemed opportunistic for the US to dislodge the Iraq government under the guise of finding and eliminating both bin Laden and his followers. Moreover, the shock and awe included a deliberate focus on destroying Baghdad's infrastructure and making it impossible to survive. This meant the deaths of an estimated 500,000 Iraqis between 2003 and 2011 (Vergano, 2013). This is a little less than the population of Surrey, BC.

In the wake of 9/11 and the Iraq war, Canadians and other Western countries became inured to what seemed to be a new reality: instead of the peace and comfort of post–World War II, life was suddenly unstable and risky again—and all of it, of course, disseminated by the media. In other words, the unstable environment that emanated from the 9/11 terror and demanded new vigilance was, as Waisbord (2011) points out, "a form of imposing order and discipline" on citizens (p. 203). This suggested there was or is no end to the possibilities of risk in a society, and we must therefore act as if we are living in a perpetual struggle among different interests, each of which may have any number of risks. The key notion here was that no one saw the risk of 9/11 emerging, and so what else could be on the horizon that could or would change our way of life? With this in mind, what has been called the **risk society** has emerged and gives governments an open door to appeal to citizens (through the media) that whatever they are proposing to do is in the name of peace and security.

In this uncertain environment, not only did the Liberal government in Canada pass a strong anti-terrorism act immediately after 9/11, it also began to adapt its legislative agenda to the needs of an ongoing "war on terror"—not a war with any particular country or at any particular time, but instead focusing on the possible risk that might have an impact on Canadian citizens. And, in reverse, anything that did not fit within the frame of a terror risk could be, and to a degree was, sidelined. One interesting and unexpected aftermath of the emergence of the "risk society" was rebuilding the strength of the state after the cutbacks in government in the 1990s. Unlike the post-war era, this did not include building up social supports for citizens, but instead making the state stronger to resist terror. Defence budgets and other government areas related to security began to grow. While post–World War II governments rebuilt the economy and made the citizenry comfortable in peacetime, a continued threat of terror lay behind most of the post-9/11 legislative activity. As Schiller (2004) pointed out, governments believed that strong legislation was needed within their own countries as a deterrent to ensure anti-terror mechanisms, security, and law and order. Although governments claimed to pass this legislation for the protection of their citizens, it was also in the interest of the government in power that citizens could see that their government was responding to issues that would keep them safe.

Before long, the Anti-terrorism Act was joined by other government actions and legislation that were either tinged with or openly included elements of security. There were two rationales for this. One was the worry of citizens after 9/11 that there could be a terror-driven incident on Canadian soil. The other was a government that needed to quash or deal with that worry while also moving ahead on its own campaign promises and its own agenda. The two elements came together and can be seen in how the government handled its communication to citizens and its legislative agenda.

To understand how the Liberal government managed the concerns of citizens after 9/11, we can look to the very beginning of the public relations industry. Public relations had its beginning in propaganda during World War I and later came into public and government usage. Moreover, many decades later, the Internet was first

BOX 9.3: MILITARIZING HOW WE TALK: CAN YOU THINK OF OTHER MILITARY LANGUAGE USED IN EVERYDAY CONTEXTS?

Ammunition	Over the top
Collateral damage	Rapid-fire questions
Drive-by	Scout out
Dug in	Shot in the dark
Entrenched	Stake out
Escalate	Suicide mission
Handcuffed	Surveillance
Juggernaut	Take down
Long shot	Take-no-prisoners approach
Mission accomplished	Targeted
Outflanked	Trial balloon

Source: Courtesy of Charles Brabazon.

developed for military and security purposes. We also use military language liberally in all walks of life, which sustains the sense of war or conflict. After 9/11, it was believed that Western countries were facing a new threat to their citizens, and the language of patriotism and war—both verbal and visual—became ubiquitous. One instance of this in the United States was the use of that country's flag in the background of television programs, including news reports and situation comedies such as *Friends*. While American news programs are usually not part of our everyday TV consumption, dramas and comedies are, and Canadians were exposed to the full extent of the anguish of Americans after 9/11 and, as good neighbours, shared and were constantly reminded of the horror.

This extended to our own government's public relations, which became entwined with the perception that more security was needed for our own country as well. In that early time after 9/11, this was reasonable given the lack of clarity of what might happen next, especially to a country so close to the US. This concern also found a place in the workings of our government in its legislation. In fact, examining the laws and how those laws are communicated to citizens can give us a sense of how the Liberal government was coping with 9/11 domestically and what kinds of messages the government wanted us to hear. Between 1997 and up to September 11, 2001, 27 of the 138 bills (19.6 percent) that were presented to Parliament for discussion by the Liberal government can be categorized as being about crime and the related issues of defence, security, and immigration—all of these areas seen by the government as key to the possibilities of further terror (Kozolanka, 2015). (Note that bills don't always become laws, so some bills can simply be a message from governments to their citizens that they acknowledge citizens' concerns about, for instance, crime issues, without actually passing a bill into law.) After 9/11 and up to February 2006, when they lost power, the Liberals submitted 59 of 217 bills (27.2 percent) related to these same intertwined subjects. Clearly, the Liberals' legislative agenda was influenced by the possible threat of terror in Canada.

Naturally, it would be expected that the new global concern about terrorism would have upped the Liberals' legislative response to 9/11, but this research did demonstrate a clear and very broad shift to what the Liberal government believed was needed in a post-9/11 way of life. Others were not as certain that some of the initiatives and clauses in the bills, from the Anti-terrorism Act (2001) to the related Public Safety Act (2002) and beyond, were necessary or needed to the extent the Liberals enacted them (Roach, 2003). For instance, as we have seen with the Sunera Thobani example, dissent can sometimes be mistaken as condoning terror during fearful times. Also, all terror-related legislation can have an important impact on a society by sending a message to citizens that their government must be concerned, if not very worried, about a future that could include unending terror and is thus needful of curtailing the rights of its citizens.

In all, the first messages that Canadians received from their government on 9/11 were swift and condemning, and this continued in the years that followed, as seen in the example of the Liberals' legislative agenda. In effect, and in addition to what they were telling Canadians directly, they were also speaking through the legislation they were passing in Parliament. While responding quickly to 9/11, they also normalized terror as an everyday part of our society. Yet the Conservative Party, the official parliamentary opposition, wanted the government to be even stronger on anti-terrorism.

Like Canada, the UK moved quickly to pass anti-terrorism legislation, with five pieces of legislation, the first even before 9/11, in 2000. The UK's second law, the Anti-terrorism, Crime and Security Act, was passed, like Canada's similar law, two months after 9/11. That may have been one of the reasons that the UK experienced the next terrorist attack in the West in 2005. If we had at all become relaxed about security, the multiple bombings in London's subway system were a reminder that everyday routines such as going to work could turn into a disaster at any time and anywhere. Once again, security measures were tightened.

A key difference between old conflicts and new ones is that in the past, wars were declared openly and were fought as full-frontal attacks on the enemy, which was then reciprocated by the other side. (There have been deviations to this unspoken rule, such as the unexpected attack in 1937 during the Spanish Civil War that bombed the small Basque town Guernica to pieces.) But in attacks that have taken place since 9/11, non-combatants—citizens—have been targeted anywhere and anytime. There is no drawing a line that separates one army from another in the way conflicts were handled in the past. That is the purpose of terrorism: the unexpected violence on the unexpected victim. To an extent, no one knows where the next (small or large) battle will take place. This prompts governments to try to cover every possible way of thwarting terror, usually, and as we have already seen, through new laws and a strong police and army presence within the country. Altogether, war is now fought in smaller areas, not in world wars, with multiple small groups, not large armies, that pop up anywhere at any time. Another difference in modern warfare is that some combatants, those whose ideas emanate from how they interpret their religious beliefs, will willingly sacrifice themselves as suicide bombers, whereas in most previous conflicts the hope was to do one's duty, but also survive the conflict.

Over the years since 9/11, there have been many flare-ups of small, localized terrorisms around the globe, from London and Bangkok to Brussels and Jakarta in just this targeted, micro-level way of warfare. Canada felt the sting of terrorism in October 2014, when a single gunman shot and killed a soldier standing guard at the war memorial in Ottawa, then breached security and entered the Parliament buildings. It was a shock that made us much more vigilant.

A SECURITY STATE?

In 2006, the Conservatives became the new federal government with a campaign that focused more on how the Liberals were seen to have been in power too long, and very little on issues regarding terror. Once in office, however, like the Liberals before them, the Conservatives were caught up in the "war on terror." It is useful to remember that over time any political party that uses the word "conservative" to describe itself usually has been seen as a party that supports the military and military actions, and Canada's Conservative Party is no different. In addition, conservative parties in Canada are historically more in sync with American foreign policy.

Within this environment, the new government was also sensitive to the safety of citizens and, like the Liberal government before it, channelled its security concerns into even more legislation. Again, just like the Liberals, the government used legislation as one way to publicize its commitment to public safety. The Conservatives had a new way to ensure that Canadians understood that they were taking security seriously: They tended to use their legislation titles as communication messages targeted at citizens. Instead of the normal title given to bills (such as the "Justice Act"), one such bill was named the "Standing Up for Victims of White Collar Crime Act," while a bill to increase prison sentences, which in the past might have simply been called the "Correctional Services Act," was named the "Serious Time for the Most Serious Crime Act." Another bill was called the "Zero Tolerance for Barbaric Cultural Practices Act." The Conservatives also linked messages and discourses on security outside Canada to crime within Canada and at one point had a government website simply called "Tackling Crime" (usually government websites carry only the name of the department). All of these can be seen as the Conservatives strategically promoting their views to the electorate through the journalists that follow politics.

While the Liberals after 9/11 proposed many bills and enacted considerable legislation on issues of crime, defence, security, and immigration to demonstrate to Canadians that they would safeguard citizens in Canada and abroad, the Conservatives poured more time and energy into their legislative agenda. Having been out of power since 1993, the new government wanted to make sure that conservative views were enacted. While the Liberals had produced 41.5 bills on crime in the four years and six months after 9/11, the Conservatives had 55.5 bills in the next four years and three months. The Liberals' legislation on defence was only 4.0, while the Conservatives had 9.0. The Liberals passed only 2.0 immigration bills, but the Conservatives had 8.0. Altogether, and as noted above, the Liberals used 27.2 percent of their bills on these intertwined subjects related to broad security issues—the Conservatives used far more, 41.2 percent (Kozolanka, 2015).

Overall, the legislation produced by the Conservatives on issues related to anti-terrorism far outweighed those of the previous Liberal government. Clearly, the Conservative government was making a strategic statement on the importance of safety and security that at the same time magnified fear of terror. Throughout this period of time, there were eruptions of terror, big and small, around the world, and it is difficult to say if the Conservatives' fulsome legislative agenda made Canadian citizens any safer. What the government did achieve was to bring terror and security to the constant attention of Canadians, fostering discourses and messages to citizens, amplified by the media, that were framed by 9/11 and our ongoing reaction to it. In the 2015 general election, the Conservatives continued with their theme of fears of terrorist attacks, while both the Liberals and the New Democrats promised to review the two new anti-terror acts enacted by the Conservatives in 2014 and 2015.

CITIZENSHIP IN FEARFUL TIMES

The terror of 9/11 and the incidents that have followed since then have had an impact on Canadians, but the responses by our governments have often been hasty and sometimes overly stringent. While trying to protect Canadians and appease their key world partners—the United Kingdom and the United States—our governments face a difficult task of deciding to what extent legislation and other measures alone can protect citizens inside our country.

Another very real and complex problem is the extent to which Canadian sovereignty is breached by international problems and decisions that are often led by the US and the UK, two superpowers with which Canada shares many values (Roach, 2003). By engaging our military in the American war in Afghanistan from 2003 to 2005, Canada was seen to have followed along behind the US. In doing so, it could be seen as having compromised a long tradition of peacekeeping and neutrality that represents our core values, as well as our independence from the US. (However, it could be said that our involvement in Afghanistan was balanced by our non-involvement in Iraq.)

The lack of world wars has inured many to smaller battles, both within and beyond our borders, as well as to a global "war on terror" that is what Artz (2011) calls "unlimited and unending and requires little justification" (p. 214). If that continues, it could upset Canada's position internationally, as well as its sense of what it means to be Canadian, both in the world and at home. As a trading nation, a peaceful global environment is essential to Canada (Sloan, 2010, p. 488).

In the 21st century, it is clear that the risk of terror and other threats will always be with us, what Dyzenhaus (2001) has called "the permanence of the temporary" (p. 22), and that we need to know how to handle them. Yet such threats also divert us from issues that make Canada the kind of country it was and still wants to be. Terror strikes should remind us of the work ahead on issues such as privacy from surveillance, civil liberties (Wark, 2015; Roach & Forcese, 2015), and democracy (Roach, 2003). These rights and freedoms, once unequivocally part of being Canadian, remain under stress in the "risk society" that has emerged in the 21st century.

THE MEDIA AND TERROR

Any hint of threats to our country are fair for the media to report in their mandate to inform citizens, and the possibilities of doing so in this ongoing era of terror are many. When events and incidents related to terror and death occur normally, there will be 24-hour coverage with both local journalists (wherever the incident is taking place) and their media subsidiaries in Canada working to get all the information they can and turn it into a concise and complete story for the audience at home. Even if there is little to say at first, the media will report it, and citizens will listen to what is being reported, sometimes many times with little additional information, as they wait for the information to be updated.

A key element in global reporting is the visuals of the incident that can be used to add to the coverage and give the viewing audience a sense of the look and the feel of what is happening. To some degree, the repetition of the horror taking place loses its shock and becomes familiar, with the audience even anticipating the moments of bloodshed. The sounds associated with terror are numerous and add to the visual tableau: screams, booms, wails, sirens. The on-site interviews of witnesses show ordinary people caught up in unique circumstances, shocked, gesturing and talking at great speed with a tinge of hysteria. Yet, as such incidents persist, they know what to say, because they have heard what others have said in the same situation. First responders—firefighters and police—are sweaty, tired, gasping and out of breath.

One key example of this spectacle is the American war against Iraq in 2003. At the time, reporters were told that they would be seeing "shock and awe," and indeed photos of that invasion are stunningly and irrevocably real.

Ongoing coverage creates opportunities for governments to demonstrate how they are handling the emergency or crisis. Heads of state look solemn in their dark suits as they decry the terrorism and the loss of life it brings. Journalist Brian Stewart (2015) notes, in these situations,

> the unprecedented influence mainstream and social media news coverage has on governments, which are determined to "seize the narrative" by promising rapid, effective action. The race is to both calm an anxious public and grab political gain by appearing bold.... The complaint is often heard that today governments seem most guided by a series of news strategies to appease a media hungry for drama and the public's demand for quick results whenever the latest headline erupts. (p. 134)

After the incident, cabinet ministers dressed informally tour the site where the terror took place, followed along by the media. Then there are the funerals, the cleanup of the debris, the accusations of fault, and last, the policy and legislative changes to ensure that it doesn't happen again. After the terror incident fades and media stories begin to wane, governments can and often do remind citizens of what happened in order to pursue their own political agendas.

The media cover it all, yet there has been much soul-searching since 9/11 about how journalists should handle such stories. As already noted, the American journalists showed their patriotism openly, and there are still lingering thoughts on what the media role should be. Unlike Americans, it can be said that Canadian society overall is less likely to trumpet the greatness of its country at any time, and even media coverage of the incidents that took place in Ottawa in October 2014 showed less flag-waving than there was deep concern that this had happened in our country. Despite that, should there be further such attacks, what is needed is a careful and judicious media every day that will serve us well in hard times.

QUESTIONS FOR DISCUSSION

1. What military and security role should Canada play in the world?
2. How far should we go to protect Canadians from terror? Would we sanction torture?
3. What are the national and international alternatives to war?
4. Living so close to the US, do we have real sovereignty in times of conflict or war?
5. How should journalists do their work during a war? What should their relationship be with the armed forces and with the government?
6. When government and the media focus on terror, what impact does that have on other national issues?

ASSIGNMENT

Divide into two sides and debate the balance between security and civil liberties in our society. One important example in Canada's history was in 1970 when then prime minister Pierre Trudeau evoked the War Measures Act, which had never previously been used in peacetime. Should we use the act in peacetime, or are there other options? If we should use it, when and to what extent?

WORKS CITED

Artz, L. (2011). The new rhetoric of the global war on terrorism. In Gerald Sussman (Ed.), *The propaganda society: Promotional culture and politics in global context* (pp. 214–228). New York, NY: Peter Lang.

Canada. Library of Parliament. (2006). The USA Patriot Act and Canada's Anti-terrorism Act: Key differences in legislative approach. Jennifer Wispinski, Law and Government Division. Retrieved from www.lop.parl.gc.ca/content/lop/researchpublications/prb0583-e.htm [May 23, 2016].

Canadian Encyclopedia. (n.d.). Old-age pension. Retrieved from www.thecanadianencyclopedia.ca/en/article/old-age-pension/ [May 10, 2016].

Dyzenhaus, D. (2001). The permanence of the temporary: Can emergency powers be normalized? In R. Daniels, P. Macklem, & K. Roach (Eds.), *The security of freedom: Essays on Canada's anti-terrorism bill* (pp. 22–37). Toronto, ON: University of Toronto Press.

Kozolanka, K. (2015). The march to militarism in Canada: Domesticating the global enemy in the post-9/11, neo-liberal nation. *Global Media Journal, Canadian Edition, 8*(1). Retrieved from www.gmj.uottawa.ca/1501/v8i1_e.html [May 20, 2016].

North Atlantic Treaty Organization (NATO). (2016). A political and military alliance. Retrieved from www.nato.int/nato-welcome/ [February 21, 2016].

Ontario Human Rights Commission. (2016). What is racial profiling? Fact sheet. Retrieved from www.ohrc.on.ca/en/what-racial-profiling-fact-sheet [May 6, 2016].

Roach, K. (2003). *September 11: Consequences for Canada.* Montreal, QC, and Kingston, ON: McGill-Queens University Press.

Roach, K., & Forcese, C. (2015). Legislating in fearful and politicized times: The limits of Bill C-51's disruption powers in making us safer. In E. M. Iacobucci. & S. Toope (Eds.), *After the Paris attacks: Responses in Canada, Europe and around the globe* (pp. 141–157). Toronto, ON: University of Toronto.

Rubin, K., & Kozolanka, K. (2014). Managing information: Too much publicity, not enough public disclosure. In K. Kozolanka (Ed.), *Publicity and the Canadian state: Critical communication perspectives* (pp. 195–214). Toronto, ON: University of Toronto Press.

Schiller, D. (2004). *Digital capitalism: Networking the global market system.* Boston, MA: MIT Press.

Sloan, E. (2010). Defense and security. In, J. Courtney & D. E. Smith (Eds.), *The Oxford handbook of Canadian politics* (pp. 488–505). Oxford, UK: Oxford University Press.

Stewart, B. (2015). Journalism and political decision-making in an age of crisis. In E. M. Iacobucci & S. Toope (Eds.), *After the Paris attacks: Responses in Canada, Europe and around the globe* (pp. 131–138). Toronto, ON: University of Toronto.

United Nations. (n.d.). Chapter 1: Purposes and principles. Retrieved from www.un.org/en/sections/un-charter/chapter-i/ [February 21, 2016].

Vergano, D. (2013, October 16). Half-million Iraqis died in the war, new study says. *National Geographic.* Retrieved from www.news.nationalgeographic.com/news/2013/10/131015-iraq-war-deaths-survey-2013/ [May 23, 2016].

Waisbord, S. (2011). Journalism, risk, and patriotism. In B. Zelizer & S. Allan (Eds.), *Journalism after September 11* (2nd ed.) (pp. 269–289). London, UK: Routledge.

Wark, W. (2015). C-51 and the Canadian security and intelligence commuity: Finding the balance for security and rights protections. In E. M. Iacobucci & S. Toope (Eds.), *After the Paris attacks: Responses in Canada, Europe and around the globe* (pp. 167–174). Toronto, ON: University of Toronto.

10 The Role and Future of Journalism in Society

> The health and quality of democracy are linked to the future of journalism in general, and accountability journalism in particular.
> —David Taras, 2015

David Taras, a distinguished Canadian professor of communication, makes an important statement when he connects journalism to democracy. As we noted in the introduction of this book, democracy doesn't spring from nowhere or grow all by itself, but is renewed by the trust we as citizens have in the information that we get from our country's media, and journalism is a key element in this state-citizen relationship in building and maintaining democracy. Some might feel it is going too far to say that journalism and the media have a sacred trust—especially because of the media's traditional role to "speak truth to power," as is often said—but there is truth in this adage. The belief of citizens, journalists, and our leaders in a healthy democracy must be nurtured constantly by journalists and in the media, a trust upon which we all depend. Without that trust relationship, the health and quality of democracy itself becomes vulnerable.

In recent times, however, in countries like Canada with long-standing traditions of independent journalism, it is also said that the news and democracy that carry that sacred trust now have only a "fragile link" (Bennett, 2012, p. 28). This is partly due to the changes to journalism culture that have become intertwined with developments taking place in the media. Many of these changes emerged after the amalgamation of media into mega-corporations, while many who work in traditional media, such as newspapers, have lost their jobs. Much of the upheaval in the media sector and in the future of journalists (and journalism) is due to the huge losses of readers and viewers since the Internet has become a quick, easy, and almost free place to find information and news at the drop of a hat.

This situation has become more troubled, as technology and its ease of information gathering has lessened the need for journalists, while those who remain have become generalists; rather than focusing on only one "beat" or subject area, they instead must cover many different beats. Is it any wonder that the changes to media institutions have had an impact on both journalists and their audiences? Given this, it is understandable that public trust in journalists, which was once seen as a cherished and important profession, is low in the contemporary views of Canadians (Delacourt, 2016).

This chapter will examine the role and history of journalism, how it has changed through history, the key relationship that journalists have with democracy, and issues facing today's journalists. The key question to ask ourselves is how, as citizens, can we identify and have confidence in the information we get from a journalism that has been degraded or swept aside by changes to media organizations and the "everyone is a journalist" ethos of the Internet?

HISTORY AND APPROACHES TO JOURNALISM

Journalism has always had a connection to democracy and citizenship, but not the kind with which we are familiar today. In fact, at the beginning, the concept of "public" itself as being somehow served by the work of journalism and the media was very vague.

In Canada, we can trace our media system back to the 17th and 18th centuries, a time when much of our lives were managed not in Canada itself, but from across the Atlantic Ocean. While the traditions and mores of France influenced Lower Canada, now Quebec, the dominant understanding of how the media worked was situated in England, where philosophers John Locke and John Stuart Mill debated a libertarian or "free press" approach in the 17th and 18th centuries. Taking a libertarian approach, which espoused total freedom of expression, Locke believed in an individual's right to life, liberty, and property, and equated freedom of the press with limitless freedom of expression and speech. Mill agreed with Locke's thinking in the latter's belief that humans were individuals with individual rights, but he added that social beings had a right as well as a social duty to freely express themselves. The newspapers that came out of these debates were to communicate all the information on a subject, and readers were supposed to choose the best ideas and values, with truth being the result. Although intended to extend the idea of the right to freedom of expression and speech, instead, newspapers turned out to be highly politically partisan, with owners divided in their affiliations between the Whigs (or liberals) and the Tories (or conservatives). At that point, journalists as we understand them today did not exist, as newspaper content was short and mostly written by owners who had their own points of view.

Many assumptions and claims underlie the free press approach to media and journalism to this day. That approach assumes that people with opposing viewpoints will be heard equally and that those with wealth and power will not take advantage of their positions to impose their views on others. It also assumes that individuality and individual expression are more important than the common good or collective expression. There is also an assumption that media have the best interest of citizens at heart, rather than their own interests and profits; can both of these goals be realized at the same time?

The United States still values the free press approach to media and journalism, but it also has a strong tradition of **muckraking**, a term that was used for American journalists in the early 1900s who pursued and wrote about social issues, as well as corruption and scandals, in order to stimulate reforms in society. Today, we call that investigative journalism. Muckrakers were responding to and often in opposition to the biased and unreliable **yellow journalism**—sensational and politically partisan journalism—that was practiced in that era.

While the free press approach remains a strong ethos in many democratic countries, especially in opposition to **totalitarianism**, in which the state itself manages information and communication, including the media, there are also approaches to media and journalism that are more democratic. For example, the United Kingdom and Canada have evolved to a social responsibility approach that emerged in the mid-20th century, prompted by the onset of the radio industry, which reached many more citizens. (Social responsibility will be elaborated on below.) It also arose along with the creation of public media through the Canadian Broadcasting Corporation (CBC). At first, that only meant radio, but later broadened to television. (Chapter 5 elaborates on the history of public media.)

In 1947, the United States took a giant step forward when its Hutchins Commission reported on how to maintain a free and responsible press. Here the addition of the word *responsible* was an important safeguard to the older libertarian approach to media and journalism. The report said the media held a privileged position and therefore must always work to be responsible to society. Hutchins also said that the goal of the media should always be to work to be responsible and accountable to society. In effect, the media are a "watchdog" for the public interest.

This is where and when that ideal of journalism as a watchdog originated. While libertarians saw the press as a watchdog against government interference, the social responsibility approach sees the press as needing government involvement of some sort—through a reciprocal journalist-government relationship, for instance—so that it can be an effective watchdog on behalf of society.

The term **social responsibility** itself was coined by the Hutchins Commission to describe the watchdog role of the media. That role includes the responsibility to report the truth, to provide a forum for the exchange of ideas, to be representative of society, to present and clarify the values of society, and to be able to have access to full information.

Here in Canada, in 1981, the Royal Commission on Newspapers (known as the Kent Report) elaborated on the same ideas as the Hutchins Commission. The Kent Report (Canada, 1981) said that it was important for the media to be free—but not free in the sense of individual freedom in the libertarian approach to media. Instead, Kent meant social responsibility in the sense of freedom of the media to report and to publish. Also, media reporting needed to serve democracy and be untainted by things such as bribes or *quid pro quo* exchanges ("you do this for me, and I will do something for you in return"). The social responsibility approach to media tends to balance an individual citizen's rights to freedom with the collective rights of society; both are important. The idea of balance here does not mean equality; instead, balance asks journalists to consider different points of view instead of only relying on and representing one view in a media story.

The social responsibility model remains a key element in today's media and journalism in Canada. While very few journalists would call themselves muckrakers these days, they do see themselves as socially responsible to the public for their reporting. That responsibility function has lessened, if not eradicated, the publisher and owner-led journalism of the past, although media owners still take a strong interest in their media, particularly on the editorial pages.

THE SHIFT TO OBJECTIVE JOURNALISM

However, objectivity in journalism was still slow to catch on: after all, why would owners fund their newspapers to publish someone else's opinions when they could publish their own? W. Lance Bennett's (2012) history of early journalism in the United States resembles the slow Canadian transition away from owner-directed content and toward a less partisan newspaper (p. 198). Historian David Mindich points out that even "the various components of objective journalism emerged at very different points in time" (in Bennett, 2012, p. 197) and lasted into the 20th century, saying that the concept of fairness in reporting occurred early on, although not the now-sacred ideal of objectivity (p. 196). Instead, as with Canada, early American news was not objective, but partisan, with the prevailing Whig and Tory political factions still funnelling their own political interests and ideologies through the newspapers they owned (p. 196).

Changes in society in the 19th century led to the growth of journalism as a fledgling profession that had its own rules and practices. Industrialization swiftly changed society, with many technological developments and inventions that fed the needs of markets for increased production of goods. In Canada, Osborne and Pike (2009) note that not only did industry expand, but rural citizens also began to migrate from farms into the cities (p. 75). Electrification also transformed both work and home life, making evening activities and night shifts possible. Modern society then developed forms of transportation such as railways to move people and goods, and—importantly—communication (see also Chapter 5). The telegraph lines, which ran along the railway lines, provided information for business, government, workers, and citizens. Telegraph development in Canada was slower than in the United States, with our first telegraph connecting Toronto and Hamilton in 1846, and further links from Hamilton to Halifax in 1849 (Kesterton, 1967). Kesterton notes that the technological and industrial revolution that was "seemingly unconnected with journalism has nonetheless affected journalism by altering the social environment of which journalism is a part" (p. 82). Along with a changing social environment, space and use of mass production allowed for the use of advertising in newspapers, which kept many newspapers publishing.

As to the media, Bennett (2012) points out that these monumental shifts in technology that began to change society also produced what he saw as "dramatic changes" in the news industry (p. 198). New printing technologies and transportation through telegraph wires disseminated news and information faster and across vast areas, which was particularly welcome in large countries like Canada and the United States. Kesterton (1967) also notes that the increase in literacy in Canada "enlarged potential readership"; however, at the same time, "mailing costs were high" and, far too often, money for subscriptions, which was collected after the fact, was never paid (p. 24). Despite the perils of newspaper publishing, by 1900, Canada had 1,226 newspapers, after having merely 23 in 1864 (p. 39). At that time, they were still run by publishers, and 84 of them were weeklies, not dailies.

The telegraph itself had an important impact on how journalists conducted their daily work. With news and information moving swiftly through the railway and telegraph network, in 1846, a group of American newspaper owners formed the Associated Press and used these technological developments to standardize and distribute the same news to all its subscribers across the nation (p. 198). These "wire services" were also used in Canadian media before the Canadian Press was set up in 1907 (Kesterton, 1967, p. 159). A further development that emerged from the use of the telegraph for communicating news was the "five Ws," that is, the use of key questions (who, what, why, when, where, and sometimes how) to standardize the dissemination of information to readers simply and quickly. One development was specifically important: with larger readership, standardized news needed to be less partisan. Kesterton (1967) notes that by 1900, several informal professional organizations for journalists had come into being, starting with the Canadian Press Association (CPA) in 1859. The CPA worked to "overcome the factious and divisive spirit which characterized both the political and journalistic life of the country at the time" (pp. 55–56). In this way, journalism became less tied to owners and their personal beliefs and began to become "objective," which usually meant having more than one point of view in a news story. The ideal of objectivity, which remains strong in journalism and to journalists to this day, is nonetheless still an ethos that is controversial: Aren't there more than two points of view on an issue? And are all equally important?

Although objectivity is practiced throughout journalism today, it should also be stated that the media are owned by individuals or groups that can decide to publish their personal views on an issue. This is usually done through editorials, but those who analyze media output often characterize where individual media come down ideologically. For instance, the *Globe and Mail* is mostly seen as a "conservative" newspaper, while the *Toronto Star* is mostly seen as "liberal."

One important historical development in Canadian journalism took place in 1866, when the newly built Parliament buildings included space for the media in their gallery overlooking the House of Commons (Canadian Parliamentary Press Gallery, 2016). The history of the Parliamentary Press Gallery (PPG), a voluntary and self-governing entity (Kesterton, 1967, p. 162), indicates that foreign correspondents were accommodated, although no female journalist was allowed in until 1922! The space given to journalists in the House when the Parliament buildings were built marked the approval of the growing need for politicians to let citizens across the country know what their governments were doing in Ottawa. Altogether, the PPG assisted in broadening specifically Canadian reporting.

A key point in the history of journalism encompasses both American and Canadian shifts in reporting over time. Not only was reporting now standardized through journalism's standards and codes of ethics, but the need to keep newspapers afloat also required reporting that was more objective, which required a larger fleet of reporters. A further consideration was the need for reporters who could tell objective stories using the five Ws (rather than opinion), which would sell more newspapers and not alienate readers. Over time, "overlapping effects of communication technology, economic development, and social change gave rise to large-scale news gathering and news-marketing organizations," while journalism itself was seen as a profession that "developed a set of business practices first" (Bennett, 2012, pp. 198–199). In other words, business still came before journalism. Even when some newspapers could be seen to lean to one political point of view over another, for the most part, those views were left to the editorial pages.

EARLY JOURNALISM AND INVESTIGATIVE JOURNALISM

According to Cecil Rosner (2008), the first person who could be called an investigative reporter was hired by Canada's first newspaper, the *Halifax Gazette*, which began publishing in 1752—not that the owner knew that Isaiah Thomas had already worked for a Boston newspaper that was "a hotbed of republican ideology" (p. 16). It was to be a short career, as the Canadian authorities questioned him after seeing his work and then sent him back to Boston.

The first long-lasting journalists of the early 1800s in Canada were William Lyon Mackenzie, publisher and owner of the *Welland Canal* in southern Ontario, and Fleury Mesplet, who published *La Gazette littéraire* in Montreal. Mesplet brought with him from France a particularly "revolutionary fervour" (Rosner, 2008, p. 17), which quickly got him into trouble when he challenged a local judge's decision in the *Gazette* and was arrested. What Canadian authorities didn't understand or take into consideration was that the winds of democracy were in the air, as the revolutions in America in 1776 and in France in 1789 had made for more democratic societies.

Rosner (2008) notes that in Upper Canada and Lower Canada, the magistrates who were the authorities were harsh with their penalties for muckraking, but they were even more so in the Maritimes. Malicious intent and criminal libel were the common accusations made against publishers and editors. In this harsh environment, in 1835, the *Novascotian* printed a letter addressed to its publisher, Joseph Howe, that was signed "The People." The letter included many grievances that the authors laid on the heads of the magistrates who controlled Halifax. Instead of seeking out the authors who wrote the letter, the magistrates arrested Howe for seditious libel. Howe's six-hour oration to the jury became a key moment for democracy in litigation in Canada. Howe was acquitted by the jury after only 10 minutes of deliberation and "rightly proclaimed a victory for press freedom" (Rosner, 2008, p. 20).

The work of William Lyon Mackenzie offers a second important example of early journalism in Canada. Unlike Howe's showy oration, Mackenzie followed what we today would think of as investigative journalism. He considered the ruling class—the **Family Compact** government—to be "avowed enemies of common schools, of civic and religious liberty, of all legislative or other checks to their own will" (Rosner, 2008, p. 21), but he also focused his exposés on banks, the government, and the police. These were often the targets of investigative journalism at the time, but Mackenzie also investigated how Upper Canada and America treated their Black citizens (p. 23). Later on, and still a journalist, Mackenzie was elected to the Legislative Assembly in 1828 and continued to be active in his muckraking, often using one of his two professions to assist the other (p. 23). The rebellions of 1837 and 1838 against the government quashed most of the muckraking impulse, and Mackenzie, who had led the rebellion in Upper Canada, left for the United States (p. 26).

WOMEN AND JOURNALISM

Although it started as a male-dominated profession—let's face it, so did most professions—today's journalists tend to be women. And just as it was for other professions, women had to push their way through the **glass ceiling**.

Although not formerly labelled as a muckraker, and though her contribution is often forgotten, American-born Mary Anne Shadd Cary became the first female editor in North America by running an anti-slavery newspaper, the *Provincial Freeman*, based in Windsor, Ontario. She and her family had moved to Canada from the United States in 1853. Although her time in Canada was relatively short—after her husband died in 1860, she returned to the United States—she travelled across both countries advocating for racial integration.

Sara Jeanette Duncan worked her first few years in the 1880s as a journalist in her hometown of Brantford, Ontario, then at *The Globe* in Toronto, and later wrote a column for *The Star* (Montreal) on social events. By the time she was 24, she was a reporter with the *Washington Post*. Susan Crean writes in her 1985 book *Newsworthy: The Lives of Media Women* that Duncan's biographer said she was "amusing, opinionated and steely" and "the range of her subject matter was broad, her tone cosmopolitan … [and] she was thoroughly modern and adamant" (p. 17). (Later, in 1904, Sara Jeanette Duncan wrote *The Imperialist*, one of the first novels that could be considered Canadian.) Kit Coleman immigrated to Canada in 1884 and got a job editing a weekly women's page at *The Mail* (Toronto)—a first for a woman. Her space in the newspaper became popular and was quickly expanded to a full page, and its scope broadened from "just" a women's page to items that included travel and eyewitness reports (Freeman, 1989). Her "Woman's Kingdom," as she called it, "became one of the most distinctive sections of the newspaper and was read avidly by men as well as women" (p. 19). Cora Hind, as a young orphan in the care of her aunt, moved from Ontario to a Winnipeg that in 1882 was just beginning to become a city. As a young woman, she earned a living by learning how to type on a new machine called the typewriter and eventually had her own business as a public stenographer. Crean says Hind learned to type up the reports of meetings of farmers and wranglers, which the *Winnipeg Free Press* would then publish. Her break into journalism came when she was asked to gather information on a crop in a farm field. By 1901, she was the agriculture editor and her annual accurate estimate of crop yields became famous. Crean (1985) points out that Hind was also a feminist and a suffragist, ready to help with campaigns for women's rights "anywhere in the Dominion [of Canada]" (p. 26).

While Duncan, Coleman, and Hind became journalists, they were not allowed into the inner sanctums of editing or publishing. However, their work gave credence to issues and information that normally had not been seen in newspapers previously. Still, the impact of a small number of gutsy women journalists was limited, as they were mostly trying to achieve what the male journalists did (such as Hind, who even wore men's clothes in her travels)—although Coleman's women-focused pages slowly chipped away at male privilege in her profession and in society. As Crean notes about these pioneering women journalists, "with each new invention, new organizations were set up and new standards were devised, by men. Each time, women had to start over again at the bottom" (p. 12).

JOURNALISM AS A PROFESSION

Throughout this same era and well into the 20th century, journalism was establishing its own rules as a fledgling profession. Kesterton (1967, p. 39) indicates that between 1857 and 1900, periodicals in British North America (Canada) grew from 291 to 1,226. Different bodies, such as the Canadian Press Association (1859), the Parliamentary Press Gallery (1867), the Canadian Press (1907), and the United Press International of Canada (1907) were formed and marked the institutionalization of journalism and its growing professionalism.

Yet journalism was still not considered to be a noble profession. The muckrakers had rankled the authorities, and there was an ongoing adversarial relationship with anyone in power. However, journalists who covered parliamentary news were considered to be at the peak of their profession, and in covering the politicians in Ottawa, often created strong relationships with them. This would benefit both the politicians, who would get their messages out to the public, and the journalists, who would have a story to file. This relationship remains strong to this day, although much tempered by both sides, who know they have to keep the relationship healthy and serve the public.

Two important areas have marked the historical development of journalism as a profession: the norms of the profession and the education of journalists. Early journalists had established their own personal styles of writing, but the later use of the five Ws to organize the content of media stories was the first important step in journalists standardizing their stories. Later innovations such as a concise first sentence also focused the reader on the key point of a news story. The long and detailed storytelling of early print media gave way to shorter stories with less flowery descriptions, while the personal opinions of the writer ceded to reporting the facts—a new concept that was intended to make a story accurate rather than personal and subjective. Over the late 19th century and into the 20th, news values were developed that helped journalists and editors to triage the importance of their stories and arrange them accordingly in their newspapers. As literacy grew in a population, and there was more demand for news, different areas of public interest were organized into sections of the newspaper. Reporters became specialists in different areas on these so-called beats, which ranged from municipal news to business to the women's page.

As mentioned above, a further and important norm of journalism was objectivity. The new journalists did not seek to insert their own views or commentary into their stories, but instead looked to present different points of view to their readers, leaving readers to make their own decisions on what had happened or who was right in the story. In itself, objectivity was a key element that would demonstrate that journalists were not the lackeys of newspaper owners and publishers, but were an intermediary reporting the facts and letting readers use their own judgment. For a very long time, the ethos of objectivity was the core of modern journalism and signalled that it was an actual profession because stories included different points of view and not simply someone's (maybe even just the journalist's) personal opinions.

The need for objectivity has strong advocates and perhaps just as many strong critics. Objectivity suggests that sources need to be found, interviewed, and sourced in media stories for the different ideas expressed. It also suggests that there are usually only two solid sides to a story and that both sides need to have equal space or perhaps be balanced in a media story. Further, sources that are used need to be authoritative, usually through their employment status or because they were an eyewitness. This raises some questions. Does the source who is articulate and has a good employment status have a better chance to get into a media story than a mere eyewitness? In other words, are all sources equal and treated equally? What if the event or whatever happened had two eyewitnesses, each with a different sense of what happened—or perhaps there was no eyewitness? These are the kinds of issues that make journalism difficult in practice. Here, Bennett (2012) suggests that clinging to objectivity actually results in the "most serious biases" precisely because journalists "default to authorities and officials as surrogates for objectivity" (p. 188). Bennett and others prefer concepts such as *accuracy, balance, fairness,* and even *comprehensiveness* to describe good reporting (p. 195). (Interestingly, the use of *objectivity* to describe good journalism goes back to the time in the mid- to late 19th and early 20th centuries when journalists aspired to be seen as professionals and so had to jettison their own partisan political roots (Bennett, 2012, p. 198).

As reporting became codified and journalists more organized, a further mark of journalism as a profession was the onset and growth of schools to train journalists. This also had the result of synchronizing and setting out a canon to standardize journalism itself. The first Canadian program in journalism began at Carleton College (now Carleton University in Ottawa) in 1946 (Kesterton, 1967, p. 164). By 2016, Canada had 67 undergraduate journalism programs in colleges and universities across the country, as well as 12 masters programs (Universities Canada, 2016).

Another tangible sign of the development of journalism as a profession was the printing of a style guide in 1940, published by the Canadian Press (CP), that has been updated in many editions since then, although now it is online. The foreword of the 1974 version says the CP is "[r]esponsible to the public and to its members for an accurate and impartial picture of the world's news" and that it "strives also for a report forcefully written and in conformity with good taste." It has a companion guide, *Caps and Spelling*. The style guide was also translated into French as *Guide du journaliste* (1978).

THE NEW "JOURNALISMS"

Journalism has evolved from its initial one-person owner-writer setup to encompass many different ways to produce and share information with citizens. It has evolved over time for many reasons that range from war to technology. Along the way, media history has also been populated by outstanding journalists whose careers moved the initial partisanship of journalism forward and opened the way for new "journalisms."

As journalists themselves have coalesced into their own professional organizations, they have explored new ways of "doing" journalism. They engage in different kinds of media work, serving broader interests of their publishers and editors yet also needing to keep the public trust. Moreover, in a fast-paced world, they have to be flexible to survive. This last point has been taken up by the Pew Center, an American non-partisan "fact-tank" that conducts research on journalism in the US. In a fast-paced and digital world, the centre maintains that new kinds of journalism are needed. Two ways to achieve a new journalism that would work in the 21st century stand out: *public (or civic) journalism* and *citizen journalism* that would renew journalism.

Over time, there have been rumbles about the state of journalism by journalists themselves. In the 1990s, Jay Rosen (1999), a writer on media and a professor at New York University, asked a deceptively simple question: What are journalists for? Even before asking that question, he had a sense that the public that was at the core of theories on democracy did not resemble how the public actually acted. If that was the case, then the ideal of the media's role of informing the public didn't exist either. Further, if we couldn't say that there was a public ready to absorb what journalists—the intermediary between the public and the world in which it lives—were producing, what did that say about our democracy? Rosen felt that informing people wasn't the journalist's first step; instead, it was to improve the chances that a real public might emerge. Only then could a real public be truly informed. This was the ideal of public (or civic) journalism.

By public journalism, Rosen meant that there was more to journalism than the traditional norms of observation and objectivity. Instead, he believed journalists should foster public participation by using their professional expertise and knowledge of audiences to enrich their stories. In other words, they should serve the public, including becoming part of communities, and should do this by building on eyewitness accounts from those communities. The key was that public journalists should actively engage citizens in the democratic process at the grassroots level. An example of public journalism could be identifying an issue of importance with the help of a community—for example, vandalism at a community centre—and holding a community meeting to discuss the problem and work on a solution. The journalist would then cover the meeting, its decisions, and its plan of action. Public journalism was a mixed bag: it opened a way for the public to participate in community and news making, but journalists, not the public, still set the agenda.

A different kind of journalism, called citizen journalism, arose in the early 2000s, with its key element as "user-generated content," that is, ordinary citizens (users) acting spontaneously as journalists. An example was the huge amount of smartphone traffic and social media by citizens during the attacks on September 11, 2001, which updated what was happening in real time in New York as the World Trade Center towers collapsed. Usually the real-time sharing of images and other information online emanates from people at or close to the scene of the event.

The key point of citizen journalism was that it empowered citizens to act as on-the-scene reporters, facilitated by their own hand-held technology (for example, smartphones). Dan Gillmor, author of the book *We the Media: Grassroots Journalism by the People, for the People* (2004), says this in effect empowers citizens to take charge of what is happening within their own environments. He suggests that these interventions by ordinary citizens form "the first draft of history" (p. xx) to which other citizen journalists can then add their own facts and commentary. One example is the unauthorized photos taken of captured Iraqi soldiers being humiliated and tortured that leaked out of the Abu Ghraib prison near Baghdad, Iraq, in 2006. Another example is when, in Minnesota in 2016, a Black driver who was stopped by a White police officer because of a broken tail-light live-streamed the officer shooting her Black boyfriend five times, even though her boyfriend said clearly that he was reaching for his wallet after the officer demanded some identification. The incident was flashed quickly around the country and also appeared in Canadian newscasts.

This first-person media-making has become normal, but seldom is as tragic or as important as these examples. A limitation of citizen journalism is that people often want to hear from other people just like them, rather than professional journalists. In this way, they may not hear the different points of view that journalists can bring to an issue. A persistent problem is that many hand-held amateur videos are of poor quality or of little consequence beyond the people who make them. Citizen journalism's impact on formal journalism is challenging, as it tends to increase the work of professional journalists, because they now need to monitor and use social media along with the rest of their work.

Public journalism and citizen journalism renewed journalism by mostly influencing media content, that is, the types of stories themselves. A later and more critical form of journalism focused instead on media *systems* and organizations (corporations). In other words, these critical alternative media recast journalism by going beyond the often mainstream media focus on content only ("what happened?") and instead considering why and how the *society* we live in plays a role in what has happened. (For more understanding of alternative journalism, see Chapter 2.)

This recasting of journalism goes beyond merely renewing journalism itself. Instead, those who can be called "advocacy journalists" or "justice journalists" go beyond changing media practice (although that is a goal as well) and want to restructure media systems to be more democratic—to be open and inclusive of many different views and organize the system itself to accommodate them.

An important aspect of alternative journalism is the rejection of objectivity found in mainstream media. Instead, these media have a clear interest in a democratic society where democratic media cannot be neutral, nor do those in alternative media want it to be so. Their work is to foster a more democratic society through progressive media. Again, to do that, they go beyond merely changing *content* and focus on democratizing the media *system* through the way they themselves produce their stories.

One well-known alternative journalism outlet is Rabble.ca, a not-for-profit organization founded in 2001. It encourages readers to be contributors, as well as to engage in dialogues with the writers online. Its mandate is clear in that it "delivers intentionally progressive journalism" (Rabble.ca, n.d.) and details its journalistic principles. Rabble.ca carries newswire lists of other alternative media in Canada, which include Toronto Media Co-op, *Briarpatch*, Alternet, TheTyee.ca, and *Canadian Dimension* (see the chapter on alternative media). In the US, the radio show *Democracy Now!* is prominent and its feed can be found on stations across Canada. In addition, OpenMedia.org lobbies for an open, equally accessible and affordable, and surveillance-free Internet.

JOURNALISM AND MEDIA LITERACY TODAY

While the profession of journalism has grown and matured over the years, the current state of the media hampers its future. The diagnosis for newspapers is grim: corporate media continue to consolidate while shrinking newsroom capacities (Watson, 2016) and, at the same time, the accelerated 24-hour news cycle demands constant updating. The journalists that are left after the downsizing of media operations have to multi-task on multiple media platforms, as well as constantly update their stories. This may include having their own websites, blogging and engaging in social media, as well as responding to the constant pings that signal new emails. In 2018, as a sign of changing times, the journalism program at Carleton University exchanged its print community newspaper with its 15,000 circulation in downtown Ottawa for an entirely online, modified version called CentreTownNews.ca.

What will journalism be like today? The concern is that when journalism falters or is curtailed, media literacy—the way we see and act based on what information we receive from the media—is also diminished. Frederick Fletcher (2014), a professor emeritus at York University, has studied journalism and the media for many years. He has a broad concern for democracy in an environment that fragments and "erodes common understanding of the public sphere" (pp. 39–40). He specifically notes how the more minimalized role of journalists "reduces the range of perspectives needed to promote democratic debates and places limits on the kind of journalism that holds governments to account" (p. 36).

Bennett (2012) also laments the ongoing fragile link between news and democracy, asking a key question: "Why is something as important as public information left to the current turbulent mix of business profit imperatives, political spin techniques and consumer tastes?" (p. 28). Yet journalists continue to need to work in environments that are strapped by these blockages to good journalism.

But has there ever been a time that needs journalism and media literacy more? Gidengil's (2012) research shows that the Canadian public is "not simply uninformed about politics; they are *mis*informed about basic policy-relevant facts" (p. 43), while Alboim (2012) reports that only 30 percent of Canadians are active in civic life. Taras (2015) calls it a politics of "mutual withdrawal" (p. 244) by both journalists and citizens. Is there a remedy for this? Fletcher (2014) maintains that journalism needs to engage citizens and inform them through

BOX 10.1: HOW CAN CITIZENS THINK MORE CREATIVELY ABOUT INFORMATION THEY SEE IN THE MEDIA?

W. Lance Bennett (2012, pp. 266–272) suggests some key ways that we can understand and assess media output. The five keys below can be useful in deciding if a media story ensures that those consuming the media can distinguish a complete and useful story from one that is lacking:

1. Recognize stereotypes and plot formulas.
2. Look for information that doesn't fit the plot.
3. Recognize spin and news control in action.
4. Learn to become self-critical.
5. Find sources of perspective, such as political comedy.

critical assessments (p. 42). This might happen less through traditional media as we know it, and more through alternative media or social media innovations. But either way, a strong democracy along with public trust will always demand good journalism, and good journalism needs to be based on the strength and calibre of media literacy.

QUESTIONS FOR DISCUSSION

1. Do journalists play a role in enforcing the rules of society by pointing out problems that arise and helping to change society (such as through partnerships with local citizen groups)? Should they? Or is their role only to identify the problems they report on and leave them for others to resolve?
2. Have you ever been interviewed by a journalist, and if so, how did the actual finished story compare to the interview? Was the focus of the story where you expected it to be? Was it factually accurate and did it tell a complete story? Would you do or say anything different the next time you get interviewed?
3. How much do we need to know about the personal lives of politicians and other public figures, and should journalists report on them?
4. How are ordinary citizens portrayed in the media compared to other sources? How can the media increase public discussion? How can citizens themselves have their voices heard?

ASSIGNMENTS

1. Choose an event that took place locally or nationally. Research two or three different media on the event, and analyze the similarities and differences using the following: length of the story, placement of the story on the page (for a newspaper) or in the lineup on the main page (for a website), who wrote the story, differences in language. Some different media could be: online news, a newspaper, a radio story, or a local community newspaper. How are they different and how are they the same? Think about interviews (who and how many), as well as photos and other graphics (or there may be none). What can each of these media tell us about what is important and needed in their work?
2. Either by yourself or in a small group, research a local mainstream media journalist. Monitor changes to their stories and commentary over a period of two or three days. How often does the journalist update their stories, add to social

media, and respond to readers/viewers? (It would be good to communicate in advance with the journalist you choose, who, for instance, might be open to sharing numbers or issues in emails from readers.) Share your research and compare information found by all groups. How much time do the journalists spend on responding to emails and social media every day? How does this compare to the amount of time they work on their main story of the day? Discuss issues facing today's journalists.

WORKS CITED

Alboim, E. (2012). On the verge of total dysfunction: Government, media, and communications. In D. Taras & C. Waddell (Eds.), *How Canadians communicate IV: Media and politics* (pp. 45–54). Athabasca, AB: Athabasca Press.

Bennett, W. L. (2012). *News: The politics of illusion* (9th ed.). Glenview, IL: Pearson.

Canada. Royal Commission on Newspapers (Kent Report). (1981). Retrieved from http://epe.lac-bac.gc.ca/100/200/301/pco-bcp/commissions-ef/kent1981-eng/kent1981-eng.htm [July 19, 2016].

Canadian Parliamentary Press Gallery. (2016). History of the press gallery. Retrieved from www.press-presse.ca/en/information/history-of-the-press-gallery [July 9, 2016].

Canadian Press. (1974). *CP style book: A guide for writers and filing editors*. Ottawa, ON: The Canadian Press. (Original work published 1940).

Crean, S. (1985). *Newsworthy: The lives of media women*. Toronto, ON: Stoddart.

Delacourt, S. (2016). Who do we trust? Journalists, maybe. Politicians, not so much. *iPolitics*. Retrieved from ipolitics.ca/2016/04/26/who-do-we-trust-journalists-maybe-politicians-not-so-much.html [June 16, 2016].

Fletcher, F. J. (2014). Journalism, corporate media, and democracy in the digital age. In K. Kozolanka (Ed.), *Publicity and the Canadian state: Critical communication perspectives* (pp. 27–48). Toronto, ON: University of Toronto Press.

Freeman, B. (1989). *Kit's kingdom: The journalism of Kathleen Blake Coleman*. Ottawa, ON: Carleton University Press.

Gidengil, E. (2012). The diversity of the Canadian political marketplace. In A. Marland, T. Giasson, & J. Lees-Marshment (Eds.), *Political marketing in Canada* (pp. 39–56). Vancouver, BC: UBC Press.

Gillmor, D. (2004). *We the media: Grassroots journalism by the people, for the people*. Sebastopol, CA: O'Reilly Media.

Kesterton, W. (1967). *A history of journalism in Canada*. Toronto, ON: McClelland & Stewart.

La Presse Canadienne. (1978). *Guide du journaliste*. Montreal, QC: The Canadian Press.

Osborne, B., & Pike, R. (2009). Lowering "the walls of oblivion": The revolution in postal communications in central Canada, 1851–1911. In D. J. Robinson (Ed.), *Communication history in Canada* (2nd ed.) (pp. 71–79). Don Mills, ON: Oxford University Press.

Rabble.ca. (n.d.). Journalistic policy. Retrieved from http://rabble.ca/about/journalistic-policy.

Rosen, J. (1999). *What are journalists for?* Boston, MA: Yale University Press.

Rosner, C. (2008). *Behind the headlines: A history of investigative journalism in Canada.* Don Mills, ON: Oxford University Press.

Taras, D. (2015). *Digital mosaic: Media, power, and identity in Canada.* Trent, ON: University of Toronto Press.

Universities Canada. (2016.) Programs search results with keyword "journalism." Retrieved from www.universitystudy.ca/search/?q=journalism [July 21, 2016].

Watson, H. G. (2016). Media concentration climbs in Canada as newsrooms shrink. *J-Source.* Retrieved from www.j-source.ca/article/media-concentration-climbs-canada-newsrooms-shrink [June 16, 2016].

GLOSSARY

Basques: Members of a people living in the Basque Country of France and Spain. Culturally one of the most distinct groups in Europe, the Basques were largely independent until the 19th century.*

Bias: An inclination toward a certain perspective, or a personal and sometimes unreasoned judgment.

British North America Act (BNA Act) of 1867: Legislation of the British Government that allowed four British colonies (Nova Scotia, New Brunswick, Quebec, and Ontario) to become four provinces in the new Dominion of Canada. The BNA Act became a major part of Canada's original Constitution, and defined its federal structure and justice system. It also outlined certain conditions the federal government must adhere to in relation to First Nations peoples.

Climate Change: Changes in the Earth's weather patterns; 97 percent of scientists claim that it is currently happening because of an increase of certain gases in our atmosphere that trap infrared radiation. An increase in carbon dioxide from the burning of fossil fuels is believed to be the main cause of climate change today.

Colonialism: A policy of acquiring or maintaining colonies; the exploitation or subjugation of a people by a larger or wealthier power, sometimes through the creation of colonies.*

Colonization: The act of controlling a people through influencing their thinking, experiencing, and social arrangements, often through educational means and transforming their language, system of governance, and cultural and religious practices.

Conservatism: A political ideology that supports traditional social hierarchies along axes of gender, race, and social class. Although there are different interpretations in different locations, in general it supports religion, monarchy, and property rights, and is opposed to minority rights. By the late 20th century, it had adopted *neoliberalism* as its economic doctrine.

Cultural Genocide: Actions by a powerful group over a people that have the aim or effect of depriving the latter of their integrity as a distinct people, or of their cultural values. It usually involves the eradication of cultural artifacts, the suppression of cultural activities, and the dispossession of the land and resources of the oppressed people.

Cultural Studies: An innovative interdisciplinary field of research and teaching that investigates the ways in which "culture" creates and transforms individual experiences, everyday life, social relations, and power. Cultural studies is also a field of theoretically, politically, and empirically engaged cultural analysis that concentrates upon the political dynamics of contemporary culture, its historical foundations, defining traits, and conflicts.

Enlightenment: Also known as the Age of Reason, it was an intellectual and philosophical movement that dominated European thought during the 18th century. The ideas were based on reason as the primary source of authority and legitimacy. It advanced ideals like liberty, progress, tolerance, and the separation of church and state. Science and the scientific method undermined the authority of the church.

Ethnological: The branch of knowledge that deals with the characteristics of different peoples and the differences and relationships between them.*

Family Compact: A name given to the ruling class in Upper Canada in the early 19th century, especially to the members of the legislature and executive councils.*

Filter Bubble: The intellectual isolation that can occur when websites make use of algorithms to selectively assume the information a user would want to see, and then give information to the user according to this assumption. Websites make these assumptions based on the user's browsing history and location. For that reason, the websites are more likely to present only information that will abide by the user's past activity. A filter bubble can cause users to get significantly less contact with contradicting viewpoints, causing the user to become intellectually isolated.

Glass Ceiling: An invisible barrier that keeps women and minorities from receiving their due status in society because they are seen as inferior to privileged groups.

Hegemony: The social, cultural, ideological, or economic influence exerted by a dominant group through persuasion or coercion. Power is gained by the dominant group through the acceptance by the masses of its interests as universal interests.

Identity Politics: A tendency for people of a particular religion, race, social background, etc., to form exclusive political alliances, moving away from traditional broad-based party politics.*

Intersectionality: The complex, cumulative ways in which multiple forms of discrimination (such as racism, sexism, classism, and homophobia) combine, overlap, or intersect, especially in the experiences of marginalized individuals or groups.

Islamophobia: Dislike of or prejudice against Islam or Muslims, especially a political force.*

Keynesian Economics: An economic doctrine developed by British economist John Maynard Keynes that encourages government intervention in order to stimulate the capitalist economy. This includes spending on public works. Franklin D. Roosevelt's New Deal is an example of Keynesian economics put into practice.

Liberalism: A political ideology founded on democratic ideals and the rights of the individual. Although there are different interpretations in different locations, in general it supports democracy, freedom of speech, freedom of the press, freedom of religion, and human rights, including minority rights. Free markets or laissez-faire economics is considered to be part of classical liberalism, but in the 20th century reformed liberalism accepted *Keynesian economics* and the social welfare state. In the late 20th century, it has mostly adopted *neoliberalism* as its economic doctrine.

Libertarian: An advocate of liberty, especially of an almost absolute freedom of expression and action, and/or a believer in free will.*

Meritocracy: A system in which it is believed that people are chosen and moved ahead of others on the basis of their talent, skill, or achievement.

Muckrake: To search out and reveal scandal, especially among famous people.*

Multicultural: Designing or pertaining to a society consisting of many culturally distinct groups; advocating or receptive to the establishment of a multicultural society; consisting of individuals from various, culturally distinct groups.*

Neoliberalism: An economic paradigm that promotes corporate power through tax cuts, privatization of the commons, deregulation of private industry, regulation of the public sector, and diminished collective bargaining rights of workers. Also known as the corporate agenda, it is very similar to the laissez-faire economics of the Industrial Revolution. In the West it is strongest among English-speaking nations, most likely because of American *hegemony*.

Panama Papers: An example of investigative journalism involving dozens of media outlets across several countries, it includes 11.5 million documents that detail financial information for over 200,000 offshore entities, including many shell companies. The documents belong to the Panamanian law firm Mossack Fonseca, which coordinated tax havens for wealthy politicians, athletes, artists, business people, and corporations. The purpose of this arrangement was to avoid paying taxes.

Partisanship: A firm adherence to a particular party, ideology, or cause, usually exhibiting blind, prejudiced, and unreasoned allegiance.

Péquistes: Members of the Parti Québécois (Quebec Party) in Canada.

Postmodernism: A late 20th-century style and concept in the arts, architecture, and criticism that represents a departure from modernism and has at its heart a distrust of grand theories and ideologies as well as a problematical relationship with any notion of "art."

Poststructuralism: A school of thought based in mid-20th-century European and especially French philosophy. It is related to *postmodernism* in its claim that there are multiple interpretations of a text, but puts much more emphasis on power in language itself, and its role in influencing social relations and what constitutes the truth.

Propaganda: Ideas, allegations, opinions, or facts deliberately spread to either further a particular cause or to damage an opposing cause; it especially applies to public discourse.

Racial Profiling: The use of race or ethnicity as grounds for suspecting someone of having committed an offence.

Risk Society: In 1986, Ulrich Beck coined the term *risk society*, saying that it follows the 20th century's period of industrialization and is based on threats to advanced industrial society that were created through industrialization and its knowledge itself.

Royal Proclamation of 1763: A decree by King George III to manage newly acquired French colonies that forbade expansion of White settlements west of the Appalachian Mountains. The proclamation is important to First Nations people today as it acknowledges their system of nations, and provides legal support for land *treaties* and Aboriginal *title*.

Social Democracy: A political ideology that is considered to be a hybrid of *liberalism* and *socialism*, it supports minority rights and democracy, but offers stronger support for the commons, workers' rights, and *Keynesian economics* than liberalism. In Canada the New Democratic Party is a social democratic party. The Nordic states of Norway, Sweden, Denmark, and Finland are considered to be true social democracies as conservative parties in those countries adhere to social democratic principles.

Social Responsibility: An ethical framework that has an obligation to act for the benefit of society at large.

Socialism: A political ideology that supports public ownership of major industries, and a commitment to a strong commons, including public education and public healthcare. Although there are different interpretations in different locations, in general it supports democratic control of the means of production. Cuba after the 1959 Cuban Revolution is considered to be very close to a true socialist state. State-owned industry, and strong public education and healthcare systems, are hallmarks of post-revolution Cuba.

Socialization: The process of learning to behave in a way that is acceptable to society.

Status Quo: From Latin, a term that indicates the existing state of affairs.

Stereotype: A mostly unfounded belief or perspective that many people have about other people or things that share a common characteristic; quite often these views are untrue and unfair.

Systemic Bias: Burdens or obstacles that make it difficult for some individuals or groups to have equal or full access to the rights and freedoms that other citizens have, because of, for example, gender, race, poverty, dis/ability or health, country of origin, and education. For example, a woman may be seen as unable to successfully perform in a job that requires a certain level of physical strength (such as a firefighter), but isn't given a test to find out whether she can do so. Or new citizens might not be able to find jobs, even though they have occupational skills that are needed in their new country. This becomes systemic when it is repeated over time and about the same groups, which then becomes normalized in society. For example, "all women are weaker than men" or "we don't have the space for a wheelchair ramp" or "his university degree can't be as good as the ones we have in Canada."

Title: Aboriginal or Indigenous title is a common law doctrine set out in the *Royal Proclamation of 1763* and the *British North America Act of 1867*. It provides a legal basis for Indigenous peoples to continue to use the lands of their ancestors to support their communities, most often through hunting and fishing.

Totalitarianism: A centralized dictatorial form of government requiring complete subservience to the state.*

Treaty: A formal agreement between two or more groups, usually sovereign bodies or nations. Historically treaties with First Nations in Canada were agreements with the federal government to clear the land for White settlement, resource extraction, and railways in exchange for education, medicines, and farm equipment. In negotiating treaties, the government must acknowledge the *title* of First Nations to their lands.

Truth and Reconciliation Commission of Canada (TRC): The TRC was part of a comprehensive response to the abuse inflicted upon Indigenous peoples through the racist residential school system, and the harmful legacy of those schools. It was established in 2008 and completed its work in 2015. The commission spent six years travelling across Canada and listened to the testimonies of approximately 6,000 Indigenous survivors of residential schools. In its final report, the TRC stated, "Reconciliation must support Aboriginal people as they heal from the destructive legacies of colonization that have wreaked such havoc in their lives."

Watergate: A major political scandal that occurred in the United States in the early 1970s, following a break-in at the Democratic National Committee headquarters at the Watergate office complex in Washington, D.C., in 1972, and Republican president Richard Nixon's administration's attempted cover-up of its involvement. The scandal led to the discovery of multiple abuses of power by the Nixon administration, an impeachment process against the president that led to articles of impeachment, and the resignation of Nixon in August 1974. The story of the Watergate scandal is considered to be an example of excellent investigative journalism.

Yellow Journalism: Journalism that is based on sensationalism and crude exaggeration.

Zapatistas: Members of a Mexican revolutionary force working for social and agrarian reforms, which launched a popular uprising in the state of Chiapas in 1994.

Note: Definitions with asterisks (*) are from the *Canadian Oxford Dictionary*.

ABOUT THE AUTHORS

Kirsten Kozolanka
Professor Emerita, Carleton University

Kirsten Kozolanka has taught in both the communication and journalism programs in the School of Journalism and Communication at Carleton University. She is the author of *The Power of Persuasion: The Politics of the New Right in Ontario* (2007), the co-editor of *Alternative Media in Canada* (2012), and the editor of *Publicity and the Canadian State: Critical Communication Perspectives* (2014). Previously, she worked for a party leader on Parliament Hill, a minister of culture and communication in the Ontario Legislature, and in a strategic communication directorate in the Government of Canada.

Paul Orlowski
Associate Professor, University of Saskatchewan

Paul Orlowski received his PhD in 2004 from the University of British Columbia in social studies education and the sociology of education. He was the department head of the Teacher Education Program at the University of the Fraser Valley in Chilliwack, British Columbia, for four years. He is currently an associate professor in the College of Education at the University of Saskatchewan in Saskatoon, and is the author of *Teaching about Hegemony: Race, Class, and Democracy in the 21st Century* (2011). Paul's research areas focus on neoliberalism, democracy, the media, environmental education, and teaching for political consciousness.

INDEX

ABC, 124
Aboriginal peoples. *See* Indigenous peoples
Aboriginal Peoples' Television Network (APTN), 188
Aboriginal title, 171–179
Abu Ghraib prison, 222
access
  to the media, 126–131
  to scientific research, 133–134
active citizenship, 47
activism, 33, 35–39
AdBusters, 33
The Advancement for Sound Science Coalition (TASSC), 126, 128
advocacy journalists, 223
AEI. *See* American Enterprise Institute (AEI)
Affordable Healthcare Act, 83–84
Afghanistan, 205–206
Africa, 35
African Americans, 153
agency, 100
Aird, John, 107
Aird Commission, 107, 108, 109, 110
Al Jazeera, 185
algorithms, 61
All the President's Men, 65
al-Qaeda, 198, 200
alternative facts, 73–75
alternative journalism, 223
alternative meaning system, 30
alternative media, 31–33
  activism and, 33
  in Canada, 36–37
  challenges for, 39–41
  defining alternative media, 33
  existence of, 25
  lack of own history, 41
  need for, 34–35
  participatory nature of, 32
  role in democratic society, 34
  and social movements, 35
  structure of, 32–33
Alternative Media (Atton), 33

Alternative Media in Canada (Kozolanka, Mazepa, and Skinner), 32
Alternet, 223
Ambrose, Rona, 132–133, 134
American Civil Liberties Union (ACLU), 157
American Constitution, 86
American Enterprise Institute (AEI), 126, 129
American Petroleum Institute, 128–129
American Press (AP), 104
Americans for Prosperity, 129
anarchism, 92
anti-science strategy, 128–129
anti-terror bill, 4
Anti-terrorism, Crime and Security Act, 203
Anti-terrorism Act, 149, 194, 195–198, 202
AP. *See* American Press (AP)
APCO, 128
Apple, 87
The Apprentice, 70
Arar, Maher, 149–150, 154, 196, 198
Arctic Air, 153
The Art of the Deal (Trump), 70
Artz, Lee, 198
Asians, 153
Associated Press, 47, 215
The Atlantic, 132
Attallah, Paul, 114
attitudes, 166
Atton, Chris, 33
austerity *versus* extraction, 138
authoritarian regimes, 81

Bad Teacher, 18
Bannon, Steve, 81
barbaric, 169
Basques, 30, 228
BBC, 49, 53
BC NDP, 164, 174
BC Social Credit government, 164
Beck, Glenn, 127
Belfast Telegraph, 51
Bell Media, 25, 104

Bennett, R. B., 108
Bennett, W. Lance, 213, 224
Bernstein, Carl, 49
Beyak, Lynn, 178, 187
bias, 63, 71–72, 228
bias of communication, 102–103
big media, 28
Big Oil, 127, 129–133
bilingualism, 147
Bill C-51, 4, 60–61
bin Laden, Osama, 198
Black, Conrad, 125
Black Lives Matter (BLM) movement, 38, 57, 59, 63, 157–158, 167, 170
Blatchford, Christie, 183
blindspots, 34
BLM. *See* Black Lives Matter (BLM) movement
Board of Broadcast Governors, 108–109
Boston Globe, 65, 86
Bowling Green massacre, 83
The Brass Check: A Study of American Journalism (Sinclair), 48
Brave New World (Huxley), 1
Breitbart News, 80, 82, 167
Breitbart.com, 56, 85
Brexit, 45
Briarpatch, 36, 223
bribes, 213
Bridgegate, 49
Britain, 60
British Columbia, 164, 170, 173–174
British Columbia Civil Liberties Association, 197
British Colonist newspaper, 173
British Columbian newspaper, 173–174
British Journalism Award, 49
British North America Act (BNA Act) of 1867, 164, 172, 173, 228
broadcast networks, 85
Broadcasting Act, 108–109, 110, 115
broadcasting legislation, 110
Brulle, Robert, 127, 130
Buckingham, David, 15
building Canada, 146–148
Bulgaria, 34
bundling, 46
Bush, George W., 4, 16, 83, 87, 131, 198
Buzzfeed, 78

C-38, 181–182
C-45, 39, 181–182
Calder Decision, 164
Canada-US border issue, 196
Canadaland, 36
Canadian Arab Association, 197
Canadian Broadcasting Corporation (CBC), 26, 29, 49, 107, 108, 109, 110, 111–116, 153, 177, 184, 212
Canadian Centre for Policy Alternatives, 90, 199
Canadian Civil Liberties Association, 157
Canadian content quotas, 109, 111
Canadian Dimension, 223
Canadian Encyclopedia, 147
Canadian Federation of Civil Liberties and Human Rights Associations, 157
Canadian Human Rights Act, 155
Canadian identity, 105–108
Canadian Media Concentration Research Project, 3, 53
Canadian Media Guild, 112
Canadian Muslims, 153–154
Canadian National Railway (CNR), 106
Canadian Pacific, 104
Canadian Press (CP), 47, 215, 220
Canadian Press Association (CPA), 215, 218
Canadian Radio Broadcasting Act, 108, 110
Canadian Radio League, 108
Canadian radio system, 108
Canadian Radio-television and Telecommunications Commission (CRTC), 109, 110
Canadian Taxpayers Association, 199
Caps and Spelling, 220
carbon dioxide (CO_2), 120–121
Carleton College, 220
carré rouge, 38
Cassidy, John, 75
Cato Institute, 129
CBC. *See* Canadian Broadcasting Corporation (CBC)
CBS, 124
censorship, 134
Center for North American Energy Security, 131
CentreTownNews.ca, 224
Century of Human Rights, 6
Charter of Rights and Freedoms, 155, 172
charter schools, 17

Cheney, Dick, 131–132
Chevron Oil, 131
Chile, 10
China, 61, 81, 169
Chomsky, Noam, 14–15, 51–52, 55, 59, 72, 132
Chrétien, Jean, 111–112
CIA, 55, 60, 61
cigarette slogans, 156
citizen journalism, 221, 222
civic engagement, 47
civic journalism, 221–223
civil society, 7, 88, 125
civilized, 169
Clark, Glen, 174
classical liberalism, 5
The Clean Air Act, 16
Clear Skies Act, 16
clicktivism, 38, 41, 61
climate change, 119, 120, 228
    access to the media, 126–131
    access to scientific research, 133–134
    climate change denial movement, 126–131, 135–136
    climate science, 122–123
    corporate media's coverage of, 123–125
    global warming, 120–121
    greenhouse effect, 121
    greenhouse gases, 120–121
    implications for citizens, 135–136
    and the media, 123–131
    media, new role for, 137–138
    oil versus state, 131–133
climate disinformation, 129
climate science, 122–123
Climategate, 49
Clinton, Hillary, 52–53, 58–59, 71, 81–82, 83, 84, 124
CNN, 53, 85
CNR. *See* Canadian National Railway (CNR)
coal, 122
Coleman, Kit, 218
Columbia School of Journalism, 130
colonialism, 171, 228
colonization, 171, 179, 184, 228
colour-blind discourse on race, 169–170
Comey, James, 76
Competitive Enterprise Institute, 128, 129
concentration of Canadian media ownership, 13–14, 56

conservatism, 5, 8, 92, 228
Conservative government, 26, 60, 111, 115, 133, 134, 138, 204
Conservative Party, 53, 56, 124, 129, 132, 133, 182, 184, 187
Conservative Political Action Conference, 62
Conservative think tanks, 127
Conway, Kellyanne, 74, 82, 83
Cook, Tim, 87
Cooney, Phil, 128–129
Copenhagen Summit, 125
Corbyn, Jeremy, 60
Corcoran, Tom, 131
corporate media, 3, 13–15, 55, 135
    see also mainstream media
corporations as job-creators discourse, 12
Council of Canadians, 90
counter-hegemonic perspectives, 8
Coyne, Andrew, 114
CPA. *See* Canadian Press Association (CPA)
Crash to Paywall (Gorman), 65
Crean, Susan, 217–218
Cree, 175
critical race theory, 185
critical theory, 4
CRTC. *See* Canadian Radio-television and Telecommunications Commission (CRTC)
CSIS, 60
cultural analysis, 50
cultural-deficit discourse, 169
cultural genocide, 177, 228
cultural issues, 27
cultural paradigm, 2
cultural studies, 29, 228–229
The Current, 178

The Daily Show, 78
Daily Xtra, 36
Dakota Access Pipeline, 39
Dale, Daniel, 77
Davey Committee, 110
Davey Report, 54
Davin Report, 176
de Beauvoir, Simone, 154–155
Debbs, Eugene, 58
defence budgets, 200
Defense Intelligence Agency, 76
definitional advantage, 3, 15

deforestation, 121
democracy, 5, 136
　and fake news, 75–77, 85–87, 91–92
　media landscape and, 62–64
　social democracy, 6, 231
　and social media, 56–59
　weakening of democracy, 79–81
Democracy Now!, 223
democratic communication, 100
Democratic Party, 52, 58, 59, 65, 133
democratic socialist, 52
Denmark, 52, 57, 125
Denver, 47
Department of Agriculture, 134
dependency, 178
deregulation
　of the American financial sector, 45, 46
　of industry, 11
Desmond, Viola, 158
Detroit, 57
Directorate of National Intelligence, 83
discrimination, 6
Dobbin, Murray, 54
the dominant ideology, 14
Doublespeak, 16
Douglas, James, 173
Douglas Treaties, 173
Dufour, Paul, 133
Duncan, Sara Jeanette, 217–218
Dunlap, Riley, 125

early journalism, 216–217
echo chambers, 78
economic elites, 13
economic issues, 26–27
Edelman Trust Barometer, 45–46
educasters, 110
education
　and Aboriginal title, 172
　and Prairie treaty promises, 176–179
Education Week, 18
educational broadcasting, 109–111
egalitarianism, 9
elections, 53
Electric Telegraph Companies Act, 104
emancipation of the masses, 5
enemy propaganda, 80
English, Kathy, 77
Enlightenment, 5, 229

Environics for the Canadian Race Relations
　Foundation, 153–154
Environmental Protection Agency (EPA),
　128, 132, 134
equality, 9
essentialist discourse on race, 167–169, 171
ethnic mosaic, 148
ethnological, 229
ethnological approach, 155
European Court of Human Rights, 34
exclusionary, 181
existential crises, 136
Exxon, 127, 129
ExxonMobil, 127, 128, 130–132

Facebook, 18, 44, 46, 50, 54, 56–57, 58, 59,
　61, 63, 82, 88
fact-checking sites, 88–89
FactCheck.org, 89
fake news, 46, 71
　in Canadian politics, 84
　and civil society, 85–87
　and democracy, 75–77, 85–87, 91–92
　examples of, 81–85
　facts about fake news, 77–79
　resisting, necessity of, 85–87
　and social media, 63, 82
　strategies for resisting, 87–90
　students' assessment of, 79
　tips for exposing fake news, 90
false political consciousness, 4
Family Compact, 217, 229
Fan, Jiayang, 85
FBI, 60, 76–77, 82
FCC. *See* Federal Communications
　Commission (FCC)
fearful citizens, 205–206
Federal Communications Commission
　(FCC), 60
Fessenden, Reginald, 106
filter bubbles, 61, 229
Finland, 89
First Amendment, 86, 88, 92
First Nations. *See* Indigenous peoples
First Nations in the Royal Proclamation of
　1763, 172
first-person media-making, 222
Flanagan, Tom, 182–183
Fleishman-Hillard, 129

Fleras, Augie, 151
Fletcher, Frederick, 224
Florida, 82
Flynn, Michael, 76
Fontaine, Tina, 184
foreign media, 113
Fort McMurray, 119, 136
Fowler Commission, 110
Fox News, 81, 82, 83, 85, 124, 128, 167
Frank, Thomas, 4
Frankenberg's taxonomy, 167–169, 169
Fraser Institute, 127
free press approach, 31, 211, 212
freedom, 9
Friedman, Milton, 10
Friends of Canadian Broadcasting, 112
Friends of Science, 129
Fueling U.S. Forward, 127

Gallup polls, 45
Gay Pride Parade, 157–158
Gaza, 58
Gen Why Media, 112
genocide, 6
Georgia Straight, 36, 40
German Canadians, 153
Germany, 80
Gillmor, Dan, 222
Gitlin, Todd, 40
glass ceiling, 217, 229
global capitalism, 54
global warming, 120–121
Globe and Mail, 54, 56, 169, 172, 182–183, 215
glossary, 228–233
Godfrey, Paul, 53
Godwin, Mike, 94
Godwin's Law, 94
Goebbels, Joseph, 80
Google, 46, 88
Gorman, Brian, 65
greenhouse effect, 121
greenhouse gases, 120–121
Greenpeace, 127
Guantanamo Bay, 83
Guardian, 47, 49, 126

Habermas, Jürgen, 100
Halifax Gazette, 216

Halliburton, 132
Hamas, 59, 84
Hannity, Sean, 82
Harcourt, Mike, 174
Harper, Stephen, 39, 53, 54, 56, 60, 111, 115, 129, 132, 133, 134, 182–184
Harper's Magazine, 128
Harvey, David, 13
Hayek, Fredrick, 10
healthcare system, 12
The Healthy Forests Act, 16
Heartland Institute, 129
Heat: How to Stop the Planet from Burning (Monbiot), 126
Hedges, Chris, 55
hegemony, 3–4, 30, 229
hegemonic device, 15, 47, 61
Heritage Foundation, 129
Herizons, 36
Herman, Edward, 14, 51, 55
Hezbollah, 59
High-Level Commission on Carbon Prices, 136
Hind, Cora, 218
Hitler, Adolf, 80, 92
Hoaxy, 88
Hotter Than Hell (Tushingham), 134
House Committee on Science, Space and Technology, 130–131
House of Commons, 215
House Intelligence Committee, 76
House Permanent Select Committee, 76
Howe, John, 216–217
Huffington Post, 129
human rights, 7, 9
Hungary, 114
Huntington, Samuel P., 150
Hutchins Commission, 212, 213
Huxley, Aldous, 1–2

identity politics, 158, 229
ideology, 4
Idle No More, 39, 57, 59, 170, 181–183, 186
IMF. *See* International Monetary Fund (IMF)
immigration to Canada, 146–147
Imperial Oil, 132
Inauguration Day, 73–74
inclusive media, 41

India, 84, 169
Indian Act, 6, 176–179
Indiana University, 88
Indigenous peoples, 39
   Aboriginal title, 171–179
   British Columbia's contrarian views, 173–174
   Idle No More, 39, 57, 59, 170, 181–183, 186
   Indigenous women, 155, 157, 183–185
   land treaties, 171–179
   murdered and missing Indigenous women, 183–185
   Prairie treaties of the 1870s, 175–176
   residential schools, 176–179
   squaw stereotype, 184
   stereotypes in mainstream media, 179–181
   traditions, maintenance of, 6
individual rights, 6–7
individualism, 6–7
Industrial Revolution, 122
informed citizenry, 2, 3
   and mainstream media, 50–56
   and media landscape, 62–64
   media output, assessment of, 224
   social media and, 59–62
Innis, Harold, 102, 104
Institute for Energy Research/American Energy Alliance, 129
institutional racism, 166
interests of the elites, 51
International Consortium of Investigative Journalists, 49
International Monetary Fund (IMF), 12
Internet, 44, 46, 60
   see also social media
Internet taxes, 60
internment of Canadians, 152–153
intersectionality, 170, 229
intimidation, 130
investigative journalism, 216–217
investigative journalist, 48–49
invisible hand, 11
Iran, 81
Iraq, 45, 87, 132, 198, 199–200, 207
Irwin, Will, 48
ISIS, 83
Islamophobia, 151, 229
Israel military, 58
Israeli government, 58

Jacobson, Mark, 136
Japan, 34, 114, 169
Japanese Canadians, 153
journalism, 45–47
   approaches to, 211–213
   citizen journalism, 221, 222
   early journalism, 216–217
   free press approach, 31, 211, 212
   history of, 211–213
   investigative journalism, 48–49, 216–217
   the new journalisms, 220–223
   newsroom staffs, 27
   objective journalism, 213–216
   as profession, 218–220
   public (or civic) journalism, 221–223
   today, 223–225
   women, and journalism, 217–218
Joystick Warriors, 156
Juneau, Pierre, 109
junk science, 128, 131
justice journalists, 223

Kennedy, John F., 86
Kent Report, 110, 213
Kent Royal Commission on Newspapers, 54
Kentucky, 83
Keynesian economics, 5, 7, 12, 13, 15, 19, 229
Khadr, Omar, 196–197, 198
Kiedrowski, Jonas, 18
Kilbourne, Jean, 2
Kill the Messenger, 55
Killing Us Softly (Kilbourne), 2
Kim's Convenience, 153
King, Thomas, 179, 188
Klein, Naomi, 123, 137
Koch brothers, 126, 130
Koch Industries, 127
Komagata Maru freighter ship, 152
Kouvalis, Nick, 84
Krugman, Paul, 52
Kyoto Protocol, 129

La Gazette littéraire, 216
La Ligue des droits et libertés, 197
laissez-faire economics, 5, 11
Lakoff, George, 16
land treaties, 171–179
Latinos, 91, 153
Latvia, 114

Laurier, Wilfrid, 106
Layton, Jack, 94
Leadnow, 112
left-wing ideas, 9
legacies, 166
Leitch, Kellie, 84
LGBTQ+, 159
Liberal government, 26, 60, 112, 198–199, 200, 202
Liberal Party, 10, 53, 60, 124, 184
liberalism, 5, 92, 230
libertarian theory, 31
libertarians, 7, 230
Lincoln Report, 110
literacy, 214
literary freedom, 134
Little Mosque on the Prairie, 153
local community *versus* corporate power, 138
local news, 47
Locke, John, 211
lone gunman, 145
Los Angeles Times, 53, 80, 130
Lügenpresse, 79–81, 92

MacBride, Sean, 102
MacBride Commission, 100, 102
MacDonald, John A., 174
Mackenzie, William Lyon, 216, 217
mainstream media
   and Aboriginal title, 172
   access to scientific research, 133–134
   bias, 63
   in Canada, 25–29
   and climate change, 123–131, 137–138
   definitional advantage, 3
   dominance of, before social media, 47
   and global capitalism, 54
   as a hegemonic device, 15, 47, 61
   Indigenous peoples, stereotypes of, 179–181
   informed citizenry, obstacles to, 50–56
   media output, assessment of, 224
   muzzling of scientists, 134
   and neoliberalism, 54, 137–138
   and powerful interests, 3
   progressive binaries, 138
   propaganda, 63
   public interest, watchdog for, 212–213
   regulation of, 108–109
   representatives of cultural groups, 2–3
   sophisticated citizenry, contributions to, 48–50
   and terror, 206–207
   Trump, resistance to, 91–92
mainstream society, 30
Manhattan Institute, 129
Mansbridge, Peter, 153
manufacturing consent, 14
Manufacturing Consent: The Political Economy of the Mass Media (Herman & Chomsky), 51
Many Voices, 102
MAPL system, 111
Marconi, Guglielmo, 106
Marcuse, Herbert, 1–2
Martin, Lawrence, 3
Martin, Paul, 111–112
Marx, Karl, 5, 14
mass media. *See* mainstream media
Massachusetts, 130
Massachusetts Institute of Technology (MIT), 14
Massey Commission, 110
Mayer, Jane, 126
McCain, John, 53
McChesney, Robert, 59–60, 137
McCue, Duncan, 179, 180, 185
McKibben, Bill, 136
meaning systems, 29–31
media giants in Canada, 25
media landscape, assessment of, 62–64
media literacy
   deconstruction of false political consciousness, 4
   for an informed citizenry, 3
   main categories of, 2
   political ideology, understanding on, 18–19
   related concepts, 2–4
   relevant theory, 2–4
   today, 223–225
media think, 14
Media Think (Winter), 13–14
MediaBiasFactCheck.com, 89
MediaMatters.org, 89
Medicare, 12
Meet the Press, 74
mega-spin, 15–16
Melfort Journal, 177
meritocracy, 166–167, 230

Index

Merriam-Webster Dictionary, 74
Mesplet, Fleury, 216
methane, 120, 121
Metro, 32
Mexico, 30
MI5, 60
MI6, 60
Middle East Monitor, 59
militarization in Canada, 199–204
military language, 201, 202
Mill, John Stuart, 211
Milloy, Steve, 128
Mills, C. Wright, 55
Mindich, David, 213–214
Mohawk First Nation, 179–180, 188
Monbiot, George, 123, 126–127, 128
Morris, Alexander, 175, 177
muckraking, 212, 230
multicultural, 103, 230
multiculturalism, 50, 147
multiplicity, 100
murdered and missing Indigenous women, 183–185
Murdoch, Rupert, 83, 124
music in Canada, 111
Muslim-bashing, 83
Muslim countries, 82
Muslims, 91
mutual withdrawal, 224
muzzling of scientists, 133–134

Namibia, 114
Nanos Research, 114
NASA, 120
nation building, 101–105
The National, 114
National Action Committee on the Status of Women (NAC), 155
National Association of Women and the Law, 197
National Campus and Community Radio Association, 36
National Citizens' Coalition, 199
National Day of Action, 39
National Library and Archives, 41
National Observer (Canada), 36–37
National Policy, 105
National Post, 54, 56, 125, 183
National Security Agency, 61
nations, 171

NATO. *See* North Atlantic Treaty Organization (NATO)
Nazis, 80, 92
NBC, 124
NDP. *See* New Democratic Party (NDP)
Negin, Elliott, 129–130
neoliberalism, 2, 5, 8–13, 51, 135, 230
 and mainstream media, 54, 137–138
 and public education, 17–18
Nepal, 35
New Democratic Party (NDP), 10, 53, 94, 124, 164, 174, 184
New Internationalist, 34, 35
the new journalisms, 220–223
New York, 130
New York Times, 47, 52, 53, 55, 58, 73, 80, 85, 126, 128, 130, 153
Newspeak, 4, 12, 19
newsroom staffs, 27
Newsworthy: The Lives of Media Women (Crean), 217
Nicaragua, 55
niche television channels, 113
Niinistö, Sauli, 89
Nineteen Eighty-Four (Orwell), 1, 19
Nisga'a people, 164–165, 174
Nisga'a Treaty, 165, 174
nitrous oxide, 120
Nixon, Richard, 49, 74
NOAA. *See* US National Oceanic and Atmospheric Administration (NOAA)
Noack, Rick, 80
North Atlantic Treaty Organization (NATO), 194, 195
North of 60, 153
Novascotian, 216
Nunes, Devin, 76

Obama, Barack, 65, 71, 73, 74, 76, 82, 83, 84, 91, 124, 132
objective journalism, 213–216
objectivism, 7
objectivity, 219–220
Obomsawin, Alanis, 188
Observatory on Social Media, 88
Occupy Wall Street movement, 12–13, 57–58
Office of the Auditor General, 115
official languages, 103
Official Secrets Act, 149

Oil Eight, 129–130
oil *versus* state, 131–133
oil subsidies *versus* green job support, 138
Ojibway, 186
Oka, Quebec, 179–180, 186, 188
Olbermann, Keith, 88
The Onion, 78
online alternative media outlets, 63
online political polls, 61
Ontario, 105, 110, 174
OpenMedia.org, 223
oppositional meaning system, 30
Organization for Economic Cooperation and Development, 155
Orwell, George, 1–2, 4, 14, 15, 19, 73
"Othering," 154–158, 168
ozone, 120

pack journalism, 72–73
Pai, Ajit, 60
Palestinian activists, 58
Panama Papers, 49, 230
Panamagate, 49
Paris Agreement, 122, 129
Parliamentary Press Gallery (PPG), 215, 218
participation, 33
partisanship, 71–72, 230
Patriot Act, 195
patriotism, 202
Paulsen, Morten, 129
PBS. *See* Public Broadcasting Service (PBS)
peacekeeping, 193–194, 195
Pegida, 80
Péquistes, 30, 230
performativity, 18
personal hand-held devices, 113
perspective, 34
Peru, 35
Pew Research Center, 47, 153, 221
Pew Research Center for the People and the Press, 45
Philip Morris, 128
Plaunt, Alan, 108
poisoning *versus* poverty, 138
political blogs, 50
political economy, 52, 59–60
political ideology, 4–8
　corporate media, 3
　social media and, 72

　teaching for comprehension of, 9–10
　understanding of, and media literacy, 18–19
political issues, 26
political partisanship, 72, 78
PolitiFact.com, 89
Pope Francis, 83
Postmedia, 53–54, 56
postmodernism, 113, 230
poststructuralism, 1, 230–231
post-truth, 77
Powell, Lewis, 126
power, 60
power-blind, 170
PPG. *See* Parliamentary Press Gallery (PPG)
Prairie treaties of the 1870s, 175–176
prevailing orthodoxy, 73
Pride Toronto, 157–158
princesses in Disney, 156
private media, 100–101
privatization, 18
professional journalist, 48
profound distrust, 178
Project Censored, 35
propaganda, 15–16, 63, 72–73, 80, 231
propagandists, 16
Provincial Freeman, 217
Pruitt, Scott, 132
the public, 99–101
Public Broadcasting Service (PBS), 110–111
public education, 17–18
public interest, 99–101, 107
　media as "watchdog," 212–213
　regulation of media, 108–109
public journalism, 221–223
public media, 99
public relations spin doctoring, 16
Public Safety Act, 202
public service broadcasting, 100
publishing houses, 127–128

Qatar, 185
QMI, 25
quality, 100
Qu'Appelle Valley, 176
Quebec, 30, 38–39, 147, 179
Quebec City, 145, 148
quid pro quo exchanges, 213

Rabble.ca, 37, 39, 54, 56, 63, 223
Raboy, Marc, 100, 115–116
race-cognizance discourse, 170–171
race theory, 165–171
racial discourses, 167–171
   colour-blind discourse on race, 169–170
   essentialist discourse on race, 167–169
   race-cognizance discourse, 170–171
racial hierarchy during British Empire, 168
racial profiling, 196, 197, 231
racially marginalized Other, 168
racism, 7
   forms of racism, 166–167
   institutional racism, 166
   systemic racism, 153, 166
racist cultural ranking system, 169
radical social movements, 32
radio, 105–108
Radio-Canada, 110, 113
Radiotelegraph Act, 106
railway, 103, 106
Rand, Ayn, 7
RCAP. *See* Royal Commission on Aboriginal Peoples (RCAP)
RCMP, 60, 183
real fake news, 78
The Real News Network, 37
Rebel Media, 56, 63, 167
RedState Gathering, 127
reform liberalism, 5
reformist left, 5
regulation of media, 108–109
ReimagineCBC, 112
religious freedom, 34
Report of the Royal Commission on Radio Broadcasting, 110
Reporting in Indigenous Communities (McCue), 180
Republican Party, 70–71, 122, 133
residential schools, 176–179
Reuters, 47
Reuters U.K., 131
Revkin, Andrew, 128
rhetoric, 15
Rice, Condoleeza, 131
Ricochet, 37
right wing, 9
rights revolution, 50
risk society, 200, 231
Roach, Kent, 195–196

Robogate, 49
Rocky Mountain News, 47
Rogers, 25
Rorty, Richard, 8
Rosen, Jay, 221
Rosner, Cecil, 216
Royal Commission on Aboriginal Peoples (RCAP), 180–181, 186
Royal Commission on Bilingualism and Biculturalism, 147
Royal Commission on Broadcasting, 110
Royal Commission on Corporate Competition, 110
Royal Commission on National Development in the Arts, Letters and Sciences, 110
Royal Commission on Newspapers, 213
Royal Commission on Radio Broadcasting, 106–108
Royal Commission on the Status of Women, 155
royal commissions, 110
Royal Proclamation of 1763, 171–173, 231
rugged individual discourse, 7
Russia, 81, 89
Russian propaganda, 89
Ryan, Paul, 127

San Jose Mercury News, 55
Sanders, Bernie, 8, 13, 19, 52, 58–59
Saskatchewan, 12, 177
satire, 78
Saturday Night Live, 78
savage, 169
School of Communication at Simon Fraser University, 34
Science magazine, 126
scientific research, 133–134
SDS. *See* Students for a Democratic Society (SDS)
Seattle, 47
Seattle Post-Intelligencer, 47
Second Jen, 153
The Second Sex (de Beauvoir), 154
security state, 204–205
Seeing Red: A History of Natives in Canadian Newspapers (Anderson & Robertson), 181
segregated education, 176–179
Senate Transport and Communications Committee Report, 110

September 11th attack, 45, 147, 148–150, 150–151, 222
Serious Time for the Most Serious Crime Act, 204
Shadd Cary, Mary Anne, 217
Shameless, 37
Shaw, 25
Siddiqui, Haroon, 50
Sikh immigrants, 152
Silverman, Craig, 78, 81
Simpson, Leanne, 182
The Simpsons, 18
Sinclair, Murray, 178
Sinclair, Upton, 48
Sinclair Media Group, 47
Slovenia, 114
smallpox, 173
Smith, Adam, 11
Smith, Lamar, 130
Snopes.com, 89
Snowden, Edward, 61
social construction of knowledge, 3
social democracy, 6, 231
social justice, 9
social media, 44, 46, 50
   advertising and marketing, 63
   allegiance to political ideology, 72
   and contemporary political scene, 86–87
   fake news, 63, 82
   mainstream media, effect on, 47
   as panacea for ailing democracy, 56–59
   partisanship, 63
   popularity, effect of, 63
   shortcomings for informed citizenry, 59–62
   see also specific social media platforms
social movements, 35–39, 40
social responsibility, 212, 213, 231
socialism, 5–6, 92, 231
socialization, 155
South Africa, 114
South Sudan, 35
space bias, 102, 104
Spain, 30
Spanish Civil War, 203
Special Senate Committee on the Mass Media, 110
specialty channels, 113
Spence, Theresa, 183
Spencer, Herbert, 169

Spicer, Sean, 73, 74, 80
spin, 15–16, 73
spin doctors, 16, 73
Spotlight, 65
Spry, Graham, 108
squaw stereotype, 184
Standing Committee on Canadian Heritage, 110
Standing Rock Indian Reservation anti-pipeline protest, 39, 57, 167
Standing Up for Victims of White Collar Crime Act, 204
Stanford University, 136
Stanford University's Graduate School of Education, 78–79
status quo, 29, 231
Stephens, Bret, 74–75
stereotypes, 179, 231
stereotyping, 197
Stewart, Brian, 207
Stiglitz, Joseph, 136
Straight Goods, 37
structure, 33
Students for a Democratic Society (SDS), 40
subprime mortgage scandal, 45
Suez Canal crisis, 193
Suzuki, David, 197
Sweden, 82–83
symbolic power, 2
Syria, 58
systemic bias, 151–153, 232
systemic racism, 153, 166

Tackling Crime, 204
Talaga, Tanya, 186
Taras, David, 210
tariff, 105
Task Force on Broadcasting Policy, 110
TASSC. *See* The Advancement for Sound Science Coalition (TASSC)
tax reform, 9
Tea Party movement, 8
Teach For America, 17, 18
Teach For Canada, 17
Télé-Québec, 110
telegraph, 103–104, 214–215
Telus, 25
terror, and the media, 206–207
terror strikes, 206
terrorist stereotype, 183

TFO (Télévision française de l'Ontario), 110
TheTyee.ca, 37, 56, 63, 223
This Hour Has 22 Minutes, 78
This Magazine, 37
Thobani, Sunera, 198, 202
Tillerson, Rex, 132
Titanic, 106
title, 171, 232
Toronto Media Co-op, 223
Toronto Police Force, 157–158
Toronto Star, 49, 50, 54, 75, 167, 215
totalitarian regime, 86
totalitarianism, 212, 232
transatlantic radio, 106
TRC. *See* Truth and Reconciliation Commission (TRC)
treaty, 171, 232
trickle-down theory, 12
Trudeau, Justin, 84, 133
Trudeau, Pierre, 54
Trump, Donald, 4, 46, 53, 60, 62, 70–71, 73–75, 75, 76, 78, 79, 80, 81, 82, 85, 86–87, 91, 94, 122, 124, 131, 132, 167, 188
Trump, Eric, 81
Trump wiretapping lie, 76–77
Trump's travel ban policy, 83
trust, 186
Trutch, Joseph, 174
Truth and Reconciliation Commission (TRC), 165, 171, 177, 178, 184, 185, 187, 232
Tushingham, Mark, 134
TVOntario (TVO), 110, 111
Twain, Mark, 158
Twitter, 18, 44, 46, 50, 54, 56–57, 57, 58, 59, 61, 62, 63, 74, 80, 86–87, 88

UNESCO. *See* United Nations Education, Scientific and Cultural Organization (UNESCO)
Union of Concerned Scientists, 129, 130
United Kingdom, 54, 203
United Nations, 169, 193, 194, 195
United Nations Climate Change Conference, 125
United Nations Education, Scientific and Cultural Organization (UNESCO), 100, 101, 102
United Press International of Canada, 218

United States, 8
American Constitution, 86
charter schools, 17
climate change, 119
free press approach, 212
left wing perspective in, 10
mainstream media, and neoliberalism, 54
media, and control, 86
"melting pot" approach, 146
radio ads, 106
voucher schools, 17
Universal Declaration of Human Rights, 6, 169
"Unreliable Sources: How the News Media Help the Kochs and ExxonMobil Spread Climate Disinformation" (Negin), 129
unreported year, 34
UN's Intergovernmental Panel on Climate Change, 122
US Congress, 130
US Department of Defense, 124
US National Oceanic and Atmospheric Administration (NOAA), 121
user-generated content, 222

Vancouver Sun, 164–165
victimhood, 184
"visible minority" groups, 153
voucher schools, 17

Wall Street, 52
War Measures Act, 153
war on terror, 4, 20, 204, 206
warrior stereotype, 183
Washington Post, 47, 49, 52, 55, 58, 76, 80, 130
Watergate, 49, 232–233
Watergate Scandal, 49, 74
"ways of seeing" (Berger), 24
We the Media: Grassroots Journalism by the People, for the People (Gillmor), 222
The Wealth of Nations (Smith), 11
Webb, Gary, 55
Welland Canal, 216
Westwood, Sean, 72
What's the Matter with Kansas? (Frank), 4
White House, 71, 85, 87, 94, 129
White House Council on Environmental Quality, 128

White privilege, 167, 170
White supremacy, 177
Williams, Raymond, 29–31, 101
Winter, James, 13–15
women
   glass ceiling, 217, 229
   Indigenous women, 155, 157, 183–185
   and journalism, 217–218
   murdered and missing Indigenous women, 183–185
   women's rights, 155–156
Women's March on Washington, 74
Woodward, Bob, 49
World Glacier Monitoring, 126
World of Life church, 34
World Trade Center. *See* September 11th attack
World War II, 108, 136, 153, 169
World Wide Web, 32

Yale University, 79
yellow journalism, 212, 233
Yemen, 58

Zapatistas, 30, 233
Zero Tolerance for Barbaric Cultural Practices Act, 204
Zika virus, 136
Zinke, Ryan, 132
Zuckerberg, Mark, 46